Understanding Art

Tenth Edition

Lois Fichner-Rathus

Australia • Brazil • Japan • Korea • Mexico • Singapore • Spain • United Kingdom • United States

Understanding Art: Tenth Edition

Understanding Art, 10th Edition
Lois Fichner-Rathus

Senior Manager, Student Engagement:

Linda deStefano

Janey Moeller

Manager, Student Engagement:

Julie Dierig

Marketing Manager:

Rachael Kloos

Manager, Production Editorial:

Kim Fry

Manager, Intellectual Property Project Manager:

Brian Methe

Senior Manager, Production and Manufacturing:

Donna M. Brown

Manager, Production:

Terri Daley

For product information and technology assistance, contact us at
Cengage Learning Customer & Sales Support, 1-800-354-9706

For permission to use material from this text or product,
submit all requests online at **cengage.com/permissions**
Further permissions questions can be emailed to
permissionrequest@cengage.com

This book contains select works from existing Cengage Learning resources and was produced by Cengage Learning Custom Solutions for collegiate use. As such, those adopting and/or contributing to this work are responsible for editorial content accuracy, continuity and completeness.

Compilation © 2014 Cengage Learning

ISBN-13: 978-1-305-29560-5
ISBN-10: 1-305-29560-9

WCN: 01-100-101

Cengage Learning
5191 Natorp Boulevard
Mason, Ohio 45040
USA

Cengage Learning is a leading provider of customized learning solutions with office locations around the globe, including Singapore, the United Kingdom, Australia, Mexico, Brazil, and Japan. Locate your local office at:
international.cengage.com/region.

Cengage Learning products are represented in Canada by Nelson Education, Ltd.

For your lifelong learning solutions, visit **www.cengage.com/custom.**
Visit our corporate website at **www.cengage.com.**

CONTENTS

PART III. TWO-DIMENSIONAL MEDIA

ABOUT THE AUTHOR

Lois Fichner-Rathus is Professor of Art in the Art Department of The College of New Jersey. She holds a combined undergraduate degree in fine arts and art history, an M.A. from the Williams College Graduate Program in the History of Art, and a Ph.D. in the History, Theory, and Criticism of Art from the Massachusetts Institute of Technology. Her areas of specialization include contemporary art, feminist art history and criticism, and modern art and architecture. She has contributed to books, curated exhibitions, published articles in professional journals, and exhibited her large-format photographic prints. She is also the author of *Foundations of Art and Design*. She resides in New York.

Everyone wants to understand art. Why not try to understand the song of a bird? Why does one love the night, flowers, everything around one without trying to understand them? But in the case of a painting, people have to understand.

—Pablo Picasso

WHAT IS ART?

1

Beauty, truth, immortality, order, harmony—these concepts and ideals have occupied us since the dawn of history. They enrich our lives and encourage us to extend ourselves beyond the limits of flesh and blood. Without them, life would be but a mean struggle for survival, and the value of survival would be unclear.

In the sciences and the arts, we strive to weave our experiences into coherent bodies of knowledge and to communicate them. Many of us are more comfortable with the sciences than with the arts. Science teaches us that the universe is not ruled purely by chance. The sciences provide ways of observing the world and experimenting so that we can learn what forces determine the courses of atoms and galaxies. Even those of us who do not consider ourselves "scientific" recognize that the scientific method permits us to predict and control many important events on a grand scale.

The arts are more elusive to define, more difficult to gather into a conceptual net. We would probably all agree that the arts enhance daily experience; some of us would contend that they are linked to the very quality of life. Art has touched everyone, and art is all around us. Crayon drawings, paper cutouts, and the like are part of the daily lives of our children—an integral function of both magnet and refrigerator door. We all look for art to brighten our dormitory rooms, enhance our interior decor, beautify our cities, and embellish our places of worship. We are certain that we do not want to be without the arts, yet we are hard-pressed to define them and sometimes even to understand them.

BARBARA KRUGER. *Money Makes Money and a Rich Man's Jokes Are Always Funny, and You Want It. You Need It. You Buy It. You Forget It.* (2010). Guild Hall, East Hampton, NY.

*The beautiful is in nature, and it is encountered in the most diverse forms of reality.
Once it is found, it belongs to art, or, rather, to the artist who discovers it.*
—Gustave Courbet

In fact, the very word *art* encompasses many meanings, including ability, process, and product. As ability, art is the human capacity to make things of beauty and things that stir us; it is creativity. As process, art encompasses acts such as drawing, painting, sculpting, designing buildings, and using the camera to create memorable works. This definition is ever expanding, as materials and methods are employed in innovative ways to bring forth a creative product. As product, art is the completed work—an etching, a sculpture, a structure, a tapestry. If as individuals we do not understand science, we are at least comforted by the thought that others do. With art, however, the experience of a work is unique. Reactions to a work will vary according to the nature of the individual, time period, place, and culture. And although we may find ourselves standing before a work of art that has us befuddled, saying, "I hate it! I don't understand it!," we suspect that something about the nature of art transcends understanding.

This book is about the visual arts. Despite their often enigmatic nature, we shall try to share something of what is known about them so that understanding may begin. We do not aim to force our aesthetic preferences on you; if in the end you dislike a work as much as you did to start, that is completely acceptable. But we will aim to heighten awareness of what we respond to in a work of art and try to communicate why what an artist has done is important. In this way, you can counter with, "I hate it, but at least I understand it."

As in many areas of study—languages, computers, the sciences—amassing a basic vocabulary is intrinsic to understanding the material. You will want to be able to describe the attributes of a work of art and be able to express your reactions to it. The language or vocabulary of art includes the visual elements, principles of design, style, form, and content. We shall see how the visual elements of art, such as line, shape, and color, are composed according to principles of design into works of art with certain styles and content.

We shall examine many mediums, including drawing, painting, printmaking, the camera and computer arts, sculpture, architecture, ceramics, and fiber arts.

When asked why we should study history, the historian answers that we must know about the past in order to have a sense of where we are and where we may be going. This

1 in.

1-1 LEONARDO DA VINCI. *Mona Lisa* (c. 1503–1505). Oil on wood panel. 30¼" × 21". Louvre, Paris, France.

argument also holds true for the arts; there is more to art history than memorizing dates! Examining a work in its historical, social, and political context will enable you to have a more meaningful dialogue with that work. You will be amazed and entertained by the ways in which the creative process has been intertwined with world events and individual personalities. We shall follow the journey of art, therefore, from the wall paintings of our Stone Age ancestors through the graffiti art of today's subway station. The mediums, the forms, the styles, and the subjects may evolve and change from millennium to millennium, from day to day, but uniting threads lie in the persistent quest for beauty, or for truth, or for self-expression.

Many philosophers have argued that art serves no function, that it exists for its own sake. Some have asserted that the essence of art transcends the human occupation with usefulness. Others have held that in trying to analyze art too closely, one loses sight of its beauty and wonderment.

These may be valid points of view. Nevertheless, our understanding and appreciation of art often can be enhanced by asking the questions "Why was this created?" and "What is its purpose?" In this section, we shall see that works of art come into existence for a host of reasons that are as varied as the human condition. Perhaps we will not arrive at a single definition of art, but we can come to understand art by considering our relationship to it.

ART AND BEAUTY

Art and beauty have been long intertwined. At times, the artist has looked to nature as the standard of beauty and has thus imitated it. At other times, the artist has thought to improve upon nature, developing an alternative standard—an idealized form. Standards of beauty in and of themselves are by no means universal. The Classical Greeks were obsessed with their idea of beauty and fashioned mathematical formulas for rendering the human body in sculpture so that it would achieve a majesty and perfection unknown in nature. The sixteenth-century artist Leonardo da Vinci, in what is perhaps the most famous painting in the history of Western art, enchants generations of viewers with the eternal beauty and mysteriousness of the smiling *Mona Lisa* (Fig. **1-1**). But appreciation of the stately repose and refined features of this Italian woman is tied to a Western concept of beauty. Elsewhere in the world, these features may seem alien, unattractive, or undesirable. On the other hand, the standard of beauty in some non-Western societies that hold scarification, body painting, tattooing, and adornment (Fig. **1-2**) both beautiful and sacred may seem odd and unattractive to someone from the Western world. One art form need not be seen as intrinsically superior to the other; in these works, quite simply, beauty is in the eye of the society's beholder.

1-2 Kenyan woman, Masai tribe.
Standards for beauty can differ from culture to culture.

ART AND UGLINESS

The images of the Mona Lisa and the Masai woman challenge our fixed notions of classical beauty, but they nonetheless reflect someone's, some era's, some culture's standard of beauty. But need art be equated with beauty? Since the nineteenth century, grotesque images have been an inextricable part of art. They reflect the dark or comical side of human experience, provide a vehicle for artistic expression that is not limited to replicating visual reality, and challenge preconceived notions and standards of beauty.

Much in the modern era provided impetus for the development of the grotesque in art—world wars with their mass destruction and genocide, theories of human psychology, uses and misuses of technology, the birth of science fiction, and more. Characteristics of the grotesque in art are, like imagination, almost limitless. Grotesque art has in common, however, a deviation from and distortion of what is considered by most to be ideal form. Artists typically combine a variety of components in unpredictable ways to create deformities that signify their individual styles. Their images can be, on balance, humorous, as in *The Apparition* by George Condo (Fig. **1-3**), or nightmarish, as in Otto Dix's *The Skat Players* (Fig. **1-4**). The result is typically defined as ugly—a subversion of the long-standing association of art with beauty and a challenge to conventional theories of aesthetics.

1 ft.

1-4 OTTO DIX. *The Skat Players* (1920). Oil and collage on canvas. 43⁵⁄₁₆" × 34¼". Galerie der Stadt Stuttgart, Stuttgart, Germany.

ART AND TRUTH

What does it mean for art to "speak a truth"? The concept of truth in art is subjective; it can mean many and different things to each viewer. Does it mean true to nature, true to human experience, true to materials? The answer is yes to all of these and more. Art can be used to replicate nature, or reality, in the finest detail. Renaissance painters came up with techniques and devices to create a convincing illusion of three-dimensionality on two-dimensional surfaces. Artists throughout history have used their rendering skills to trick the eye into perceiving truth in imitation. Sometimes the tales of their virtuosic exploits survive the work, as in anecdotes recorded on the subject of the ancient Greek painter Apelles. In one such story, we are told that the artist, fearful that other painters might be judged more superior at realistic representation, demanded that real horses be brought before paintings of horses that were entered into a competition. When the horses began to neigh in front of Apelles' work, he received the recognition he deserved.

Artists have sought to extract universal truths by expressing their own experiences. Sometimes their pursuit has led them to beauty, at other times to shame and outrage. The

1-3 GEORGE CONDO. *The Apparition* (2009). Oil on canvas. 40" × 36". The Living and the Dead, Gavin Brown's enterprise, NY.

FOR CENTURIES, ARTISTS have devoted their full resources, their lives, to their work. Orlan has also offered her pound of flesh—to the surgeon's scalpel. Orlan (Fig. 1-5) is a French multimedia performance artist who has been undergoing a series of cosmetic operations to create, in herself, a composite sketch of what Western art has long set forth as the pinnacle of human beauty: the facial features that we find in classic works such as Botticelli's *The Birth of Venus* (Fig. 1-6), Leonardo's *Mona Lisa* (Fig. 1-1), and Boucher's *Europa*, or, more specifically, Venus's chin, the Mona Lisa's forehead, and Europa's mouth.

Most people undergo cosmetic surgery in private, but not Orlan. Several of her operations have been performances or media events. Her first series of operations were carried out in France and Belgium. The operating rooms were filled with symbols of flowering womanhood in a form compatible with medicine: sterilized plastic fruit. There were huge photos of Orlan, and the surgeons and their assistants were decked out not in surgical greens but in costumes created by celebrated couturiers. A recent operation was performed in the New York office of a cosmetic surgeon and transmitted via satellite to the Sandra Gering Gallery in the city's famed SoHo district. Orlan did not lie unconscious in a hospital gown. Rather, she lay awake in a long, black dress and read from a work on psychoanalysis while the surgeon implanted silicone in her face to imitate the protruding forehead of *Mona Lisa*.

When will it all end? Orlan says that "I will stop my work when it is as close as possible to the computer composite,"* as the lips of Europa split into a smile. ●

---

* Margalit Fox, "A Portrait in Skin and Bone," *New York Times*, November 21, 1993, V8.

1-5 French performance artist Orlan, who has dedicated herself to embodying Western classic beauty as found in the works of Leonardo, Botticelli, and Boucher through multiple plastic surgeries. Here Orlan is being "prepped" for one in a series of operations. © 2011 Artists Rights Society (ARS), NY/ADAGP, Paris.

1-6 SANDRO BOTTICELLI. *The Birth of Venus* (1486). Detail. Tempera on canvas. 5′ 8⅞″ × 9′ 1⅞″. Galleria degli Uffizi, Florence, Italy.

It is the glory and good of Art,
That Art remains the one way possible
Of speaking truths, to mouths like mine at least.
—Robert Browning

"ugly truth," just like the beautiful truth, provides a valid commentary on the human condition.

In her self-portraits, the Mexican painter Frida Kahlo used her tragic life as an emblem for human suffering. At age 18, she was injured when a streetcar slammed into a bus on which she was a passenger. The accident left her with many serious wounds, including a fractured pelvis and vertebrae, and chronic pain. Kahlo's marriage to the painter Diego Rivera was also painful. She once told a friend, "I have suffered two serious accidents in my life, one in which a streetcar ran over me. . . . The other accident was Diego."[2] As in *Diego in My Thoughts* (Fig. **1-7**), her face is always painted with extreme realism and set within a compressed space, requiring the viewer to confront the "true" Frida. When asked why she painted herself so often, she replied, "*Porque estoy muy sola*" ("Because I am all alone"). Those who knew Kahlo conjecture that she painted self-portraits in order to "survive, to endure, to conquer death."

Zhang Xiaogang's (b. 1958) *Big Family* (Fig. **1-8**) features a passage of bright red in a sea of monotonous beige and gray tones. For this Chinese artist, the uniformity of a drab palette reflects the appearance—indeed the lives—of what he calls a typical revolutionary family: "asexual, dressed in Mao suits, their gaze glassy and dismal. . . . They could be clones."[3] Red as a signifier of Chinese Communist culture creates points of narrative and visual emphasis, but there is more to the print than its design elements. The work addresses a truth of contemporary Chinese life: this "big" family is as big as a family is permitted to get in this overpopulated country, given its one-child policy. And because of sexism, abortion is not uncommon when an early sonogram reveals that the fetus is female. Chinese social critics worry that the country seems to be headed toward a surplus of males and a resultant era of social instability.

Modern artists who discarded the practice of manipulating materials and techniques to create illusionistic surfaces built their compositions instead on the principle of "truth to materials." Paint retained its identity as paint, rather than pretending that it was cloth or glass or leaves. Modern architects also championed truth to materials by making visible the raw, structural elements of a building and arguing their aesthetic validity.

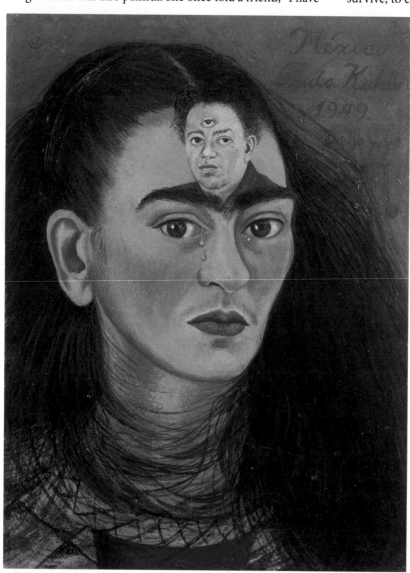

1 in.

1-7 FRIDA KAHLO. *Diego in My Thoughts (Diego y yo)* (1949). Oil on canvas, mounted on Masonite. 24" × 36". Collection of Mary-Anne Martin/Fine Arts, NY. © 2011 Banco de México Diego Rivera Frida Kahlo Museums Trust, Mexico, D.F./Artists Rights Society (ARS), NY.

[2] Martha Zamora, *Frida Kahlo: The Brush of Anguish* (San Francisco: Chronicle Books, 1990), 37.
[3] M. Nuridsany, *China Art Now* (Paris: Flammarion, 2004), 114.

1 in.

1-9 ANDY WARHOL. *Four Marilyns* (1962). Synthetic polymer paint and silkscreen ink on canvas. 30" × 23⅞". © 2011 The Andy Warhol Foundation for the Visual Arts/ Artists Rights Society (ARS), NY.

ART, IMMORTALITY, AND GLORY

In the face of certain death, an artist such as Robert Mapplethorpe can defy mortality by creating a work that will keep his talents and his tragedy in the public's consciousness for decades. Human beings are the only species conscious of death, and for millennia they have used art to overleap the limits of this life.

In *Four Marilyns* (Fig. 1-9), Pop artist Andy Warhol participated in the cultural immortalization of a film icon of the 1960s by reproducing a well-known photograph of Monroe on canvas. Proclaimed a "sex symbol" of the silver screen, she rapidly rose to fame and shocked her fans by taking her own life at an early age. In the decades since Monroe's death, her image is still found on posters and calendars, books and songs are still written about her, and the public's appetite for information about her early years and romances remains insatiable. In other renderings, Warhol arranged multiple images of the star as if lined up on supermarket shelves, commenting, perhaps, on the ways in which contemporary flesh peddlers have packaged and sold her—in death as well as in life.

The lines between life and death, between place and time, are temporarily dissolved in the renowned

1 in.

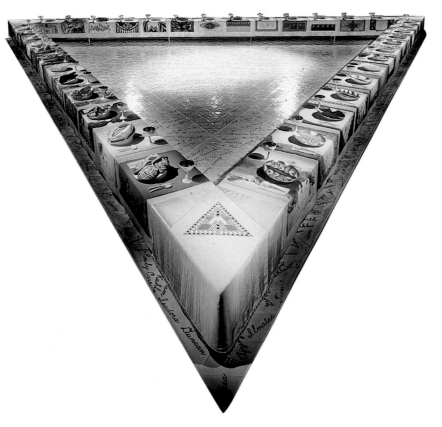

1-10 JUDY CHICAGO. *The Dinner Party* (1974–1979). Painted porcelain and needlework. 48' × 48' × 48' × 3'. Brooklyn Museum, Brooklyn, NY. © 2011 Judy Chicago/Artists Rights Society (ARS), NY.

1-11 Column of Trajan, Forum of Trajan, dedicated 112 CE. 128' high. Rome, Italy.

installation *The Dinner Party* (Fig. **1-10**) by feminist artist Judy Chicago. The idea for this multimedia work, which was constructed to honor and immortalize history's notable women, revolves around a fantastic dinner party, where the guests of honor meet before place settings designed to reflect their personalities and accomplishments. Chicago and numerous other women artists have invested much energy in alerting the public to the significant role of women in the arts and society.

The desire to immortalize often goes hand in hand with the desire to glorify. Some of art history's wealthiest patrons, from the Caesars of ancient Rome and the Vatican's popes to emperors around the world, commissioned artists to create works that glorified their reigns and accomplishments. The Roman emperor Trajan's tomb (Fig. **1-11**), 128 feet high, is covered with a continuous spiral relief that recounts his victories in military campaigns in great detail. Centuries later, the French would adapt this design for a column erected to glorify the victories of the emperor Napoleon Bonaparte.

In China during the early third century BCE, the first emperor of Qin prepared a tomb (Fig. **1-12**) for himself that was filled not only with treasure, but also with facsimiles of more than 6,000 soldiers and horses, along with bronze chariots. The site, which is still being excavated, was probably

1-12 Terra-cotta warriors. Pit No. 1 (Han Dynasty c. 210 BCE). Museum of the First Emperor Qin, Shaanxi Province, China.

intended to recreate the emperor's lavish palace. The sheer manpower that was necessary to create the imperial funerary monument—literally thousands of workers and artists—is a testament to the emperor's wealth, power, and ambition.

ART AND RELIGION

The quest for immortality is the bedrock of organized religion. From the cradle of civilization to the contemporary era, from Asia to the Americas, and from the Crimea to the Cameroon, human beings across time and cultures have sought answers to the unanswerable and have salved their souls with belief in life after death. In the absence of physical embodiments for the deities they fashioned, humans developed art forms to visually render the unseen. Often the physical attributes granted to their

gods were a reflection of humans. It has been said, for example, that the Greeks made their men into gods and their gods into men. In other societies, deities were often represented as powerful and mysterious animals, or composite men-beasts. Ritual and ceremony grew alongside the establishment of religions and the representation of deities, in actual or symbolic form. Until modern times, one could probably study the history of art in terms of works expressing religious values alone.

The *North Wind Mask* (*Negakfok*) (Fig. **1-13**), is one of a series of masks from the Yup'ik speaking Inuit of western Alaska, worn during rituals designed to mediate the spirit world—in this case the spirits of the north, east, and south winds—and the human and animal worlds. Dancers, adorned with such masks and elaborate costumes, were believed to be transformed into spirits. The spirit of the north wind is associated with snowstorms and frigid cold temperatures. White spots painted on the mask may allude to snowflakes; the sound created by the clanking of the wood pieces that hang from the mask suggests the whooshing of cold winds.

Another artist of color, Aaron Douglas, translated a biblical story into a work that speaks to the African American

1-13 *North Wind Mask* (*Negakfok*) (early 20th century). Wood, paint, and feathers. 45¼" × 21⅜" × 17⅞". The Michael C. Rockefeller Memorial Collection, Purchase, Nelson A. Rockefeller Gift, 1961 (1978.412.76a, b). The Metropolitan Museum of Art, NY. © The Metropolitan Museum of Art.

1-14 AARON DOUGLAS. *Noah's Ark* (c. 1927). Oil on Masonite. 48" × 36".

Muhammad petitioned God to reduce the number of obligatory daily prayers from fifty to five. Gabriel is the central figure, identified by his wings and intricate apparel. Moses is shown on the left, standing next to a throne, and Muhammad stands to the right in a green tunic. His face, in compliance with proscriptions for representing the Prophet, appears blocked out in white. Muslims believe that Abraham was the first prophet, that Jesus was also a prophet, and that Muhammad was the last prophet, completing God's revelation.

ART AND IDEOLOGY

Throughout history, works of art have been used to create or reinforce ideology. Defined as an organized collection of ideas, ideologies articulate the way societies look at things. These ideas spring from commonly held beliefs or are imposed on members of society by ruling or dominant classes. The degree

sensibility. In his *Noah's Ark* (Fig. **1-14**), one of seven paintings based on James Weldon Johnson's book *God's Trombones: Seven Negro Sermons in Verse*, Douglas expressed a powerful vision of the great flood. Animals enter the ark in pairs as lightning flashes about them, and the sky turns a hazy gray purple with the impending storm. African men, rendered in rough-hewn profile, ready the ark and direct the action in a dynamically choreographed composition that takes possession of and personalizes the biblical event for Douglas's race and culture.

Traditions in Islamic art vary, reflecting regional styles, different eras, and the embracing or prohibition of representational imagery. For the Islamic artist, expression of religious beliefs can be seen in simple yet elegant calligraphic renderings of sacred text or, as in the miniature depicting Muhammad with Moses and the angel Gabriel (Fig. **1-15**), a narrative of significance in the life of the Prophet. The exquisitely painted miniature depicts a vision of Muhammad in which he is led through seven heavens by Gabriel. On this journey he meets Moses, who asks Muhammad about his prayer obligations to God. It is written in the Qur'an—the Muslim holy book—that, upon Moses' recommendation,

1-15 *Prophets Moses and Muhammad with the Angel Gabriel.* Miniature. 12¼" × 8¹⁄₁₆". Museum of Islamic Art, Berlin, Germany.

1 ft.

1-16 MASACCIO. *Expulsion from the Garden of Eden* (c. 1424–1428). Fresco. 7' × 2' 11". Brancacci Chapel, Santa Maria del Carmine, Florence, Italy.

1-17 SUZANNE VALADON. *Adam and Eve* (1909). Oil on canvas. 6⅓" × 5⅛". Musee National d'Art Moderne, Centre Georges Pompidou, Paris, France.

to which an ideology is perpetuated depends on the degree to which members of a society subscribe to it.

When it comes to ideology, sometimes images speak louder than words. Think of representations of Adam and Eve. Every time you see Eve tempting Adam with an apple, you are witnessing the representation of an ideology in art, in this case that Eve (and, by extension, women in general) was responsible for humankind's fall from grace and loss of paradise. For hundreds of years, Christianity perpetuated a negative view of women based on this ideological position. Masaccio's fifteenth-century version of the expulsion from the Garden of Eden (Fig. 1-16) illustrates the distraught first couple being forcibly cast into the wilderness at swordpoint. Adam holds his head in his hands, shielding his eyes while Eve, her head thrown back in desperate weeping, covers her body in shame. It is as if the artist is suggesting, in these gestures, that Adam's was a sin of the mind (he made a decision to succumb to temptation) whereas Eve's was a sin of the flesh (her uncontrolled passion and weakness led to their predicament). In the twentieth century, Suzanne Valadon subverted the traditional assignment of blame and guilt in a new version of the story of Eden in which Adam appears to lead Eve's hand toward the apple (Fig. 1-17). His body parts, not hers, are covered in shame by a strategically placed vine.

ART AND FANTASY

Art also serves as a vehicle by which artists can express their innermost fantasies. Whereas some have labored to reconstruct reality and commemorate actual experiences, others have used art to give vent to their imaginary inner lives. There are many types of fantasies, such as those found in dreams and daydreams or simply the objects and landscapes that are conceived in the imagination. The French painter Odilon Redon once said that there is "a kind of drawing which the imagination has liberated from any concern with the details of reality in order to allow it to serve freely for the representation of things conceived" in the mind. In an attempt to cap-

ture the inner self, many twentieth-century artists looked to the psychoanalytic writings of Sigmund Freud and Carl Jung, who suggested that primeval forces are at work in the unconscious reaches of the mind. These artists sought to use their art as an outlet for these unconscious forces, as we shall see in Chapters 20 and 21.

1 ft.

1-18 MARC CHAGALL. *I and the Village* (1911). Oil on canvas. 6'3⅝" × 4'11⅝".
The Museum of Modern Art, NY.

1 ft.

1-19 MAX BECKMANN. *The Dream* (1921). Oil on canvas. 73⅛" × 35".
The Saint Louis Art Museum, Saint Louis, MO.

1-20 BARBARA KRUGER. *Money Makes Money and a Rich Man's Jokes Are Always Funny, and You Want It. You Need It. You Buy It. You Forget It.* (2010). Guild Hall, East Hampton, NY.

Marc Chagall's self-portrait *I and the Village* (Fig. **1-18**) provides a fragmented image of the artist among fantasized objects that seem to float in and out of one another. Fleeting memories of life in his Russian village are assembled like so many pieces of a dreamlike puzzle, reflecting the fragmentary nature of memory. Chagall's world is a happy, though private, one; the strange juxtaposition of images is reconciled only in the artist's own mind.

A similar process of fragmentation and juxtaposition was employed by German artist Max Beckmann in *The Dream* (Fig. **1-19**), but with a very different effect. The suggestion of space and atmosphere in Chagall's painting has given way to a claustrophobic room in which figures are compressed into a zigzag group. The soft, rolling hills and curving lines that gave the village painting its pleasant, dreamy quality have been forfeited for harsh, angular shapes and deformations. Horror hides in every nook and cranny, from the amputated and bandaged hands of the man in red stripes to the blinded street musician and maimed harlequin. Are these marionettes from some dark comedy or human puppets locked in a world of manipulation and hopelessness?

ART, INTELLECT, AND EMOTION

Art has the power to make us think profoundly, to make us feel deeply. Beautiful or controversial works in all mediums can trigger many associations for us: gazing at a landscape painting may remind us of a vacation past, puzzling over a work of geometric abstraction may bring back memories of tenth-grade math, or a quilt may have the power to evoke family ties and traditions. It is almost impossible to truly confront a work and remain unaffected. Art can ask us to consider our definitions of self and the world. Art can demand us to consider and reconsider our preconceived notions of the definition and parameters of art. Art and idea, it seems, are inseparable. Yet sometimes they are purposefully separated to great effect.

Consider Barbara Kruger's installation of graphic text on the walls and ceiling of East Hampton's Guild Hall in the summer of 2010 (Fig. **1-20**). As an example of **conceptual art**, it prioritizes the *idea* of the work over the object, emphasizing the artist's thinking and often de-emphasizing traditional artistic techniques. The visual aspect of Kruger's text relates to the billboards, magazines, and commercial advertising that saturate our cultural landscape and remind us of the constant media bombardment in our lives. The work forces us to think about the impersonal information systems of our era and the degree to which we are affected by their subliminal messages. In this piece, Kruger asks the viewer to think about the cult of materialism and the adage "Money talks." The scale of the type and almost claustrophobic installation make confronting ourselves, our morals, and our way of life inescapable.

ART, ORDER, AND HARMONY

Artists and scientists have been intrigued by, and have ventured to discover and describe, the underlying order of nature. The Classical Greeks fine-polished the rough edges of nature by applying mathematical formulas to the human figure to perfect it; the nineteenth-century painter Paul Cézanne once remarked that all of nature could be reduced to the cylinder, the sphere, and the cone.

One of the most perfect expressions of order and harmony is found in the fragile Japanese rock garden (Fig. **1-21**). Also known as "dry landscape," they are frequently part of a pavilion complex and are tended by the practitioners of **Zen**, a Buddhist sect that seeks inner harmony through introspection and meditation. The gentle, raked pattern of the stones symbolizes water and rocks, with mountains reaching heavenward. Such gardens do not invite the observer to mill about; their perfection precludes walking. They are microcosms, really—universes unto themselves.

When can order pose a threat to harmony and psychological well-being? Perhaps this is the question that Laurie Simmons set out to answer in her color photograph called *Red Library #2* (Fig. **1-22**). Here, in a compulsively organized library, where nothing is a hair out of place, a robotlike woman assesses her job well done. She has become one with her task; even her dress, hair, and skin match the decor.

1-22 LAURIE SIMMONS. *Red Library #2* (1983). Color photograph. 48½" × 38¼".

1 ft.

1-21 Ryogintel Rock Garden, Kyoto, Japan.

THE *PIANO LESSON*(S) BY MATISSE AND BEARDEN

FREQUENTLY AN ARTIST WILL USE COMPOSITION, or the arrangement of elements, to impose order. In Henri Matisse's *Piano Lesson* (Fig. **1-23**), every object, every color, every line seems to be placed to lead the eye around the canvas. The pea green wedge of drapery at the window is repeated in the shape of the metronome atop the piano, the wrought-iron grillwork at the window is complemented by the curvilinear lines of the music desk, and the enigmatic figure in the upper-right background finds her counterpart in a small sculpture placed diagonally across the canvas. Through contrast and repetition, unity within the diversity is achieved. The painting exudes solitude, resulting from the regularity of the compositional elements more than the atmosphere in the room. The boy's face appears quite tense, in fact, under the watchful eye of the seated woman behind him.

With Matisse's painting in mind, does Romare Bearden's *Piano Lesson* (Fig. **1-24**) appear then to be an example of disharmony, of disorder? Certainly it is a cacophony of shapes, lines, and unpredictable vantage points. But as in Matisse's painting, color repetition draws the composition's disparate

1-24 ROMARE BEARDEN. *Piano Lesson* (1983). Oil with collage. 29" × 22". The Walter O. Evans Collections of African American Art, SCAD Museum of Art, Savannah, GA. Art © Romare Bearden Foundation/Licensed by VAGA, NY.

1-23 HENRI MATISSE. *Piano Lesson* (1916). Oil on canvas. 8'½" × 6'11¾". The Museum of Modern Art, NY. © 2011 Succession H. Matisse/Artists Rights Society (ARS), NY.

parts together—the red of the background is balanced by the touches of red in the costumes of the figures up front; an undulating green strip on the piano is echoed in the billowing green drapes beyond. Ironically, there seems to be a more genuine feeling of serenity, despite the jumbled atmosphere. Is it because Matisse's seated woman—not touching? not feeling?—has a more flesh-and-blood counterpart in Bearden's work—a teacher? a mother?—who guides the young girl with the loving placement of a hand on her shoulder? When seen side by side, these paintings convey two different experiences. Matisse's piano student seems a product of his surroundings, a child of privilege partaking in an obligatory cultural ritual. Bearden's student, an African American girl in an apartment decorated catch-as-catch-can, seems to be breaking the bonds of her surroundings through the transcendence of music. ●

ART AND CHAOS

Just as beauty has its dark side and the intellect is balanced by the emotion, so, too, do order and harmony presume the existence of chaos. Artists have portrayed chaos in many ways throughout the history of art, seeking analogies in apocalyptic events such as war, famine, or natural catastrophe. But chaos can be suggested even in the absence of specific content. In *Eclipse* (Fig. **1-25**), without reference to nature or reality, Native American artist Jaune Quick-to-See Smith creates an agitated, chaotic atmosphere of color, line, shape, and movement. The artist grew up on the Flathead Indian reservation in Montana and uses a full vocabulary of Native American geometric motifs and organic images from the rich pictorial culture of her ancestors.

1-26 LOUISA CHASE. *Storm* (1981). Oil on canvas. 90" × 120". Denver Art Museum, Denver, CO.

1-25 JAUNE QUICK-TO-SEE SMITH. *Eclipse* (1987). Oil on canvas. 60" × 60". Flomenhaft Gallery, NY.

ART, EXPERIENCE, AND MEMORY

From humanity's earliest days, art has been used to record and communicate experiences and events. From prehistoric cave paintings, thought to record significant events in the history of Paleolithic societies, to a work such as the Vietnam Memorial in Washington, D.C.—installed in honor of American service personnel who died during this country's involvement in that war—art has been used to inform future generations of what and who have gone before them. Art also conveys the personal experiences of an artist in ways that words cannot.

American painter Louisa Chase was inspired to paint nature's unbridled power as revealed in waves, waterfalls, and thunderstorms, although the intensity of her subjects is often tempered by her own presence in the piece. In *Storm* (Fig. **1-26**), a cluster of thick, black clouds lets go a torrent of rain, which, in league with the decorative **palette** of pinks and purples, turns an artificial blue. The highly charged images on the left side of the canvas are balanced on the right by the most delicate of ferns, spiraling upward, nourished by the downpour. Beneath the sprig, the artist's hand cups the raindrops, becoming part of the painting and part of nature's event as well. Chase said of a similar storm painting, "During the [marking] process I do become the storm—lost—yet not lost. An amazing feeling of losing myself yet remaining totally conscious."[4]

The photographer Alfred Stieglitz, who recognized the medium as a fine art as well as a tool for recording events, happened upon the striking composition of *The Steerage* (Fig. **1-27**) on an Atlantic crossing aboard the *Kaiser Wilhelm II*. He rushed to his cabin for his camera, hoping that the upper and lower masses of humanity would maintain their balanced relationships to one another, to the drawbridge that divides the scene, to the stairway, the funnel, and the horizontal beam of the mast. The "steerage" of a ship

was the least expensive accommodation. Here the "huddled masses" seem suspended in limbo by machinery and by symbolic as well as actual bridges. Yet the tenacious human spirit may best be symbolized by the jaunty patch of light that strikes the straw hat of one passenger on the upper deck. Stieglitz was utterly fascinated and moved by what he saw.

More than 80 years after Stieglitz captured the great hope of immigrants entering New York harbor, African American artist Faith Ringgold tells the story of life and dreams on a tar-covered rooftop. *Tar Beach* (Fig. **1-28**) is a painted patchwork quilt that stitches together the artist's memories of family, friends, and feelings while growing up in Harlem. Ringgold is noted for her use of materials and techniques associated

[4] Louisa Chase, journal entry for February 20, 1984, in *Louisa Chase* (New York: Robert Miller Gallery, 1984).

1-27 ALFRED STIEGLITZ. *The Steerage* (1907). Photograph. 12 11/16" × 10 3/16".

1-28 FAITH RINGGOLD. *Tar Beach* (1988). Acrylic paint on canvas and pieced fabric. 74" × 68½". Solomon R. Guggenheim Museum, NY.

with women's traditions as well as her use of narrative or storytelling, a strong tradition in African American families. A large, painted square with images of Faith, her brother, her parents, and her neighbors dominates the quilt and is framed with brightly patterned pieces of fabric. Along the top and bottom are inserts crowded with Ringgold's written description of her experiences. This wonderfully innocent and joyful monologue begins:

> I will always remember when the stars fell down around me and lifted me up above the George Washington Bridge . . .

ART AND THE SOCIAL AND CULTURAL CONTEXT

Faith Ringgold's *Tar Beach* tells us the story of a young girl growing up in Harlem. Her experiences take place within a specific social and cultural context. In recording experi- ence, artists frequently record the activities and objects of their times and places, reflecting contemporary fashions and beliefs, as well as the states of the crafts and sciences.

The architecture, hairstyles, hats, and shoulder pads, and even the price of cigars (only five cents), all set Edward Hopper's *Nighthawks* (Fig. **1-29**) in an unmistakably Ameri- can city during the late 1930s or 1940s. The subject is com- monplace and uneventful, though somewhat eerie. There is a tension between the desolate spaces of the vacant street and the corner diner. Familiar objects become distant. The warm patch of artificial light seems precious, even precarious, as if night and all its troubled symbols are threatening to break in on disordered lives. Hopper uses a specific sociocultural context to communicate an unsettling, introspective mood of aloneness, of being outside the mainstream of experience.

In Richard Hamilton's *Just What Is It That Makes Today's Homes So Different, So Appealing?* (Fig. **1-30**), the aims are identical, but the result is self-mocking, upbeat, and alto- gether fun. This little collage functions as a veritable time cap- sule for the 1950s, a decade during which the speedy advance

1 ft.

1-29 EDWARD HOPPER. *Nighthawks* (1942). Oil on canvas. 30" × 60". The Art Institute of Chicago, Chicago, IL.

of technology finds everyone buying pieces of the American dream. What is that dream? Comic books, TVs, movies, and tape recorders; canned hams and TV dinners; enviable physiques, Tootsie Pops, vacuum cleaners that finally let the "lady of the house" clean all the stairs at once. Hamilton's piece serves as a memento of the time and the place and the values of the decade for future generations.

We more commonly think of visual art (painting and sculpture, for example) when we consider the connection between art and social or cultural context, but art history is full of examples of architecture that reflect or embody the ideas or beliefs of a people at a point in time. Think of the Parthenon in Classical Athens or Chartres Cathedral in the Middle Ages. Symbolism is often disguised in architecture, but sometimes it is the essence of its design. Zaha Hadid's Sheikh Zayed Bridge (Fig. **1-31**), connecting Abu Dhabi island to the mainland, is composed of sweeping, irregular rhythms of arches. Hadid has acknowledged the influence of Arabic calligraphy on the flowing forms of her structures, but in this work, the arches—

1 in.

1-30 RICHARD HAMILTON. *Just What Is It That Makes Today's Homes So Different, So Appealing?* (1956). Collage. 10¼" × 9¾". Kunsthalle Tübingen, Tübingen, Germany.

1-31 ZAHA HADID. Sheikh Zayed Bridge, 2006. Abu Dhabi, United Arab Emirates.

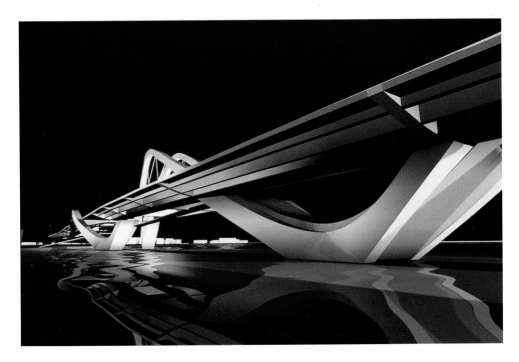

each different from one another in height and span—reflect the dunes of the nearby topography, thus connecting it (metaphorically and literally) to a specific place and time.

ART AND SOCIAL CONSCIOUSNESS

As other people have, artists have taken on bitter struggles against the injustices of their times and have tried to persuade others to join them in their causes, and it has been natural for them to use their creative skills to do so.

The nineteenth-century Spanish painter Francisco Goya used his art to satirize the political foibles of his day and to condemn the horrors of war (see Fig. 19-6). In the twentieth century another Spanish painter, Pablo Picasso, would condemn war in his masterpiece *Guernica* (see Fig. 20-9).

Goya's French contemporary Eugène Delacroix painted the familiar image of *Liberty Leading the People* (Fig. 1-32) in order to keep the spirit of the French Revolution alive in 1830. In this painting, people of all classes are united in rising up against injustice, led onward by an allegorical figure of liberty. Rifles, swords, a flag—even pistols—join in an upward rhythm, underscoring the pyramid shape of the composition.

Suzanne Lacy and Leslie Labowitz's performance *In Mourning and in Rage* (Fig. 1-33) was a carefully orchestrated media

1 ft.

1-32 EUGÈNE DELACROIX. *Liberty Leading the People* (1830). Oil on canvas. 8'6" × 10'10". Louvre, Paris, France.

1-33 SUZANNE LACY AND LESLIE LABOWITZ. *In Mourning and in Rage* (1977). Performance at Los Angeles City Hall, Los Angeles, CA.

1-34 BETYE SAAR. *The Liberation of Aunt Jemima* (1972). Mixed media. 11¾" × 8" × 2¾". University of California, Berkeley Art Museum, Berkeley, CA.

event reminiscent of ancient public rituals. Members of feminist groups donned black robes to commemorate women who had been victims of rape-murders and to protest the shoddy media coverage usually given to such tragedies.

Millions of us have grown up with a benevolent, maternal Aunt Jemima. She has graced packages of pancake mix and bottles of maple syrup for generations. How many of us have really thought about what she symbolizes? Artists such as African American artist Betye Saar have been doubly offended by Aunt Jemima's state of servitude, which harks not only to the days of slavery but also to the suffocating traditional domestic role of the female. Sharon F. Patton notes:

> *The Liberation of Aunt Jemima* subverts the black mammy stereotype of the black American woman: a heavy, dark-skinned maternal figure, of smiling demeanor. This stereotype, started in the nineteenth century, was still popular culture's favorite representation of the African-American woman. She features in Hollywood films and notably as the advertising and packaging image for Pillsbury's "Aunt Jemima's Pancake Mix."[5]

The Aunt Jemima in Betye Saar's *The Liberation of Aunt Jemima* (Fig. **1-34**) is revised to reflect the quest for liberation from servitude and the stereotype. She holds a broomstick in one hand but a rifle in the other. Before her stands a portrait with a small white child violated by a clenched black fist representing the symbol of Black

1 in.

[5] Sharon F. Patton, *African-American Art* (New York: Oxford University Press, 1998), 201.

1-35 MIRIAM SCHAPIRO. *Wonderland* (1983). Acrylic and fabric collage on canvas. 90" × 144". Smithsonian American Art Museum, Washington, D.C.

Power. The image of the liberated Aunt Jemima confronts viewers and compels them to cast off the stereotypes that lead to intolerance.

ART AND POPULAR CULTURE

Have you come across embroidered dish towels or aprons with the words *God Bless Our Happy Home* or *I Hate Housework*? Miriam Schapiro's *Wonderland* (Fig. **1-35**) is a collage that reflects her "femmage" aesthetic—her interest in depicting women's domestic culture. The work contains ordinary doilies, needlework, crocheted aprons, handkerchiefs, and quilt blocks, all anchored to a geometric patterned background that is augmented with brushstrokes of paint. In the center is the most commonplace of the commonplace: an embroidered image of a housewife who curtsies beneath the legend "Welcome to Our Home."

Some of the more interesting elevations of the commonplace to the realm of art are found in the **readymades** and **assemblages** of twentieth-century artists. Marcel Duchamp's

1-36 MARCEL DUCHAMP. *Fountain* (1917). 1951 version after lost original. Porcelain urinal. 24" high. © 2011 Artists Rights Society (ARS), NY/ADAGP, Paris/Succession Marcel Duchamp.

Fountain (Fig. **1-36**) is a urinal, turned upside down and labeled. Pablo Picasso's *Bull's Head* (see Fig. 9-15) is fashioned from the seat and handlebars of an old bicycle. In **Pop Art**, the dependence on commonplace objects and visual clichés reaches a peak. Prepared foods, soup and beer cans, and media images of beautiful women and automobile accidents became the subject matter of Pop Art. As we saw in Figures 1-9 and 1-30, Pop Art impels us to cast a more critical eye on the symbols and objects with which we surround ourselves.

ART AND DECORATION

We have all decided at one time or another to change the color of our bedrooms. We have hung a poster or painting here rather than there, and we have arranged a vase of flowers or placed a potted plant in just the right spot in the room. We may not have created works of art, but we did manage to delight our senses and turn our otherwise ordinary environments into more pleasurable havens.

Works of art have been used to create pleasing environments for centuries. From tapestries that adorned and insulated the cold stone walls of medieval castles to elaborate sculpted fountains that provided focal points for manicured, palatial gardens, whatever other functions they may serve, many works of art are also decorative. Joyce Kozloff's *Galla Placidia in Philadelphia* (Fig. **1-37**), a mosaic for the Penn Center Suburban Station in that city, elevates decorative patterns to the level of fine art and raises the art-historical consciousness of the casual commuter. The original Mausoleum of Galla Placidia is the fifth-century chapel and burial place of a Byzantine empress, a landmark monument known for its complex and colorful mosaics. Kozloff's own intricate and diverse designs dazzle the eye and stimulate

1 ft.

1-37 JOYCE KOZLOFF. *Galla Placidia in Philadelphia* (1985). Mosaic installation. 13' × 16'. Penn Center Suburban Station, Philadelphia, PA.

the intellect, providing an oasis of color in an otherwise humdrum city scene.

Glass sculptor Dale Chihuly's *Fiori di Como* (Fig. **1-38**) is a 70-foot-long ceiling installation suspended above the reception area of the Bellagio Hotel in Las Vegas. Even in a city of neon and assorted trappings of excess, Chihuly's piece dazzles with its colors and textures. Reminiscent of the undulating shapes and brilliant palette of Venice's renowned Murano glass, it is another set piece in the hotel's interior decor that is intended to transport its guests to that famed small town of Bellagio on the shore of Italy's spectacular Lake Como.

ART AND THE NEEDS OF THE ARTIST

Artists may have special talents and perceptive qualities, but they are also people with needs and the motivation to meet those needs. Psychologists speak of the need for *self-actualization*—that is, the need to fulfill one's unique potential. Self-actualizing people have needs for novelty, exploration, and understanding; they also have aesthetic needs for art, beauty, and order. Under perfect circumstances, art permits the individual to meet needs for achievement or self-actualization and, at the same time, to earn a living.

1-38 DALE CHIHULY. *Fiori di Como* (1998). 70' × 30' × 12'. Bellagio Resort, Las Vegas, NV.

1-39 JOSÉ CLEMENTE OROZCO. *Epic of American Civilization: Hispano-America* (c. 1932–1934). Fresco. 10' × 9'11". Hood Museum of Art, Hanover, NH. © 2011 Artists Rights Society (ARS), NY/SOMAAP, Mexico City.

1 ft.

Murals such as José Clemente Orozco's *Epic of American Civilization: Hispano-America* (Fig. **1-39**) were created for a branch of the Works Progress Administration (WPA), a federal work-relief program intended to help people in the United States, including artists, survive the Great Depression. The WPA made it possible for many artists to meet basic survival needs while continuing to work, and be paid, as artists. Scores of public buildings were decorated with murals or canvas paintings by artists in the Fine Arts Program (FAP) of the WPA. Some of them were among the best known of their generation. Orozco's epic also met another, personal need—the need to call attention to and express his outrage at what he believed to be financial and military injustices imposed on Mexican peasants.

Creating works of art that are accepted by one's audience can lead to an artist's social acceptance and recognition. But sometimes art really is created only to meet the needs of the artist and nothing beyond—with no thought to sale, exhibition, review, or recognition. Such is the story of *outsider art*, a catchall category that has been used for works by untrained artists; self-taught artists who have been incarcerated for committing crimes and who use the circumstances of their isolation as a motive for creating; and people who are psychologically compromised and sometimes institutionalized. Works of art by these individuals and others like them are often *not* intended to be seen. Thus, in the purest sense, they come into existence to meet some essential emotional or psychological need of the artist and the artist alone.

1-40 SIMON RODIA. *Simon Rodia Towers in Watts* (1921–1954). Cement with various objects. 98' high. Cultural Affairs Department, Los Angeles, CA.

The sculptural environment known as the *Simon Rodia Towers in Watts* (Fig. **1-40**) was constructed by an Italian-born tile setter who immigrated to Watts, a poor neighborhood in Los Angeles. Rodia's whimsical towers of cement on steel frames rise to nearly 100 feet and are encrusted with debris such as mirror fragments, broken dishes, shards of glass and ceramic tile, and shells. The result is a lacy forest of spires that glisten with magical patterns of contrasting and harmonious colors. The towers took 33 years to erect and were built by Rodia's own hands. He knew nearly nothing of the world of art and, when asked why he undertook the endeavor, said "I wanted to do something big and I did it."

VISUAL ELEMENTS OF ART

2

The language of art is the language of our visual and tactile experiences in the world, and the words or vocabulary of this language consist of the visual elements of *line, shape, light, value, color, texture, space, time,* and *motion.* Line can define shape; light can reveal it. Color can describe the world we see around us and reveal the psychological worlds within us; we are blue with sorrow, red with rage. Texture is linked with all the emotion of touching, with the cold sharpness of rock or the yielding sensations of flesh. We exist in space; we occupy space and space envelops us. Time allows us to develop into what we are capable of being; time ultimately takes from us what we have been. We are all in motion through space, in a solar system that is traversing the rim of our galaxy at thousands of miles per second, or rotating on the surface of our own globe at a thousand miles per hour. Yet it is the smaller motion—the motion of lifting an arm or of riding through a field—that we are more likely to sense and hence to represent in art.

This vocabulary—*line, shape, light, value, color, texture, space, time,* and *motion*—comprises what we call the **visual elements** or **plastic elements** of art. Artists select from a variety of mediums, including, but by no means limited to, drawing, painting, sculpture, architecture, photography, textiles, and ceramics. They then employ the visual elements of art to express themselves in the chosen medium. In their self-expression, they use these elements to design compositions of a certain style, form, and content.

View of *Tall Tree and the Eye* by Anish Kapoor at the Guggenheim Museum, Bilbao, Spain.

Visual elements, design, style, form, and content—these make up the language of art. Languages such as English and French have symbols—words—that are combined according to rules of grammar to create a message. The visual arts have a "vocabulary" of visual elements that are combined according to the "grammar" of art, or principles of design. These principles include unity, balance, rhythm, scale, and proportion, among others. The composition of the elements creates the style, form, and content of the work—even if this content is an abstract image and not a natural subject, such as a human figure or a landscape. In this chapter, we explore the basic vocabulary or visual elements in the language of art.

LINE

Line is at once the simplest and most complex of the elements of art. It serves as a basic building block around which an art form is constructed and, by itself, has the capacity to evoke thought and emotion. In geometry, we learn that line is made up of an infinite number of points and that the shortest distance between two points is a straight line. In art, a line is more commonly defined as a moving dot.

Characteristics of Line

MEASURE OF LINE The **measure** of a line is its length and its width. If we conceptualize line as a moving dot, the dots that compose it can be of any size, creating a line of lesser or greater width, and of any number, creating a shorter or a longer line.

Sol LeWitt's *Lines from Four Corners to Points on a Grid* (Fig. **2-1**) consists of lines whose measures are precise and carefully plotted. Both the concept of their placement and the act of measuring to create exact mathematical relationships are intrinsic to the work and define it. LeWitt's installations are temporary and can be reproduced by permission of the owner of the instructions, in this case The Whitney Museum of American Art. Because the artist's relationship to his work begins and ends in a set of instructions, the actual implementation of the work can vary from one embodiment to another. Much Conceptual Art, of which this is an exam-

2-1 SOL LEWITT. *Lines from Four Corners to Points on a Grid* (1976), detail. A 6-inch grid covering each of four black walls. White lines to points on grids. First wall: 24 lines from the center; second wall: 12 lines from the midpoint of each of the sides; third wall: 12 lines from each corner; fourth wall: 24 lines from the center; 12 lines from the midpoint of each of the sides, 12 lines from each corner. White crayon lines and black crayon grid on black walls. Dimensions variable. Whitney Museum of American Art, NY.

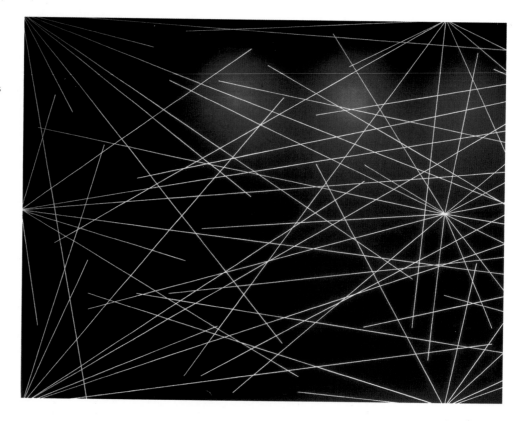

ple, challenges our notions of whether an artist is obligated to create the physical work of art to be its author or whether the idea of the work is sufficient.

By contrast, the notion of measuring the lengths of line that are both the subject and the process of Jackson Pollock's *Number 14: Gray* (Fig. **2-2**) seems ludicrous and incomprehensible. Pollock's lines weave and overlap and swell and pinch, creating a sense of infinite flow and freedom from constraint (where *constraint* is defined as logical and mathematical measurement). LeWitt's lines are precise; Pollock's are gestural, fluid, and loose. The effects of the LeWitt and the Pollock are very different. The LeWitt is static; the Pollock expands and contracts, shoots forward and recedes.

EXPRESSIVE QUALITIES OF LINE

The works by LeWitt and Pollock also reveal the expressive characteristics of line. Lines may be perceived as delicate, tentative, elegant, assertive, forceful, or even brutal. The lines in the LeWitt installation are assertive but cold. The emotional human element is missing. The work seems to express the human capacity to detach the intellect from emotional response, and perhaps to program computers (and other people) to carry out pre-

cise instructions. The lines in the Pollock work combine the apparently incongruous expressive qualities of delicacy and force. They are well rounded and human, combining intellect with passion. The LeWitt suggests the presence of a plan. The Pollock suggests the presence of a human being weaving elegantly through the complexities of thought and life.

TYPES OF LINE

The variety of line would seem to be as infinite as the number of points that, we are told, determine it. Lines can be straight or curved. They can be vertical, horizontal, or diagonal. A curved line can be circular or oval. It can run full circle to join itself where it began, thereby creating a complete shape. Curved lines can also be segments or arcs—parts of circles or ovals. As a line proceeds, it can change direction abruptly: A straight line that stops and changes course becomes a zigzag. A curved line that forms an arc and then reverses direction becomes wavy. Circular and oval lines that turn ever inward on themselves create vertiginous spirals. Art's most basic element is a tool of infinite variety.

Contour lines are created by the edges of things. They are perceived when three-dimensional shapes curve back into space. Edges are perceived because the objects differ from

2-2 JACKSON POLLOCK. *Number 14: Gray* (1948). Enamel and gesso on paper. 22¾" × 31". Yale University Art Gallery, New Haven, CT. © 2011 Pollock-Krasner Foundation/Artists Rights Society (ARS), NY.

1 in.

2-3 EDWARD WESTON. *Knees* (1927). Gelatin silver print. 6¼" × 9³⁄₁₆". San Francisco Museum of Modern Art, San Francisco, CA.

1 in.

the backgrounds in value (lighter versus darker), texture, or color. If you hold up your arm so that you perceive it against the wall (or, if you are outside, the sky), you will discriminate its edge—its contour line—because the wall is lighter or darker, because it differs from the wall in color, and because the texture of flesh differs from the wallboard or plaster or wood or brick of the wall.

Edward Weston's photograph *Knees* (Fig. **2-3**) highlights the aesthetic possibilities of contour lines. Weston was drawn to the sculptural forms of the human figure, plant life, and natural inanimate objects such as rocks. In *Knees*, the contour lines (edges) of the legs are created by the subtle differences in value (light and dark) and texture between the legs and the wall and the floor. The legs take on the abstract quality of an exercise to demonstrate how contour lines define the human form and how shading creates or *models* roundness.

Actual line can be distinguished from *implied line*. The points in **actual line** are connected and continuous. The LeWitt (Fig. 2-1) and Pollock (Fig. 2-2) are examples of works with actual line. Works with **implied line** are completed by

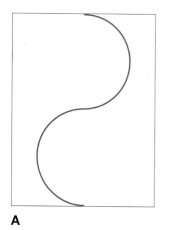

A

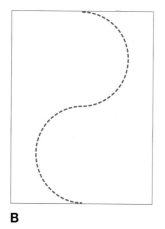

B

C

2-4 A, B, and C Actual line (A) versus two kinds of implied lines, one formed by dots (B) and the other formed by psychologically connecting the edges of a series of straight lines (C).

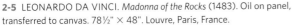

2-5 LEONARDO DA VINCI. *Madonna of the Rocks* (1483). Oil on panel, transferred to canvas. 78½" × 48". Louvre, Paris, France.

1 ft.

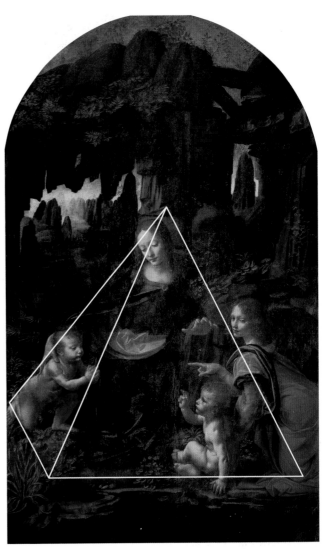

2-6 The pyramidal structure of the *Madonna of the Rocks*. Oil on panel, transferred to canvas. 78½" × 48". Louvre, Paris, France.

the viewer. An implied line can be a discontinuous line that the viewer reads as continuous because of the overall context of the image. Implied lines can be suggested by a series of points or dots, as in Part B of Figure **2-4**. They can be suggested by the nearby endpoints of series of parallel or nearly parallel lines of different lengths, as in Part C of Figure 2-4. The movements and glances of the figures in a composition also imply lines.

One of the hallmarks of Renaissance paintings is the use of implied lines to create or echo the structure of the composition. Geometric shapes such as triangles and circles are suggested through the use of linear patterns created by the position and physical gestures of the participants and, often,

glances between them. These shapes often serve as the central focus and the main organizational device of the compositions. In the *Madonna of the Rocks* (Fig. **2-5**), Leonardo da Vinci places the head of the Virgin Mary at the apex of a rather broad, stable pyramid formed not by actual lines but by the extension of her arms and the direction of her glance. The base of the pyramid is suggested by an implied line that joins the "endpoints" of the baby Jesus and the infant John the Baptist. Figure **2-6** highlights the pyramidal structure of the composition.

A mental or perceptual connection can create a **psychological line**. If a character in a painting points to an object, or if one figure gazes directly toward another—as in Emily

1 ft.

2-7 EMILY MARY OSBORN. *Nameless and Friendless* (1834–?). Oil on canvas. 34" × 44". Private Collection.

Mary Osborn's *Nameless and Friendless* (Fig. **2-7**)—we perceive the connection between the two as a psychological line, even though the artist has not created an actual or implied line. In Osborn's painting, which represents the plight of the woman artist, a small boy (her brother?) stares directly at the condescending art dealer as he feigns serious consideration of her work. The boy's unflinching glance and the dealer's face are visually connected with a psychological line. Another psychological line connects the downward face of the impoverished woman with the tip of her shoe, which emerges from the bottom of her long black skirt. She stands in judgment, fidgeting with the fringe of her shawl, not quite knowing where to look. Gestures and glances such as those in Osborn's work lead the viewer's eye around the composition. Therefore, psychological lines are also called compositional lines.

Functions of Line

The line, as an element of art, is alive with possibilities. Artists use line to outline shapes, to evoke forms and movement, to imply solid mass, or for its own sake. In groupings, lines can create shadows and even visual illusions.

TO OUTLINE AND SHAPE When you make or observe an outline, you are describing or suggesting the edge of a form or a shape. Line defines a shape or form as separate from its surrounding space; line gives birth to shape or form. Line grants them substance.

In addition to defining shape, line can also function as form itself. *Madonna and Child* (Fig. **2-8**) by Rimma Gerlovina and Valeriy Gerlovin is a revision of one of the most popular religious themes of the Renaissance. Taking their cue from works by artists such as Raphael, the Gerlovins use their signature combination of the body and braided hair to embroider a contemporary image of the Virgin Mary and the infant Jesus. The Gerlovins are the principal subjects of their work, and in this piece Gerlovina serves as the model for the Virgin. Braid extensions of her own sandy brown hair cascade from a sculptural head whose three-dimensionality stands in marked contrast to the flatness of the rippling braids. These braids flow into the contours of the Christ-child's body, nested in the palm of a sculpted hand.

TO CREATE DEPTH AND TEXTURE The face of Elizabeth Catlett's sturdy *Sharecropper* (Fig. **2-9**) is etched by a series of short, vigorous lines that are echoed in the atmosphere that surrounds her. The lines give the woman's features a gaunt, hollowed-out look and are also used to create a harsh texture in a turbulent environment. The textures of her garment, hair, and hat are also represented by series of lines.

1 ft.

2-8 RIMMA GERLOVINA AND VALERIY GERLOVIN. *Madonna and Child* (1992). 40" × 40". Chromogenic print. Collection of DZ Bank, Germany.

1 in.

2-9 ELIZABETH CATLETT. *Sharecropper* (1968). Color linocut. 26" × 22". Hampton University Museum, Hampton, VA. Art © Elizabeth Catlett/ Licensed by VAGA, NY.

A. Stippling

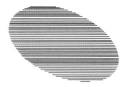

B. Hatching

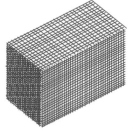

C. Cross-hatching

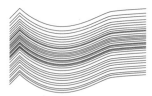

D. Contour hatching

2-10 Illusion of three-dimensionality.
Dots and lines can be used to create the illusion of three-dimensionality through shading. Part A shows the method of stippling, in which shading is represented by a pattern of dots that thickens and thins. Part B represents shading by means of hatching—that is, using a series of closely spaced parallel lines. Part C shows the method of cross-hatching, in which the series of lines intersects another series of lines. Part D shows how directional changes in hatching can define contours.

Modeling on a two-dimensional surface is the creation of the illusion of roundness or three dimensions through the use of light and shadow. As shown in Figure **2-10**, shadows can be created by the use of dots and lines. Part A shows the method of **stippling**, of using a pattern of dots that thickens and thins. Areas where the dots are thicker are darker and create the illusion of being more shaded. Part B shows the technique of **hatching**, or using a series of closely spaced parallel lines to achieve a similar effect. Areas in which lines are closer together appear to be more shaded. **Cross-hatching**, shown in Part C, is similar to hatching, but as the name implies, a series of lines run in different directions and cross one another.

Contours can be created when hatching changes direction, as in Part D. Notice how the sharecropper's face is carved by hatching that alters direction to give shape to the wells of the eyes, the nose, the lips, and the chin. Directional changes in hatching also define the prominent anatomic features of the sharecropper's neck.

TO SUGGEST DIRECTION AND MOVEMENT Renaissance artist Sandro Botticelli's *The Birth of Venus* (Fig. **2-11**) shows how line can be used to outline forms and evoke movement. In this painting, firm lines carve out the figures

1 ft.

2-11 SANDRO BOTTICELLI. *The Birth of Venus* (c. 1482). Tempera on canvas. 5'8⅞" × 9'1⅞". Galleria degli Uffizi, Florence, Italy.

1 in.

2-12 JACOB LAWRENCE. *Harriet Tubman Series, No. 4* (1939–1940). Casein tempera on gessoed hardboard. 12" × 17⅞". Hampton University Museum, Hampton, VA.

from the rigid horizontal of the horizon and the verticals of the trees. Straight lines carry the breath of the Zephyr from the left, and the curved lines of the drapery imply the movement of the Zephyrs and of the nymph to the right. Implied compositional lines give this work an overall triangular structure.

Horizontal lines, like horizon lines, suggest stability. Vertical lines, like the sweeping verticals in skyscrapers, defy gravity and suggest assertiveness. Diagonal lines are often used to imply movement and directionality, as in the directionality and movement of the breath of the Zephyr in *The Birth of Venus*. African American artist Jacob Lawrence used assertive sticklike diagonals to give the slave children in his painting *Harriet Tubman Series, No. 4* (Fig. **2-12**) a powerful sense of movement and directionality. While the horizon line provides a somewhat stable world, the brightly clad children perform acrobatic leaps, their branchlike limbs akin to the wood above. The enduring world implied by the horizon is shattered by the agitated back-and-forth of the brushed lines that define ground and sky. Such turmoil presumably awaits the children once they mature and realize their lot in life.

SHAPE, VOLUME, AND MASS

The word *shape* has many meanings. Parents or teachers may tell you to "shape up" when they are concerned about your behavior. When you started arranging things in your dorm room or apartment, you may have had thoughts as things began to "take shape." Such expressions suggest *definition*— that is, pulling things together within defined boundaries to distinguish them from what surrounds them. We say our bodies are "out of shape" when they violate our preferred physical contours. In works of art, **shapes** are defined as the areas within a composition that have boundaries that separate them from what surrounds them; shapes make these areas distinct.

Shapes are formed when intersecting or connected lines enclose space. In Botticelli's *The Birth of Venus* and in the Lawrence painting, for example, shape is clearly communicated by lines that enclose specific areas of the painting. Shape can also be communicated through patches of color or texture. In three-dimensional works, such as sculpture and architecture, shape is discerned when the work is viewed against its environment. The edges, colors, and textures of the work give it shape against the background. Theo van Doesburg's

2-13 HELENE BRANDT. *Mondrian Variations, Construction No. 3B with Four Red Squares and Two Planes* (1996). Welded steel, wood, paint. 22" × 19" × 17".

Composition (Fig. 20-17) features colorful geometric shapes of various dimensions that are created when vertical and horizontal black lines slice through the canvas space and intersect to define areas distinct from the rest of the surface.

The word **form** is often used to speak about shape in sculpture or architecture—three-dimensional works of art. Helene Brandt's *Mondrian Variations, Construction No. 3B with Four Red Squares and Two Planes* (Fig. **2-13**) is a translation into three dimensions of a composition by painter, Piet Mondrian—a contemporary of van Doesburg. Therefore, some artists and people who write about art may prefer to speak of the *form* of the Brandt sculpture rather than its shape. Others use the word *shape* to apply to both two-dimensional and three-dimensional works of art. We will use the terms interchangeably.

The word **volume** refers to the mass or bulk of a three-dimensional work. The volume of a work is the amount of space it contains. In geometry, the volume of a rectangular solid is computed as its length times its width times its height. But one may use the concept more loosely to say that a structure has a great *volume* as a way of generally describing its enormity. Gerrit Rietveldt's Schroeder House in Utrecht (Fig. **2-14**) seems to be a volumetric translation of Mondrian's geometric shapes. Here is an example of the usefulness of the term *volume* as it conveys a sense of containment.

Mass

Like volume, the term *mass* also has a specific meaning in science. In physics, the mass of an object reflects the amount of force required to move it. Objects that have more mass are harder to budge. In three-dimensional art, the **mass** of an object refers to its bulk. A solid work made of steel with the same dimensions as Helene Brandt's sculpture would have more mass.

We would be hard-pressed to conjure a better exemplar of mass than Rachel Whiteread's Holocaust Memorial in Vienna (Fig. **2-15**). It possesses the gravity of a stone pyramid and evokes the simplicity and serenity of a mausoleum. Built of concrete and weighing 250 tons, the memorial is designed as an inverted library—the "books" protrude on the outside—in recognition of the significance of study to the Jewish people, "the people of the book." But the doors to this "library" are bolted, making the books inaccessible. In the wake of the destruction of the Austrian Jewish community, there is no longer any use for them. The names of the places to which the country's Jews were deported for annihilation are inscribed in alphabetical order around the exterior. There is murder, death, and loss here, and the massiveness of the memorial shapes a sense of gloom that cannot be lifted.

ACTUAL MASS VERSUS IMPLIED MASS The Whiteread Memorial has **actual mass**. It occupies three-dimensional space and has measurable volume and weight. Objects that are depicted as three-dimensional on a two-dimensional surface (such as a drawing or a painting) have what we call **implied**

2-14 GERRIT RIETVELDT. Schroeder House (1924). Utrecht, Netherlands.

mass. That is, they create the illusion of possessing volume, having weight, and occupying three-dimensional space. Consider a two-dimensional work of art that features massive shapes, broken and fragmented and piled in a pyramidal shape, like so much fuel for a funeral pyre of art's historical icons. In *Landscape* (Fig. **2-16**), Mark Tansey meticulously portrays the remnants of colossal sculptures amid the unending sands of a bleak desert. His realistic style gives the illusion of three dimensions on the two-dimensional canvas surface and implies the extraordinary mass of the oversized stone figures. In the painting, the shapes have implied mass, whereas the sculptures they reference, in reality, have actual mass.

1 ft.

2-16 MARK TANSEY. *Landscape* (1994). Oil on canvas. 71½" × 144".

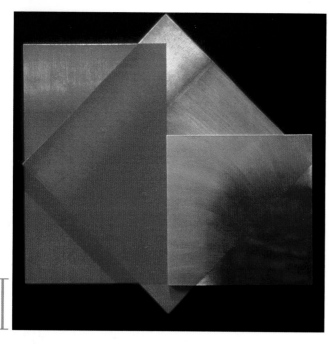

1 ft.

2-17 DOROTHEA ROCKBURNE. *Pascal's Provincial Letters* (1987). Oil on linen. 67" × 67" × 8". © 2011 Dorothea Rockburne/Artists Rights Society (ARS), NY.

Types of Shape

Shapes that are found in geometric figures such as rectangles and circles are called **geometric shapes**. Geometric shapes are regular and precise. They may be made up of straight (rectilinear) or curved (curvilinear) lines, but they have an unnatural, mathematical appearance. Shapes that resemble organisms found in nature—the forms of animals and plant life—are called **organic shapes** and have a natural appearance. Most of the organic shapes found in art are soft, curvilinear, and irregular, although some natural shapes, such as those found in the structure of crystals, are harsh and angular. Artists also work with **biomorphic** and **amorphous** shapes.

Geometric shapes can be **rectilinear** when straight lines intersect to form them. Geometric shapes can also be **curvilinear** when curving lines intersect to form them or when they circle back to join themselves and make up closed geometric figures. Geometric shapes frequently look crisp, or hard-edged, as in painter Dorothea Rockburne's *Pascal's Provincial Letters* (Fig. **2-17**). Rockburne's work has frequently been guided by her interest in mathematics, where we find a purity of form that is rare in the real world. *Pascal's Provincial Letters* is a shaped canvas constructed of overlapping geometric shapes—a rectangle and two squares. Blaise Pascal was a seventeenth-century French mathematician who made many discoveries in geometry, including the fact that the sum of the angles of a triangle equals two right angles (180 degrees). Rockburne rotates the center square, forming triangles in the overlapping shapes, parts of which are obscured. The artist redraws the hidden edges of the shapes, visually fusing the layers. The fusion is enhanced by the softness of the colors and the fluid way in which the pigment is absorbed by the linen.

Frank Gehry, the architect of the Guggenheim Museum in Bilbao, Spain (Fig. **2-18**), refers to his work as a "metallic flower." Others have found the billowing, curvilinear shapes to be reminiscent of ships, linking the machine-tooled

2-18 FRANK GEHRY. Guggenheim Museum (1997). Bilbao, Spain.

PICASSO'S *LES DEMOISELLES D'AVIGNON* WITH COLESCOTT'S *LES DEMOISELLES D'ALABAMA: VESTIDAS*

IN THE YEAR 1907, A YOUNG PABLO PICASSO unveiled a painting that he had been secretly working on for a couple of years. A culmination of what was known as his Rose Period, this new work—*Les Demoiselles d'Avignon* (Fig. **2-19**)—would turn the tide of modern painting. Picasso had studied the work of African and Iberian artists in Parisian museums and galleries. He was struck by the universality of the masks, believing that their rough-hewn, simplified, and angular features crossed time and culture. This painting launched the movement called Cubism, which geometricizes organic forms. The contours of the body in *Demoiselles* are harsh and rectilinear, forming straighter lines than are found in nature. The women in the painting are expressionless and lack identity; some of them even have rectilinear masks in lieu of faces. The intellectual exercise of transforming the human form into geometric shapes takes precedence over any interest in expressing the plight of these women, who are prostitutes in the French underworld. The "figures" in the work transcend the period and culture in which the women lived and worked.

You have probably heard the expression "Clothing makes the man." In Robert Colescott's *Les Demoiselles d'Alabama: Vestidas* (Fig. **2-20**), it could be argued that clothing makes

2-20 ROBERT COLESCOTT. *Les Demoiselles d'Alabama: Vestidas* (1985). Acrylic on canvas. 96" × 92".

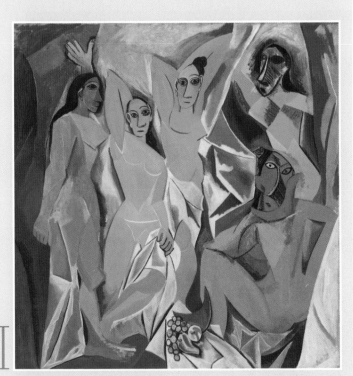

2-19 PABLO PICASSO. *Les Demoiselles d'Avignon* (1907). Oil on canvas. 8' × 7'8". The Museum of Modern Art, NY. © 2011 Estate of Pablo Picasso/ Artists Rights Society (ARS), NY.

the woman. The women in Picasso's painting are dehumanized in part by their nudity. The subjects of Colescott's painting, executed some 80 years later, are given strong individuality by their choice of costume. Colescott's painting is one of the thousands of instances in which one artist transforms the work of another in a certain way to make a certain point. Picasso's nudes have a harsh and jagged quality that gives an overall splintered effect to his work; the movement of the women seems to be abrupt and choppy. By contrast, Colescott's women are well rounded (in the literal sense) and fleshy—they are natural, organic, "real" counterparts to Picasso's geometry. The flowing, curvilinear lines of the women cause them to undulate across the canvas with fluid movement.

Whereas Picasso's rectilinear women are timeless (and "placeless"), the curvilinear, clothed women of Colescott are very much tied to their time and place—an American South full of life and spontaneity and emotional expression. Whereas Picasso seemed to relish the intellectual transformation of the prostitutes into timeless figures, Colescott seems to revel in the tangibility and sensuality of his sexy subjects. ●

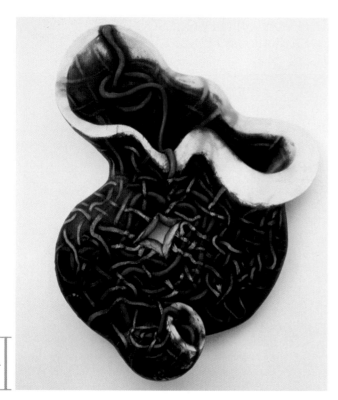

1 ft.

2-21 ELIZABETH MURRAY. *Tangled Fall* (1989–1990). Oil on canvas. 83½" × 66" × 19". © 2011 The Murray-Holman Family Trust/Artists Rights Society (ARS), NY.

2-22 HELEN FRANKENTHALER. *Bay Side* (1967). Acrylic on canvas. 6'2" × 6'9". Private Collection, NY. © 2011 Helen Frankenthaler/ Artists Rights Society (ARS), NY.

structure that is perched on the water's edge to the history of Bilbao as an international seaport. It is as if free-floating geometric shapes have collided on this site, and on another day, they might have assumed a different configuration.

Elizabeth Murray's *Tangled Fall* (Fig. **2-21**) is reminiscent of any number of bodily organs or underwater life—although no medical student or botanist could ever quite place it according to kingdom, phylum, and so on. The shape looks rawly excised from some creature. The interlacing tubes are reminiscent of veins and capillaries carrying who knows what (or who wants to know what). Such imagery is said to have a biomorphic shape—that is, it has the form (the Greek *morphē*) of biological entities. Rather than have strictly defined shapes, whose boundaries are unyielding, biomorphic shapes seem to ebb and flow, expand and contract, or metamorphose as directed by some inner life force.

Shapes need not be clearly defined or derived from nature or the laws of geometry. Many artists, such as the contemporary painter Helen Frankenthaler, create **amorphous** shapes. In *Bay Side* (Fig. **2-22**), Frankenthaler literally poured paint onto her canvas, creating a nebulous work that is dense in form and rich in texture. The "contents" of the loosely defined shapes spill beyond their boundaries, filling the canvas with irregularly shaped pools of poured paint.

1 ft.

My lordship My lancelot My crusader for peace with dignity
My Chairman of the Board My guardian of culture
My in the god
My hope My d or My ker My
lawye Mr land My er fort ly provi My
better half My wunderkind My quarterback My to the
charts My great artist My baby mogul My sugar daddy My
ticket to ride My jack of all trades My leader of the pack
My c ma at addy
My lo sh nc ader wi nity
My be M in g an lture
My professor of desire My host with the most My Dagwood
My Rambo My Popeye My pimp My doctor My banker My
lawyer My landlord My so er of fortune My provider
b un ind le
ch arti My ab ar addy My
tic to k of ll d er c ck
capo My pope My stickman My ayatollah My daddy

What big muscles you have!

2-23 BARBARA KRUGER. *Untitled (What Big Muscles You Have!)* (1985). Photograph. 60" × 80".

1 ft.

POSITIVE AND NEGATIVE SHAPES Viewers usually focus on the objects or figures represented in works of art. These are referred to as the **positive shapes**. Whatever is left over in the composition, whether empty space or space filled with other imagery, is termed the **negative shape** or shapes of the composition.

Positive and negative shapes in a work of art have a **figure–ground relationship**. The part or parts of the work that are seen as what the artist intended to depict are the figure, and the other parts are seen as the ground, or background. Barbara Kruger's *Untitled (What Big Muscles You Have!)* (Fig. **2-23**) illustrates that the figure and ground can be distinct even when the relationship between the two is not so clear-cut. Against a satirical running text of the mindless mantra of a hero-worshiper, Kruger sums up the litany with the proclamation "What big muscles you have!" The viewer identifies the larger type as figure and the smaller type of the running text as ground. Notice the visual tension between the large and small type. As we read the larger type, our eye shifts to the pattern and flow of the words behind, and vice versa. The smaller type serves as a kind of psychological wallpaper, signifying one of the horrors of an age of male supremacy that Kruger hopes we left behind in the last millennium.

For many sculptors, negative shapes, or open spaces, are part and parcel of their compositions. The positive shapes in Nancy Holt's *Sun Tunnels* (Fig. **2-24**) consist of the huge

2-24 NANCY HOLT. *Sun Tunnels* (1973–1976). Concrete. Great Basin Desert, UT.

concrete pipes she placed in the Utah desert. But the views framed by looking through the interiors of these massive structures—the voids, or negative shapes—have as much meaning as the solids, or more. The flow of air and light through the pipes—the "sun tunnels"—lends them a lightness of being that contrasts with their actual mass. The artist has, in effect, enlisted the sun as an element in her composition.

Gestalt psychologists have noted that shapes can be ambiguous, so as to encourage **figure–ground reversals** with viewers. Figure **2-25** shows a Rubin vase, which is a classic illustration of figure–ground reversals found in psychology textbooks. The central shape is that of a vase, and when the viewer focuses on it, it is the figure. But "carved" into the sides of the vase are the shapes of human profiles; when the viewer focuses on them, they become the figure and the vase becomes the ground. The point of the Gestalt psychologists is that we tend to perceive things *in context*. When we are focusing on the profiles, the vase is perceived as ground, not figure.

The Rubin vase and other psychological illusions were favorite subjects for the contemporary artist Jasper Johns. His painting *Spring* (Fig. **2-26**) shows Rubin vases on a flat canvas with muted colors, among human figures and other fragments of the psychological mind. The askew vases are ambiguous, encouraging figure–ground reversals. The shad-

2-25 A Rubin vase.
Gestalt psychologists use this drawing to illustrate the fact that humans tend to perceive objects within their context. When we focus on the vase, it is the figure, and the white shapes to the sides are part of the ground. But when we focus on the "profiles of heads" suggested by the white shapes where they intersect with the sides of the vase, the vase becomes the ground. The drawing is ambiguous; that is, it can be perceived in different ways. As a result, the viewer may experience figure–ground reversals.

2-26 JASPER JOHNS. *Spring* (1986). Encaustic on canvas. 75" × 50". The Museum of Modern Art, NY. Digital Image ©The Museum of Modern Art, NY/Art Resource, NY. Art © Jasper Johns/Licensed by VAGA, NY.

owed vase beneath them in the center right is given more prominence by its implied three-dimensionality, and therefore the viewer is not as encouraged to perceive profiles in the negative shapes to its sides. Psychology buffs will also find a well-known drawing of a younger/older woman in the purple space just below the shadowed vase. Can you see why this drawing is ambiguous and allows the viewer's perceptions to shift back and forth so that now one sees a younger woman and now an older woman?

Edward Steichen's photograph of the sculptor Auguste Rodin silhouetted against his sculpted portrait of Victor Hugo (Fig. **2-27**) creates a visual limbo between figure and ground.

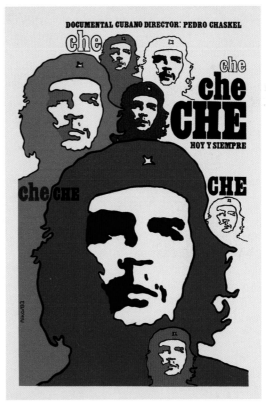

The eye readily perceives the contours of the face of Rodin sitting opposite his bronze sculpture of *The Thinker*, also set against the Hugo sculpture. The viewer's sense of what is a positive shape and what is a negative shape undergoes reversals, as the white-clouded image of the background work seems to float toward the viewer. The spectrelike image of Hugo hovers between and above the dark images, filling the space between them and pushing them visually into the background.

Shape as Icon

Some shapes have entered our consciousness in such a way as to carry with them immediate associations. They are never mistaken for anything else. We could say that they have become cultural icons in the same way that an icon of an opening folder in the toolbar of a word-processing program signifies "Click here to view a list of your files." Some of these images have symbolic resonance that raises them above their actual configuration. Consider the Christian cross, the Jewish Star of David, or the Chinese symbol of yin and yang.

Based on what has been called the most famous photograph in the world, the stylized shape of the social activist and revolutionary, Che Guevara (Fig. **2-28**), has become an icon associated with class struggle, guerilla warfare, and, in

2-28 *Che, Hoy y Siempre* Movie Poster by Niko.

2-29 An advertisement for the iPad.

general, counterculture. Although many young people wear merchandise such as wristwatches and T-shirts emblazoned with the bearded, beret-sporting Che, it is not necessarily because they are familiar with who he was and what he did (an Argentinian physician-turned-Marxist revolutionary who joined Fidel Castro's efforts to depose the U.S.-backed dictator Fulgencio Batista). From Cuba, Che went on to inspire (or incite) revolutions in Africa and Latin America, where he was captured with the help of the U.S. Central Intelligence Agency (CIA) and executed. For most young people, Che's instantly recognizable image is simply synonymous with rebellion against authority and idealistic struggle.

Similarly, the ad campaigns for iPod MP3 players, iPhones, and the iPad from Apple, Inc. have capitalized on shape—from the minimalist design of the objects themselves to the print and TV ads featuring consumers using the products (Fig. **2-29**). The shapes of Apple products—iPods, Mac computers, iPhones, and the iPad—have been so intrinsic to their appeal that financial commentators link the company's success to consumer identification with the products' shapes. Shape is a powerful visual element, and the representation of shape is a powerful design tool.

2-30 FANG LIJUN. *No. 2* (1990–1991). Oil on canvas. 31½" × 39⅓". Rheinisches Bildarchiv, Colonge, Germany.

1 ft.

2-31 A value scale of grays.

Do the circles become darker as they move to the right, or do they only appear to do so? How does this value scale support the view of Gestalt psychologists that people make judgments about the objects they perceive that are based on the context of those objects?

LIGHT AND VALUE

Light is fascinating stuff. It radiates. It illuminates. It dazzles. It glows. It beckons like a beacon. We speak of the "light of reason." We speak of genius as "brilliance." **Visible light** is part of the spectrum of electromagnetic energy that also includes radio waves and cosmic rays. It undulates wavelike throughout the universe. It bounces off objects and excites cells in our eyes, enabling us to see. Light is at the very core of the visual arts. Without light there is no art. Without light there is no life.

One of the lobes of the brain contains a theater for light. Somehow it distinguishes light from dark. Somehow it translates wavelengths of energy into colors. We perceive the colors of the visible spectrum, ranging from violet to red. Although red has the longest wavelength of the colors of the visible spectrum, these waves are measured in terms of *billionths* of a meter. And if our eyes were sensitive to light of a slightly longer wavelength, we would perceive infrared light waves. Sources of heat, such as our mates, would then literally glow in the dark. And our perceptions, and our visible arts, would be quite different.

Light makes it possible for us to see points, lines, shapes, and textures. All of these can be perceived as light against dark or, in the case of a pencil line on a sheet of paper, as dark against light. Light against dark, dark against light—in the language of art, these are said to be differences in *value*.

The value of a color of a surface is its lightness or darkness. The value is determined by the amount of light reflected by the surface: the greater the amount of light reflected, the lighter the surface. More light is reflected by a white surface than by a gray surface, and gray reflects more than black. White, therefore, is lighter than gray, and gray is lighter than black.

Infinite shades of gray lie between black and white. Consider the variations in Fang Lijun's *No. 2* (Fig. **2-30**). Figure **2-31** is a value scale of gray that contains seven shades of gray, varying between a gray that is almost black to the left and one that is slightly off-white to the right. When we describe

works of art in terms of value, not only do we distinguish their range of grays, but we also characterize their *relative* lightness and darkness, that is, their value contrast. **Value contrast** refers to the degrees of difference between shades of gray. Look again at Figure 2-31. Note that there are circles within the squares. Each of them is exactly the same value (they are all equally dark). However, their value contrast with the squares that contain them differs. The circle and square in the center are of the same value, and therefore they have no value contrast. The circles at either end of the scale have high value contrast with the squares that contain them.

Drawing objects or figures with high value contrast makes them easy to see, or makes them "pop." Consider Figure **2-32**. Part A shows a gray sentence typed on gray paper that is nearly as dark; it is difficult to read. Part B shows nearly black type on off-white paper; it is easy to read. Part C shows light

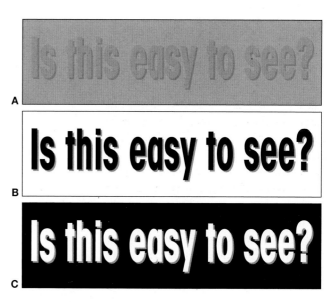

2-32 Value contrast.

Artists and designers know that figures with high value contrast are easier to see. They tend to "pop" out at the viewer. Why is Part A of this figure relatively difficult to read? Why are Parts B and C easier to read?

1 ft.

type that is "dropped out" of dark gray—it, too, pops out at the reader because of high value contrast.

We can discuss the relative lightness and darkness in a work regardless of whether it is a black-and-white or full-color composition. The term *value pattern* describes the variation in light and dark within a work of art and the ways in which they are arranged within a composition. Value patterns can be low-contrast or high-contrast. A high-contrast value pattern can be seen on the left side of David Salle's *Angel* (Fig. **2-33**), and a low-contrast value pattern can be seen on the right side.

Chiaroscuro

Artists use many methods to create the illusion of three dimensions in two-dimensional media, such as painting, drawing, or printmaking. They frequently rely on a pattern of values termed **chiaroscuro**, or the gradual shifting from light to dark through a successive gradation of tones across a curved surface. By use of many gradations of value, artists can give objects portrayed on a flat surface a rounded, three-dimensional appearance.

In *La Source* (Fig. **2-34**), Pierre-Paul Prud'hon creates the illusion of rounded surfaces on blue gray paper by using black and white chalk to portray light gradually dissolving into shade. His subtle modeling of the nude is facilitated by the middle value of the paper and the gradation of tones from light to dark through a series of changing grays. Prud'hon's light source is not raking and harsh, but diffuse and natural. The forms are not sharply outlined; we must work to find out-

1 in.

2-34 PIERRE-PAUL PRUD'HON. *La Source* (c. 1801). Black and white chalk on blue gray paper. 21³⁄₁₆" × 15⁵⁄₁₆". Sterling and Francine Clark Art Institute, Williamstown, MA.

1 in.

2-35 PABLO PICASSO. *Self-Portrait* (1900). Charcoal on paper. 8⅞" × 6½". Museu Picasso, Barcelona, Spain. © 2011 Estate of Pablo Picasso/Artists Rights Society (ARS), NY.

Descriptive and Expressive Properties of Value

Values—black, grays, white—may be used purely to describe objects, or they can be used to evoke emotional responses in the viewer.

Black and white may have expressive properties or symbolic associations. Consider the photograph of a performance piece by Lorraine O'Grady (Fig. **2-36**) staged in protest of the opening of an exhibit titled "Personae," which featured the work of nine white artists and *no* artists of color. Labeling herself "Mlle Bourgeoisie Noire" (or Miss Middle-Class Black), O'Grady appeared in an evening gown constructed of 180 pairs of white gloves and shouted poems that lashed out against the racial politics of the art establishment. Clearly, the white gloves were both evocative and provocative. They were at once a symbol of high society and servitude, of the elegant attire of the exclusive dinner party and the vaudevillian costume of blackface and white-gloved hands.

2-36 LORRAINE O'GRADY. *Mlle Bourgeoise Noire Goes to the New Museum* (1981).

lining anywhere but in the drapery and in the hair. The softly brushed edges of the figure lead your eye to perceive three-dimensional form (continuing around into space) rather than flat, two-dimensional shape.

Picasso used chiaroscuro in his *Self-Portrait* (Fig. **2-35**), sketched at age 19. Although he restricted himself to the use of charcoal, he managed to effect a more subtle gradation of tone through shading that softly delineates his facial features. Sharp contrasts are eliminated by the choice of a buff-colored paper that provides a uniform flesh tone. In effect, the sides of the nose and cheek are built up through the use of soft shadows. The chin and jaw jut out above the neck through the use of sharper shadowing. The eyes achieve their intensity because they are a dark counterpoint to the evenly modeled flesh. There is a tension between the angularity of the lines in the drawing and the modeling. If you focus on the lines, the drawing may seem to be more angular and geometric than organic, but the use of chiaroscuro creates a more subtle and human rounding of the face.

ROTHKO'S *NUMBER 22* WITH ROTHKO'S *BLACK ON GREY*

THE AMERICAN ARTIST MARK ROTHKO (1903-1970) worked in many styles during his lifetime. His early work, like that of many twentieth-century artists, was largely in a realistic vein. By the time he was 40 years old, he showed an interest in **Surrealism**, which was imported from Europe. But within a few years, he was painting the **Abstract Expressionist** color-field paintings with which he is mainly associated.

He painted *Number 22* (Fig. **2-37**) in 1949, at about the time a critic remarked that his work tended to evoke the color patterns of French Impressionists and to create "lovely moods." The realistic images of his early days and the symbols of his Surrealistic days were replaced with large, abstract fields of color, which were more or less vertically stacked. Here Rothko uses a high key palette with intensely saturated color. The values in *Number 22* are bold, jaunty, hot, and abrasive. We observe the work of an innovative 46-year-old painter coming into his own—creating his mature style, being invited to teach in academies across the country, and receiving some critical acclaim. The light values seem to imbue the work with boisterous emotion and life. Rothko was developing his signature image of "floating" rectangles that continued to be his model throughout his life's work. The canvases consisted solely of these shapes,

stacked one atop the other, varied in width and height and hue, edges softened with feathered strokes that created the illusion of subtle vibration. By not referring to any specific visual experience, the high key values of these nonobjective works seem to suggest a divine, spiritual presence. The luminosity of *Number 22* is perhaps suggestive of the birth of the universe. The red band in the middle is reminiscent of a horizon line, but all is aglow and alive.

Compare *Number 22* to a work Rothko painted some 20 years later: *Black on Grey* (Fig. **2-38**). The painting reveals one of the most dramatic and resonant uses of black in the history of abstract painting. Toward the end of the 1960s, Rothko began to simplify his color fields, stretching his rectangles out to the very edges of the canvas and effectively dividing the surface into two simple fields. He also reduced his palette to low key values—particularly grays, browns, and black. In Rothko's last painting, *Black on Grey*, created just before he took his own life in his studio on February 25, 1970, black and gray merge at a horizon punctuated by a dull light. Darkness falls heavily on the mottled gray field; note that the title, *Black on Grey*, underscores the symbolism of the encroaching of death. It is as if he has brought his life, and his life's work, to a close. The spiritual presence has flickered out.

1 ft.

2-37 MARK ROTHKO. *Number 22* (1949). Oil on canvas. 117" × 107⅛". The Museum of Modern Art, NY.

1 ft.

2-38 MARK ROTHKO. *Black on Grey* (1970). Acrylic on canvas, 80¼" × 69". The Solomon R. Guggenheim Museum, NY.

*It is only after years of preparation that the young artist should touch color—
not color used descriptively, that is, but as a means of personal expression.*
—Henri Matisse

COLOR

Color is a central element in our spoken language as well as in the language of art. The language connects emotion with color: we speak of being blue with sorrow, red with anger, green with envy.

The color in works of art can also trigger strong emotional responses in the observer, working hand in hand with line and shape to enrich the viewing experience. The Postimpressionist Vincent van Gogh often chose color more for its emotive qualities than for its fidelity to nature. Likewise in some amorphous abstract works, such as *Bay Side* (Fig. 2-22), color seems to be much of the message being communicated by the artist.

What is color? You have no doubt seen a rainbow or observed how light sometimes separates into several colors when it is filtered through a window. Sir Isaac Newton discovered that sunlight, or white light, can be broken down into different colors by a triangular glass solid called a **prism** (Fig. **2-39**).

Psychological Dimensions of Color: Hue, Value, and Saturation

The wavelength of light determines its color, or **hue**. The visible spectrum consists of the colors red, orange, yellow, green, blue, indigo, and violet. The wavelength for red is longer than that for orange, and so on through violet.

The value of a color, like the value of any light, is its degree of lightness or darkness. If we wrap the colors of the spectrum around into a circle, we create a color wheel such as that shown in Figure **2-40**. (We must add some purples not found in the spectrum to complete the circle.) Yellow is the

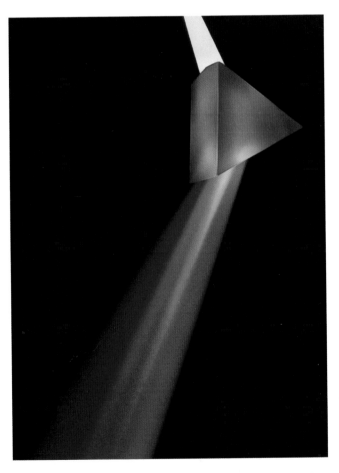

2-39 Prism.
A prism breaks down white light into the colors of the visible spectrum.

2-40 A color wheel.
The color wheel bends the colors of the visible spectrum into a circle and adds a few missing hues to complete the circle.

Color **49**

lightest of the colors on the wheel, and violet is the darkest. As we work our way around from yellow to violet, we encounter progressively darker colors. Blue-green is about equal in value to red-orange, but green is lighter than red.

The colors on the green-blue side of the color wheel are considered **cool** in "temperature," whereas the colors on the yellow-orange-red side are considered **warm**. Perhaps greens and blues suggest the coolness of the ocean or the sky, and hot things tend to burn red or orange. A room decorated in green or blue may appear more appealing on a hot day in July than a room decorated in red or orange. On a canvas, warm colors seem to advance toward the picture plane. Cool colors, on the other hand, seem to recede.

The **saturation** of a color is its pureness. Pure hues have the greatest intensity, or brightness. The saturation, and hence the intensity, decrease when another hue or black, gray, or white is added. Artists produce **shades** of a given hue by adding black, and **tints** by adding white.

Additive and Subtractive Colors

When all those years as a child you were mixing fingerpaints together, or rubbing crayons across already colored surfaces, you probably thought you were adding colors to other colors. In a piece of irony in which science contradicts common sense, it turns out that you were actually subtracting colors from one another. **Additive colors** have to do with mixing *lights*, and **subtractive colors** have to do with mixing *pigments*.

Additive colors are rays of colored light, which, when overlapped or "mixed" with other rays of color, produce lighter colors and white (Fig. **2-41**). White light can be rec-

2-42 Subtractive color mixtures.
One subtracts colors by mixing pigments.

reated by overlapping orange-red, blue-violet, and green. Because these colors cannot be derived from the mixing of other colored light, they are called **primary colors**. When they are overlapped, they form lighter colors known as **secondary colors**: the overlap of orange-red and green create yellow; the overlap of blue-violet and green create indigo (or cyan); and lights of blue-violet and orange-red "mix" to form magenta. White is at the center of the three-way overlap of these primary colors.

Subtractive color refers to the mixing of pigment rather than light and is actually more relevant to the experience of the artist (Fig. **2-42**). When you apply a pigment to a surface, as in applying paint to a canvas, you are applying a substance that causes that surface to reflect every color of the visible spectrum *except for the color you see on the surface*.

Complementary versus Analogous Colors

With pigments, red, blue, and yellow are the primary colors, the ones that we cannot produce by mixing other hues. Mixing pigments of the primary colors creates secondary colors. The three secondary colors are orange (derived from mixing red and yellow), green (blue and yellow), and violet (red and blue), and they are denoted by the number 2 on the color wheel. **Tertiary colors** are created by mixing pigments of primary and adjoining secondary colors and are denoted by a 3 on the color wheel.

Hues that lie next to one another on the color wheel are **analogous**. They form families of color, such as yellow and

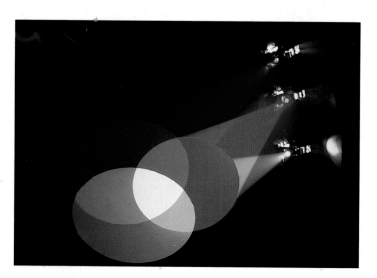

2-41 Additive color mixtures.
One adds colors by mixing lights.

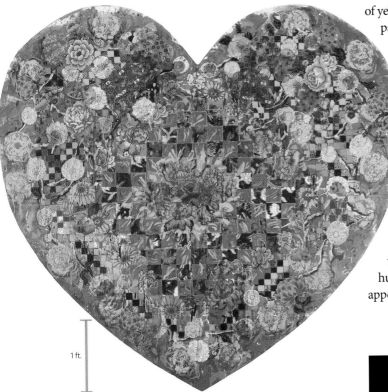

1 ft.

2-43 MIRIAM SCHAPIRO. *Atrium of Flowers* (1980). Acrylic and fabric on canvas. 64" × 60". Flomenhaft Gallery, NY.

of yellow—again, complementary colors—complete the vibrant palette. The painting serves as homage to Tintoretto, a seventeenth-century Venetian artist known as a colorist whose intense palette and dramatic lighting gave a theatrical feeling to his work.

Local versus Optical Color

Have you ever driven at night and wondered whether vague, wavy lines in the distance outlined the peaks of hills or the bases of clouds? Objects may take on different hues as a function of distance or lighting conditions. The greenness of the trees on a mountain may make a strong impression from the base of the mountain, but from a distant vantage point, the atmospheric scattering of light rays may dissolve the hue into a blue haze. Light-colored objects take on a dark appearance when lit strongly from behind. Hues fade as late

1 ft.

2-44 SANDRO CHIA. *Incident at the Tintoretto Café* (1982). Oil on canvas. 88⅝" × 130". Collection Galerie Bruno Bischofberger, Zurich, Switzerland.

orange, orange and red, and green and blue. As we work our way around the wheel, the families intermarry, such as blue with violet and violet with red. Works that use closely related families of color seem harmonious. Miriam Schapiro's *Atrium of Flowers* (Fig. **2-43**) reveals how neighboring colors can be harmoniously augmented by incorporating an array of values of each. Here a palette of reds, pinks, mauve, and peach lends an overall unity to a complicated patchwork design of flowers and quiltlike squares. The color unity that we see in Shapiro's painting is sometimes referred to as the *tonality* of a work of art. *Atrium of Flowers* has a red tonality; red dominates the composition even though other colors are evident in the work.

The dramatic contrasts found in complementary color schemes can heighten the expressive or emotional quality of a work. Italian Neo-Expressionist painter Sandro Chia confined his palette to the complementary scheme of orange and blue in his explosive painting *Incident at the Tintoretto Café* (Fig. **2-44**). An oversized orange-draped figure leaps away from the viewer toward the tumultuous blue drapery of the background. In the confusion, the candles of a swinging chandelier spew their flames and tables tip and fly. Shadows of purple and highlights

2-45 AUDREY FLACK. *Marilyn (Vanitas)* (1977). Oil over acrylic on canvas. 96" × 96". University of Arizona Museum, Tucson, AZ.

afternoon wends its way to dusk and dusk to night. **Local color** is defined as the hue of an object as created by the colors its surface reflects under normal lighting conditions. **Optical color** is defined as our perceptions of color, which can vary markedly with lighting conditions.

Audrey Flack's oversized photorealist still life paintings—such as *Marilyn (Vanitas)* (Fig. 2-45)—take advantage of local color to underscore the familiarity of her everyday objects. An orange is orange; grapes are green. Even our "concept" of lipstick is confirmed as a pillar of creamy red. The type of still life that Flack presents here is one in a long tradition of what are called *vanitas* paintings, the contents of which include objects pertaining to vanity—cosmetics, mirrors, jewelry. They are juxtaposed with objects that reference the eventuality of death: an hourglass, a pocket watch, a candle burning down. Between the objective colors and the enormous scale of the work (this painting is eight feet square), the viewer cannot escape the reality of the commonplace objects and the inevitability of fate.

Color as Symbol

The connectedness between emotion and color often explains an artist's palette choices. We all link mood with color—we are green with envy, red with anger, blue with sorrow, white with fright. Some of these descriptions may be more accu-

rate than others (faces really do turn red when angry or white when frightened), but they have in common their use of symbolism: feelings and behavior are symbolized with color.

Abstract notions and ideas also have their symbolic color coordinates. For example, what does it mean if one is true to the red, white, and blue? If you are an American citizen, it means that you are loyal to your country—the United States of America—as symbolized by the red, white, and blue colors of the flag. But this would also be true if you were, say, a British student or a French student, because their national flags (the Union Jack or the tricolor) bear the same color combination, albeit with different designs.

In a subtle but chilling commentary on issues of equality, oppression, and difference, contemporary Nigerian British artist Yinka Shonibare reworked typical Victorian costume in fabrics expressing African identity, both constructed and adopted. In *Victorian Couple* (Fig. 2-46) the profiles of the coat and bustle may seem familiar, but the colorful textiles and printed designs create a cultural disconnect with symbolic ramifications. Shonibare was born in London to Nigerian parents and spent most of his childhood in Nigeria. He returned to England to study at the University of London and

2-46 YINKA SHONIBARE. *Victorian Couple* (1999). Wax-printed cotton textile. Approx. 60" × 36" × 36" and 60" × 24" × 24".

has focused his art on issues of African identity and authenticity, in which the symbolism of color plays a central role.

This brings us to an important fact concerning color and symbolism: The symbols of colors, their meanings, are culture-specific. You may associate white with a bride in American culture, but in China, brides wear red. If you happen to spot a young Chinese American newlywed couple posing for their wedding portraits in a city park, you will likely notice that even though the bride is dressed in white, she wears a prominent red ribbon on her bodice—East meets West.

Texture is another element of art that can evoke a strong emotional response.

TEXTURE

The softness of skin and silk, the coarseness of rawhide and homespun cloth, the coolness of stone and tile, the warmth of wood—these are but a few of the **textures** that artists capture in their works. The word *texture* derives from the Latin for "weaving," and it is used to describe the surface character of woven fabrics and other materials as experienced primarily through the sense of touch.

The element of texture adds a significant dimension to art beyond representation. An artist may distort or exaggerate textures used to define a subject in order to communicate a feeling about it or an emotional state the artist was in when the work was in process. These textures can produce an empathetic response in the viewer. Consider the contrasting use of texture—and the differing emotional impact—of Leon Kossoff 's *Portrait of Mrs. Peto No. 2* (Fig. **2-47**) and Marie Laurencin's *Mother and Child* (Fig. **2-48**). The first contains thickly brushed lines and the harsh, gouged textures of impasto—that is, the thick buildup of paint on the surface

2-47 LEON KOSSOFF. *Portrait of Mrs. Peto No. 2* (c. 1972–73). Oil on board. Private collection. The Bridgeman Art Library International.

2-48 MARIE LAURENCIN. *Mother and Child* (1928). Oil on canvas. 32" × 25½". The Detroit Institute of Arts, Detroit, MI. © 2011 Artists Rights Society (ARS), NY/ADAGP, Paris.

2-49 VINCENT VAN GOGH. *Sunflowers* (1887). Oil on canvas. 1'5" × 2'. The Metropolitan Museum of Art, NY.

 1 in.

2-50 RACHEL RUYSCH. *Flower Still Life* (after 1700). Oil on canvas. 29¾" × 23⅞". The Toledo Museum of Art, Toledo, OH.

of the canvas. The overall feeling is one of anxiety or somberness. The agitated textural brushwork and the drab palette drag the emotion down.

Laurencin's *Mother and Child*, like Kossoff's *Portrait of Mrs. Peto No. 2*, is an oil painting. But here the brushstrokes are shorter and flatter, and they gradually build up the imagery rather than "carve" it. The overall texture of *Mother and Child* is soft and seems comforting, reinforcing the feeling of tenderness between mother and child. In these contrasting portraits, the role of texture surpasses the literal content of the works—that is, they are both portraits of people—to add an emotional dimension for the viewer.

Types of Texture

In three-dimensional media such as sculpture, crafts, and architecture, the materials have definable textures or *actual texture*. In a two-dimensional medium such as painting, we discuss texture in other terms. For example, the surface of a painting has an *actual* texture—it can be rough, smooth, or something in between. But we typically discuss the surface only when the texture is palpable or unusual, as when thick impasto is used or when an unusual material is added to the surface.

ACTUAL TEXTURE **Actual texture** is *tactile*. When you touch an object, your fingertips register sensations of its actual texture—rough, smooth, sharp, hard, soft. Any work of art has actual texture—whether it is the hard, cold texture of marble or the rough texture of pigment on canvas. Vincent van

1 ft.

2-51 LYNDA BENGLIS. *Morisse* (1985–1987). Copper, nickel, chrome, and gold leaf. 148" × 43" × 14". Art © Lynda Benglis/Licensed by VAGA, NY.

Gogh's *Sunflowers* (Fig. **2-49**) is rendered with a great deal of surface texture. Van Gogh used impasto—the most common painting technique that yields actual texture—to define his forms, and he often deviated from realistic colors and textures to heighten the emotional impact of his work. The surface texture of the painting goes beyond the real texture of the blossom to communicate an emotional intensity and passion for painting that is independent of the subject matter and more linked to the artistic process—that is, to the artist's method of using gestural brushstrokes to express his sensibilities.

VISUAL TEXTURE Simulated texture in a work of art is referred to as **visual texture**. Artists use line, color, and other elements of art to create the illusion of various textures in flat drawings and paintings. The surface of Rachel Ruysch's *Flower Still Life* (Fig. **2-50**) is smooth and glasslike; however, an abundance of textures is *simulated* by the painstaking detail of the flowers and leaves.

Artists employ a variety of materials to create visual texture, or the illusion of surfaces or textures far removed from their actual texture. In *Morisse* (Fig. **2-51**), for example, sculp-

tor Lynda Benglis creates the illusion of soft, pleated, billowing fabric tied in a knot. It is hard to imagine how the artist can create the impression of silk with materials such as copper, nickel, and chrome. The observer is tempted to reach out and touch the work to reconcile what the eyes are witnessing with what the museum label says. Here the visual texture is vastly different from the actual texture.

In *Gift Wrapped Doll #19* (Fig. **2-52**), Pop artist James Rosenquist uses a common medium—oil on canvas—to simulate the texture of cellophane wrapped around the head of a wide-eyed porcelain doll. The folds of the transparent wrap reflect light, tearing across the innocent face like white-hot rods. We feel, as observers, that were we to poke at the cellophane, we would hear a crackling sound and the pattern of lightning-like stripes would change direction. The image of a doll is usually that of a cuddly companion, but Rosenquist's specimen is haunting and sinister. Perhaps it is a commentary on the ways in which the Western ideal of beauty—blue eyes, blond hair, and a "Cupid's bow" mouth—can suffocate the little girls who grow into women.

The success of *Gift Wrapped Doll* is dependent on the artist's ability to fool the eye. Artists call this **trompe l'oeil**—the French phrase that literally means "trick the eye." Trompe l'oeil has made its appearance throughout the history of art, from first-century-BCE Roman wall painting to contemporary Photorealism.

1 ft.

2-52 JAMES ROSENQUIST. *Gift Wrapped Doll #19* (1992). Oil on canvas. 60" × 60". Art © James Rosenquist/Licensed by VAGA, NY.

GÉRICAULT'S *THE RAFT OF THE MEDUSA* WITH STELLA'S *RAFT OF THE MEDUSA*

IN THE YEAR 1816, off the coast of West Africa, a makeshift raft laden with Algerian immigrants was set adrift by the captain and crew of the crippled French ship *Medusa*. Two years later, the artist Théodore Géricault began what was to be his most controversial and political painting, *The Raft of the Medusa* (Fig. **2-53**). Like many of his liberal contemporaries, Géricault opposed the French monarchy and used the tragedy of the *Medusa* to call attention to the mismanagement and ineffectual policies of the French government. The plight of the survivors and victims of the *Medusa* became a national scandal, and Géricault's authentic documentation—based on interviews with the rescued—was construed as a direct attack on the government. Géricault's powerful composition is full of realistic detail and explores the full gamut of human emotion under extreme hardship and duress. The drama of Géricault's composition rests on the diagonal placement of the figures, from the corpse in the lower left that will soon slip into the dark abyss of the ocean, upward along a crescendo that culminates in the muscular torso of a black man waving a flag toward a rescue ship barely visible on the horizon. The fractured raft is tossed about mercilessly by the winds and waves; humans battle against nature, and their own, for sheer survival.

Nearly two centuries later, Frank Stella revisited the subject of the tragedy of the raft of the *Medusa* (Fig. **2-54**) in his aluminum and steel sculpture of the same title. While the heroic drama of "man against the elements" in Gericault's version is conveyed through dramatic lighting, linear forces, and realistic detail, the sense of the event is captured in Stella's work primarily through texture. The structure of the raft, parts of it turned to twisted steel by the forces of the ocean, is overrun by the coarse textures of aluminum fashioned to suggest the frothing of assaulting waves. These textures convey the uneven match between the ill-fated castaways and the unleashed power of nature. ●

1 ft.

2-53 THÉODORE GÉRICAULT. *The Raft of the Medusa* (1818-1819). Oil on canvas. 16'1" × 23'6". Louvre, Paris, France.

1 ft.

2-54 FRANK STELLA. *Raft of the Medusa, Part 1* (1990). Aluminum and steel. 167½" × 163" × 159". © 2011 Frank Stella/Artists Rights Society (ARS), NY.

1 in.

2-55 MERET OPPENHEIM. *Object* (1936). Fur-covered cup, saucer, and spoon. Overall height: 2⅞". The Museum of Modern Art, NY.

SUBVERSIVE TEXTURE Textures are sometimes chosen or created by the artist to subvert or undermine our ideas about the objects they depict. **Subversive texture** compels the viewer to look again at an object and to think about it more deeply.

You may take objects such as a cup, saucer, and spoon for granted, but not after viewing Meret Oppenheim's *Object* (Fig. **2-55**). Oppenheim uses subversive texture in lining a cup, saucer, and spoon with fur. Teacups are usually connected with civilized and refined settings and occasions. The coarse primal fur completely subverts these associations, rendering the thought of drinking from this particular cup repugnant. *Object* also shows how textures can simultaneously attract and repel us. Does Oppenheim want the viewer to ponder the violence that has enabled civilization to grow and endure?

SPACE

"Space, the final frontier." Every die-hard Trekker is familiar with the opening mantra of the hit TV and film series *Star Trek*. But it just as well describes the "mission impossible" of millennia of artists seeking to recreate three-dimensional space on a two-dimensional surface. The space explored by the starship *Enterprise* was that beyond the earth's atmosphere—the space between celestial spheres and galaxies. Artists are less ambitious. They seek to explore ways to visually and psychologically extend the space of a finite rectangle—a canvas, let's say—into nothing less than a vast universe.

If pulling three dimensions out of a two-dimensional hat seems a trick, it is. Artists have had to develop a variety of tricks over the centuries in order to create the much-sought illusion of space on a two-dimensional surface. The history of the pursuit of this illusion is long and it has taken winding turns, but we hear about it in the art of ancient Greece, we see it in ancient Rome, and we follow its path to perfection in the Renaissance. The value placed on achieving this goal is illustrated in an anecdote about the famed Greek painter Apelles. In bringing before a panel of judges an example of his painting, Apelles was admonished by the judges for setting nothing on the easel for review. Of course he had. Apelles's work was so realistic, was so remarkable in its illusionism, that it went unseen in its surroundings. The painted image blended imperceptibly with that which surrounded it in actual space. Or so we've been told. What we do know for certain is that artists, like ordinary people, have been surrounded by the reaches of space as they look into the heavens, out over

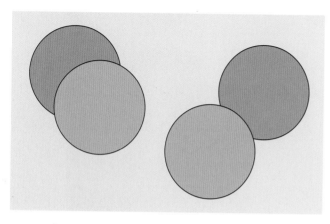

2-56 Overlapping circles and arcs.

mountains, or into the seas. They have seen fog collide with distant hills. They have seen sunlight burn at its edges. They have seen objects appear and disappear—lost in the distance, emerging from it. How can this be captured, communicated, shared? What's the trick?

However numerous and varied they are, the tricks took millennia to develop. From simple methods such as overlapping and relative size to complex systems of linear perspective, the goal of entire eras of artists was to transcend the space at their fingertips, to defy its limitations. In Chapters 9 and 11, which discuss the three-dimensional art forms of sculpture and architecture, we explore ways in which artists situate their objects in space and envelop space. In Chapter 11, we chronicle the age-old attempt to enclose vast reaches of

1 ft.

2-57 MARTINA LÓPEZ. *Heirs Come to Pass, 3* (1991). Silver dye bleach print made from digitally assisted montage. 2'6" × 4'2". Smithsonian American Art Museum, Washington, D.C.

space that began with massive support systems and currently focuses on lightweight steel-cage and shell-like structures. In this section, we examine ways in which artists who work in two dimensions create the illusion of depth—that is, the third dimension.

Overlapping

When nearby objects are placed in front of more distant objects, they obscure part or all of the distant objects. Figure **2-56** shows two circles and two arcs, but our perceptual experiences encourage us to interpret the drawing as showing four circles, two in the foreground and two in back. Likewise, this perceptual phenomenon allows an artist to create the illusion of depth by overlapping objects, or apparently placing one in front of another. Many of the works in your textbook illustrate the technique of overlapping and its effect in suggesting space—whether deep, as in Church's *The Andes of Ecuador* (Fig. 2-68), or shallow, as in Orozco's *Epic of American Civilization* (see Fig. 1-39).

Relative Size and Linear Perspective

The farther objects are from us, the smaller they appear to the eye. To recreate this visual phenomenon and to create the illusion of three-dimensionality on a two-dimensional surface, such as a canvas, artists employ a variety of techniques, among them **relative size** and **linear perspective**. For example, things that are supposed to be closer to the viewer are larger, whereas things that are supposed to be more distant are smaller. This simple principle of relative size can do wonders to suggest spatial complexity in works such as *Heirs Come to Pass, 3* (Fig. **2-57**) by Martina López.

The space in the composition is divided into three principal areas—foreground, middle ground, and background. The stagelike setting consists of a broad and minimally defined landscape that fills most of the area of the piece, leaving just a small strip for a cloud-soaked sky. With no apparent design, figures (from old family photographs) are digitally patched into the print. They range from looming to barely visible, and their size relative to one another creates whatever illusion of space there is. For López, this "visual terrain" is open, not only to her own memories, but also to those of the viewer.

2-58 LOUIS COMFORT TIFFANY. *Magnolias and Irises* (c. 1908). Leaded Favrile glass. 60¼" × 42". Anonymous Gift, in memory of Mr. and Mrs. A. B. Frank, 1981 (1981.159). The Metropolitan Museum of Art, NY. Image copyright © The Metropolitan Museum of Art / Art Resource, NY.

In the Tiffany Studios' *Magnolias and Irises* (Fig. **2-58**) there are a few different cues for perceiving depth. The flowering trees and purple irises along the edge of the water are large, brightly colored, and clearly defined. Situated in the extreme foreground as they are, the plants not only seem close to us but also frame our view of the distant hills. Their relative size accounts for our perception that the space between us and the horizon is deep. In the valley between the hills, a serpentine line—a river—leads our eyes from the reflective surface of the water in the middle ground to the hills and sunset of the extreme background. As we move from foreground to background, the imagery becomes less distinct. The vastness of space is reinforced by the use of cool blues and purples—colors which, as we have learned, tend to recede into the distance.

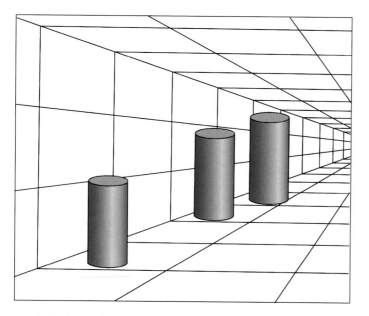

2-59 A visual illusion.

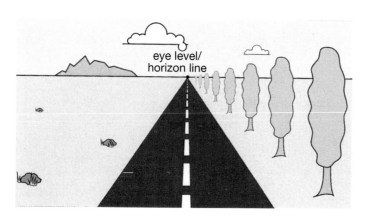

2-60 One-point perspective.

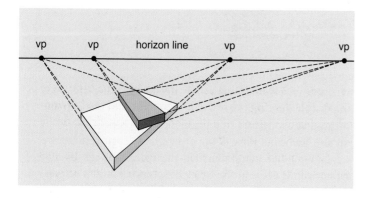

2-62 Perspective drawing of objects set at different angles.

We see this again in Figure 2-59. Note how the cylinders appear to grow larger toward the top of the composition. Why? For at least two reasons: (1) Objects at the bottom of a composition are usually perceived as being closer to the picture plane; and (2) the converging lines are perceived as being parallel, even when they are not. However, if they were parallel, then space would have to recede toward the center right of the composition, and the cylinder in that region would have to be farthest from the viewer. According to rules of perspective, a distant object that appears to be equal in size to a nearby object would have to be larger, so we perceive the cylinder to the right as the largest, although it is equal in size to the others.

Figures 2-60 through 2-63 show that the illusion of depth can be created in art by making parallel lines come together, or converge, at one or more **vanishing points** on an actual or implied **horizon**. The height of the horizon in the composition corresponds to the apparent location of the viewer's eyes, that is, the **vantage point** of the viewer. As we shall see in later chapters, the Greeks and Romans had some notion of linear perspective, but Renaissance artists such as Leonardo da Vinci refined perspective.

In **one-point perspective** (Fig. 2-60), parallel lines converge at a single vanishing point on the horizon. Raphael's (1483–1520) Renaissance masterpiece *School of Athens* (Fig. 2-64) is a monumental example of one-point perspective. Representing Philosophy, it was one of four match-

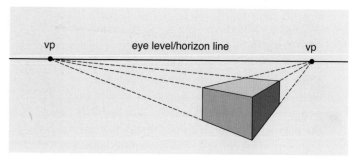

2-61 Two-point perspective.

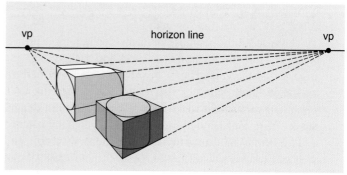

2-63 Curved objects drawn in perspective.

2-64 RAFFAELLO SANZIO (CALLED RAPHAEL). *Philosophy, or School of Athens* (1509–1511). Fresco. 26' × 18'. Stanza della Segnatura, Vatican, Rome, Italy.

1 ft.

2-65 Perspective in *School of Athens.* Raphael's painting is a powerful example of one-point perspective.

ing frescoes depicting the most valuable aspects of a pope's education. The painting is a virtual *Who's Who* of intellectual movers and shakers from antiquity to the Renaissance. Plato (left) and Aristotle (right) occupy the center of the congregation, sharing the spotlight and representing divergent philosophical perspectives. The horizon line cuts through the center of their bodies, and the vanishing point sits squarely between them (Fig. **2-65**). Converging on this point are orthogonals that can be traced from the patterns of the marble flooring below the horizon line and the horizontal entablatures sitting atop the piers that recede dramatically toward the rear of the arcade.

In **two-point perspective** (Fig. **2-61**), two sets of parallel lines converge at separate vanishing points on the horizon. You would be hard-pressed to find a clearer use of two-point perspective than in Gustave Caillebotte's *Paris Street: Rainy*

2-66 GUSTAVE CAILLEBOTTE. *Paris Street: Rainy Day* (1877). Oil on canvas. 83½" × 108¼". The Art Institute of Chicago, Chicago, IL.

2-67 Perspective in Caillebotte's *Paris Street: Rainy Day.*
The use of two-point perspective in the Caillebotte painting is powerful and obvious. It draws our attention upward from the prominent figures in the foreground.

Day (Fig. **2-66**). We see the building in the background from the eye level of the figures in the foreground. The sight lines follow the receding dual facades of the building toward two distinct vanishing points (Fig. **2-67**).

We can use additional sets of parallel lines to depict objects that are set at different angles, as shown in Figure **2-62**. Figure **2-63** shows how curved objects may be "carved out" of rectangular solids.

Atmospheric Perspective

In **atmospheric perspective** (also called *aerial perspective*), the illusion of depth is created by techniques such as texture gradients, brightness gradients, color saturation, and the manipulation of warm and cool colors. A gradient is a progressive change. The effect of a **texture gradient** relies on the fact that closer objects are perceived as having rougher or more detailed surfaces. The effect of a **brightness gradient** is due to the lesser intensity of distant objects.

Frederic Edwin Church's masterpiece, *Andes of Ecuador* (Fig. **2-68**), relies in part on atmospheric perspective to create the illusion of deep vistas. The foreground of the picture contains great botanical detail. As the vista recedes into the distance, the plants and hills become less textured and the colors become less saturated. Church belonged to the Hudson River School of nineteenth-century American painting. The group's members used landscape as a vehicle for communicating the feeling of awe they experienced when they encountered the romantic, scientific, and religious ideas of the era—a world without limits.

The haunting painting *Schunnemunk Mountain* (Fig. **2-69**) reveals Sylvia Plimack Mangold's fascination with the transitional moments of the day. Here in the evening of the Hudson River Valley, brightness gradients employing purple, navy, and cobalt set the hills beneath the sky. The dark foreground is rendered more vacant by twinkling lights that suggest habitation in the valley beyond.

1 ft.

2-68 FREDERIC EDWIN CHURCH. *Andes of Ecuador* (1855). Oil on canvas. 48" × 75". Museum of American Art, Winston-Salem, NC.

1 ft.

2-69 SYLVIA PLIMACK MANGOLD. *Schunnemunk Mountain* (1979). Oil on canvas. 60" × 80⅛". Dallas Museum of Art, Dallas, TX.

I paint with shapes.
—Alexander Calder

TIME AND MOTION

Objects and figures exist and move not only through space but also through the dimension of time. In its inexorable forward flow, time provides us with the chance to develop and grasp the visions of our dreams. Time also creates the stark limits beyond which none of us may extend.

Artists through the ages have sought to represent three-dimensional space in two-dimensional art forms as well as to represent, or imply, movement and the passage of time. Only in modern times have art forms such as cinematography and video been developed that involve *actual* movement and *actual* time.

Actual Motion

Artists create or capture **actual motion** in various ways. **Kinetic art** (from the Greek *kinesis*, meaning "movement")

and photography are two of them. Most works of art sit quietly on the wall or, perhaps, on a pedestal, but kinetic art is designed to move.

The **mobiles** of Alexander Calder are among the most popular examples of kinetic art in the twentieth century. *The Star* (Fig. **2-70**) is composed of petal-like discs of different sizes and colors that are cantilevered from metal rods in such a way that they can rotate horizontally—in orbits—in the breeze. However, the center of gravity remains stable, so that the entire sculpture is hung from a single point. The composition changes according to air currents and the perspective of the observer. The combinations of movements are for all practical purposes infinite, so that the observer will never see the work in quite the same way.

With Liz Magic Laser's *The Thing #25* (Fig. **2-71**), the work of art is the record of a moment in time choreographed for the purposes of the photograph. Many of Laser's works examine the relationship between people and liquid; her

2-70 ALEXANDER CALDER. *The Star* (1960). Polychrome sheet metal and steel wire. 35¾" × 53¾" × 17⅝". University of Kentucky Art Museum, Lexington, KY. © 2011 Calder Foundation, NY/Artists Rights Society (ARS), NY.

1 ft.

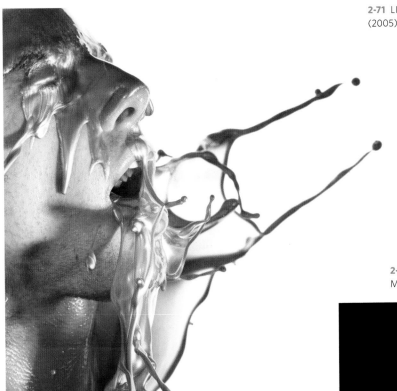

1 in.

2-72 GIANLORENZO BERNINI. *Apollo and Daphne* (1622–1624).
Marble. 7'6". Galleria Borghese, Rome, Italy.

1 ft.

subjects are typically immersed in it, spattered by it, or projecting it. What captivates the viewer, however, is the way in which time has stopped in this work, exaggerating the impact and ejection of a mysterious green goo.

Implied Motion and Time

The Thing #25 captured motion through the use of **stopped time**. Other works of art imply motion; that is, the viewer infers that motion is occurring or has occurred. **Implied motion** and **implied time** are found in Baroque sculptor Gianlorenzo Bernini's *Apollo and Daphne* (Fig. **2-72**) through the use of diagonal lines of force that help simulate movement from left to right. In the Greek myth, the wood nymph Daphne beseeches the gods to help her escape the overtures of Apollo. As Apollo gains on her, her prayer is answered in a most ironic manner because the gods choose to facilitate her "escape" by transforming her into a tree. In Bernini's sculpture, we see Daphne just at the point when bark begins to enfold her body, her toes begin to take root, and her fingertips are transformed into the branches of a laurel. The passage of time is implied as she is caught in the midst of her transformation.

The Illusion of Motion

There is a difference between implied motion and the illusion of motion. Works such as *Apollo and Daphne* imply that motion has occurred or that time has passed. In other works, artists use techniques to suggest that motion is *in the process of occurring* rather than that motion has occurred. We say that these works contain the illusion of motion.

Early experiments with photography provided an illusion of the figure in motion through the method of rapid multiple exposures. In his *Man Pole Vaulting* (Fig. 2-73), Thomas Eakins—better known for his paintings—used photo sequences to study the movement of the human body. In the wake of these experiments, several artists created the illusion of motion by applying the visual results of multiple-exposure photography to their paintings.

Marcel Duchamp's *Nude Descending a Staircase #2* (Fig. 2-74) in effect creates multiple exposures of a machine-tooled figure walking down a flight of stairs. The overlapping of shapes and the repetition of linear patterns blur the contours of the figure. Even though an unkind critic labeled the Duchamp painting "an explosion in a shingle factory," it symbolized the dynamism of the modern machine era.

The movement of the 1960s and 1970s known as **Op Art** was based on creating optical sensations of movement through the repetition and manipulation of color, shape, and line. In kinetic sculpture, movement is real, whether activated by currents of air or motors. In Op Art, bold and apparently vibrating lines and colors create the illusion of movement. Bridget Riley's *Gala* (Fig. 2-75) is composed of a series of curved lines that change in thickness and proximity to one another. These changes seem to suggest waves, but they also create a powerful illusion of rip-

2-73 THOMAS EAKINS. *Man Pole Vaulting* (c. 1884). Photograph. The Metropolitan Museum of Art, NY.

pling movement. Complementary red and green colors also contribute to the illusion of vibration. When we look at a color for an extended period of time, we tend to perceive its **afterimage**. Red is the afterimage of green, and vice versa. Therefore, there seems to be a pulsating in Riley's selection of color as well as in the tendency of the eye to perceive the lines as rippling.

If the visual elements are considered the basic vocabulary of art, principles of design may be viewed as the grammar of art. Artists use principles of design to combine the visual elements into compositions. In art, as in life, this "language" is idiosyncratic to the individual.

2-74 MARCEL DUCHAMP. *Nude Descending a Staircase #2* (1912). Oil on canvas. 58" × 35". The Philadelphia Museum of Art, Philadelphia, PA. © 2011 Artists Rights Society (ARS), NY/ADAGP, Paris/Succession Marcel Duchamp.

2-75 BRIDGET RILEY. *Gala* (1974). Acrylic on canvas. 5'2¾" square.

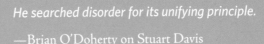
He searched disorder for its unifying principle.

—Brian O'Doherty on Stuart Davis

PRINCIPLES OF DESIGN

3

Unity is one of the principles of design, which, like visual elements, are part of the basic language of art. Just as people use principles of grammar to combine words into sentences, artists use principles of design to combine the visual elements of art into compositions that have a certain style, form, and content.

Design or **composition** is a process—the act of organizing the visual elements to effect a desired aesthetic in a work of art. Designs can occur at random, as exemplified by the old mathematical saw that an infinite number of monkeys pecking away at an infinite number of typewriters would eventually (though mindlessly) produce *Hamlet*. But when artists create compositions, they consciously draw upon design principles such as unity and variety, balance, emphasis and focal point, rhythm, scale, and proportion. This is not to say that all artists necessarily apply these principles, or even always recognize the extent of their presence in their work. In fact, some artists prefer to purposefully violate them.

CHUCK CLOSE. *Lucas II* (1987). Oil on canvas. 36" × 30". Collection of John and Mary Shirley, NY.

UNITY AND VARIETY

Unity is oneness or wholeness. A work of art achieves unity when its parts seem necessary to the composition as a whole. Artists generally prefer to place some variety within a unified composition to add visual interest, but the principle of variety is most often subservient to the sense of oneness or overall unity in a work.

Ways to Achieve Unity and Variety within Unity

Andy Warhol built *Ethel Scull Thirty-Six Times* (Fig. **3-1**) on the principle of a grid—an extreme example of unity—drawing attention to the ubiquity of mass-produced consumables of any and all types, including human beings of celebrity. Reflecting his signature compositional arrangement, the work consists of the repetition of silk-screened photo-booth-type images, in this case of Ethel Scull, an important patron of the arts in

the 1960s. An overall unity abides within the nine-by-four grid and repetitive color scheme, but the wide variety of expressions create a multidimensional view of Scull's appearance and personality. Warhol's multiportrait serves as an excellent illustration of variety within unity. The more you look at works of art, the better you will become at sensing the unity of compositions and at pinpointing the ways that artists achieve it. Sometimes the techniques will be obvious, and at other times they will be subtler.

Archibald Motley Jr.'s *Saturday Night* (Fig. **3-2**) offers the viewer a captivating array of characters—from the dining and drinking patrons and the waiters balancing their orders on tottering trays to one particularly flamboyant woman in a flame red costume who seems lost in the expressive rhythms of her solo dance. Yet this cacophony of sights and sounds and movements achieves a sense of oneness through a unified color field. To be sure, there is also some variety in the color scheme: the eye leaps from patches of black to black and from white to white, mimicking the riot of movement

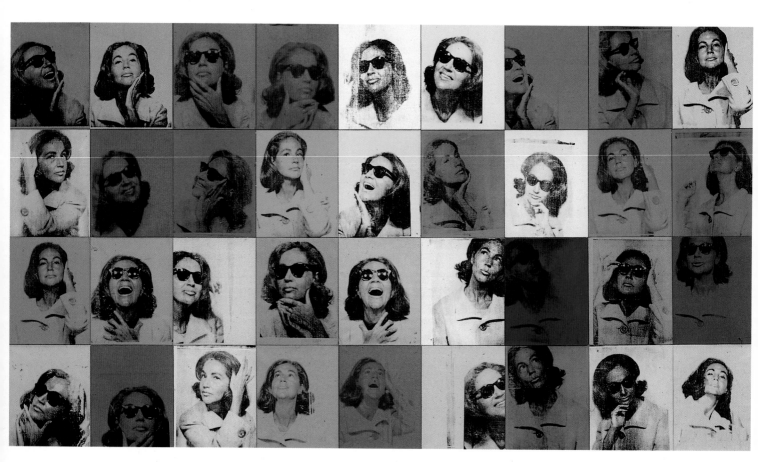

3-1 ANDY WARHOL. *Ethel Scull Thirty-Six Times* (1963). Synthetic polymer paint silkscreened on canvas. 79¾" × 143¼". Whitney Museum of American Art, NY. © 2011 The Andy Warhol Foundation for the Visual Arts/Artists Rights Society (ARS), NY.

1 ft.

in the nightclub. However, the overall composition is unified by the pulsating reds that seem to emanate from the center of the dance floor and bathe the atmosphere with emotion, energy, and an almost mystical glow.

Although color harmonies also contribute to a sense of oneness in Thomas Hart Benton's *Palisades* (Fig. **3-3**), the curvilinear rhythms of shape and line are the strongest purveyors of unity in this work. Here the diversity of the players in this mythologized narrative of American history—the Spanish conquistador, the European colonizer, the Native American—are joined symbolically and pictorially by the echoing shapes and lines and rhythms that define and distinguish the figures and landscape elements. The emergence of a visual pattern of similar elements dominates the individual parts.

When working with the principles of variety and unity, an artist will often keep one or more aspects of the work constant so that despite the multiplicity of images or elements, the composition's overall unity will not be compromised. The device of continuity to effect unity is also seen in a

1 ft.

work that is, literally, a world apart—Delilah Montoya's *Los Jovenes* (Youth) (Fig. **3-4**). It too features eight figures (and here a hovering image of the Virgin of Guadalupe), some interacting, some not; some confronting the viewer, some not the least bit interested in doing so. Continuity is reflected in the ages of the youths, their ethnicity, and a suggested bond of friendship. As in *Palisades*, our eye can travel from one side of the photograph to the other, picking out lights and darks, shifts in foreground and background, and the prominence of hand gestures and positions. The visual flow is effortless.

All of the works we have discussed have **visual unity**; most embrace the principle of variety within unity. There is, however, a way to achieve unity in a composition that does not rely on the consistency or repetition of the elements of art. Sometimes artists pursue, instead, a unity of ideas and impose a **conceptual unity** on their work. They will recognize that the strength of a composition lies in the diversity of elements and their juxtaposition. They reject visual harmonies in favor of discordant punctuations and focus on the relationships between the meanings and functions of the images. Emma Amos's *Measuring Measuring* (Fig. **3-5**) offers an example of conceptual unity. The "ideal" human form is represented by works of art from the Western canon flanking the seminude figure of an African woman. "Measuring" has at least a double meaning—the measure of the African standard of beauty against that of the Western tradition and the measure of black against white. The images are physically incongruous, and the elements of the composition do not

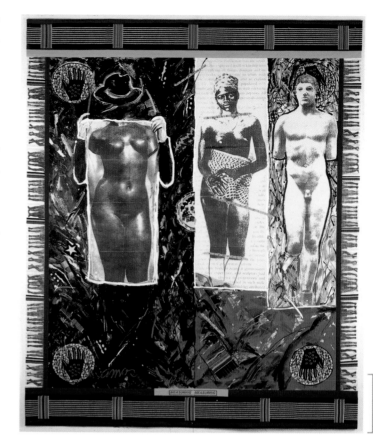

3-5 EMMA AMOS. *Measuring Measuring* (1995). Acrylic on linen canvas, African fabric, laser-transfer photographs. 84" × 70". Flomenhaft Gallery, NY.

3-4 DELILAH MONTOYA. *Los Jovenes* (Youth) (1993). Collotype. 9 3/16" × 10". Smithsonian American Art Museum, Washington, D.C.

encourage visual unity. What unites this composition is the concept behind the work: the challenge to address the standard and the canon.

Emphasis on Variety

When artists emphasize variety, they are usually exaggerating differences rather than similarities among their images. Palmer Hayden's painting called *The Subway* (Fig. **3-6**) is a demographic and ethnic cross section of the strap-hanging population of 1930s New York City. Even though they are unified by the common need to move efficiently from place to place beneath the streets of the metropolis, this fact is not the main theme of the work. Rather, the artist builds his painting around the individuality and diversity of the riders. Hayden's emphasis on variety is signified in the juxtaposition of the light and dark hands at the center of the painting. This snapshot of subway life hasn't changed much in three-quarters of a century. The underground in New York City remains a great equalizer, and as one surveys the contemporary scene, one finds an even greater human diversity, with even more emphasis on variety.

3-6 PALMER HAYDEN. *The Subway* (c. 1930). Oil on canvas. 31" × 26½". New York State Office of General Services, Adam Clayton Powell, Jr., State Office Building, NY.

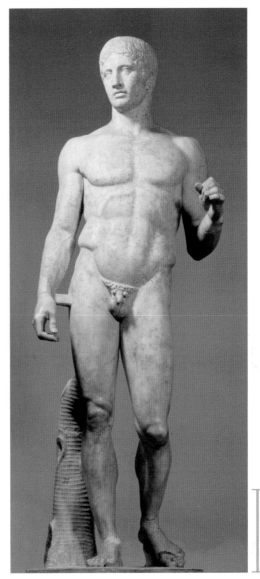

3-7 POLYKLEITOS. *Doryphoros* (c. 450–440 BCE). Roman copy after bronze Greek original. Marble. 6'6". Museo Archeologico Nazionale, Naples, Italy.

BALANCE

Most people prefer to have some stability in their lives, to have their lives on a "firm footing." In the same way, most people respond positively to some degree of balance in the visual arts. When we walk, run, or perform an athletic feat, balance refers to the way in which our weight is distributed, or shifts, so that we remain in control of our movements. **Balance** in art also refers to the distribution of the weight— of the actual or apparent weight of the elements of a composition. As the athlete uses balance to control movement, so might the artist choose to use balance to control the distribution or emphasis of elements such as line or shape or color in a composition.

The Classical Greek artist Polykleitos was perhaps the first artist to observe the body's shifting of weight in order to achieve balance and to develop a set of rules to apply this observation to representations of the figure. In his *Doryphoros* (Fig. **3-7**), or Spear Bearer, Polykleitos featured his weight-shift principle. He observed that when the body is at rest, one leg bears the weight of the body and the other is relaxed. Further,

in order for the body to balance itself, the upper torso shifts, as if corresponding to an S curve, so that the arm opposite the tensed leg is tensed, and the one opposite the relaxed leg is relaxed. Thus, with the weight-shift principle, tension and tension and relaxation and relaxation are read diagonally across the body. Overall figural balance is achieved.

Actual Balance and Pictorial Balance

Sculptures such as *Doryphoros* have *actual weight* and may thus also have actual balance. Even though actual weight and **actual balance** are not typically at issue in two-dimensional works such as drawings, paintings, and prints, we nonetheless do speak of balance in these compositions. **Pictorial balance** refers to the distribution of the apparent or *visual weight* of the elements in works that are basically two-dimensional, and there are many ways to achieve it.

Symmetrical Balance

You can divide the human body in half vertically, and in the ideal, as in Leonardo da Vinci's most famous drawing, *Proportion of the Human Figure* (Fig. **3-8**), there will be an exact correspondence between the left and right sides. **Symmetry** refers to similarity of form or arrangement on either side of a dividing line or plane, or to correspondence of parts in size, shape, and position. When the correspondence is exact, as in Leonardo's drawing, we refer to it as *pure* or *formal symmetry*. In reality, nature is not as perfect as Leonardo would have had it.

Examples of pure or formal symmetry appear no more frequently in art than in nature. More typically, **symmetrical balance** is created through *approximate* symmetry, in which the whole of the work has a symmetrical feeling, but slight variations provide more visual interest than would a mirror image. When the variations to the right and left side of the composition are *more* than slight, yet there remains an overall sense of balance, there is said to be **asymmetrical balance**.

In *pure* or *formal symmetry*, also known as **bilateral symmetry**, everything in a composition to either side of an actual or imaginary line is the same. The regularity and predictability of symmetry cannot help but conjure a sense of peace, calm, comfort, and order. The effect of repetition can be mesmerizing. In architectural works like the U.S. Capitol Building (Fig. **3-9**)—the house in which the laws of the land are created—repetition and symmetry can imply rationality and decorum, tying the structure of the building to a certain symbolic ideal. The design of the Capitol consists of a solid rectangular structure flanked by identical wings that extend from the central part of the building, project forward at right angles, and culminate in "temple fronts" that echo the main entrance beneath a hemispherical dome. An ordinary citizen of the republic takes pride in the architectural grandeur, feels secure in the balance of all of the parts, and—with the obvious references to Greek architecture of the Golden Age—feels a part of the history of democracy. It is no coincidence that, for the nation's Capitol, our founders adapted structures such as the Parthenon of Athens in the hope of associating the new republic with the ancient birthplace of democracy.

In many works of art, the symmetry is *approximate* rather than exact. For example, the overall impression of William Wegman's *Ethiopia* (Fig. **3-10**) is that of symmetry, primarily attributable to the echoing shapes of the Weimaraners' heads and the firm vertical line that bisects the composition. Yet there are elements that break the monotony of the symmetry, such as the juxtaposition of near-complementary shades of red and green, and the contrast of the clear, detailed face of the dog on the right with ghostlike iteration on the left.

Asymmetrical Balance

When your eyes are telling you that the elements of a composition are skewed but your brain is registering overall balance, chances are you are witnessing asymmetrical balance. There is probably a human tendency to effect balance at any cost. Sometimes the right and left sides of a composition bear visibly different shapes, colors, textures, or other elements, yet they are arranged or "weighted" in such a way that the impression, in total, is one of balance. In such cases, the artist has employed the design principle of *asymmetrical* or *informal balance*.

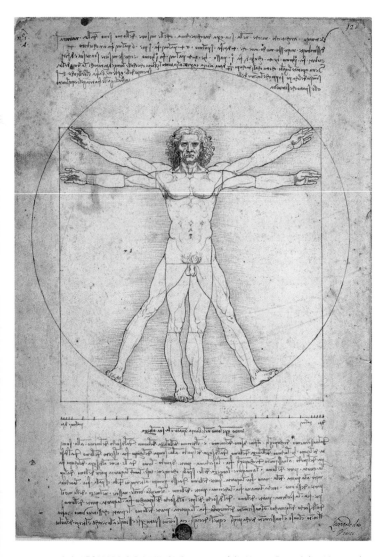

3-8 LEONARDO DA VINCI. *Proportion of the Human Figure* (after Vitruvius) (c. 1485–1490). Pen and ink. 13½" × 9¾". Accademia, Venice, Italy.

3-9 The U.S. Capitol Building, Washington, D.C.

1 ft.

3-10 WILLIAM WEGMAN. *Ethiopia* (2006). Pigment print. 36" × 44".

In Wu Jide's *River Dwellers* (Fig. **3-11**), patches of white and well-placed touches of color are responsible for the overall visual balance in an asymmetrical and essentially monochromatic composition. Like a movie within a movie, the large, square canvas sail of a small boat is printed with a scene of another boating party. The bright colors of the sail dominate the ocher atmosphere of the woodcut, as does the scale of the figures therein. Asymmetrical balance is achieved as the artist picks up the reds and yellows and blues of the sail and adds them as almost random touches to other parts of the composition. The stark white of the sail, which provides a luminous backdrop for the boating group, is echoed in scattered bits and pieces that float like large snowflakes or a torn love note and tie the entire work together.

In Deborah Butterfield's *Verde* (Fig. **3-12**), the mane and head of the horse are defined by greenish strips of steel that enframe void space. (The title *Verde* calls our attention to the finish of the steel, a greenish coating referred to as *verdigris*.) The *actual weight* of this upper part of the horse is negligible. The body, on the other hand, is composed of heavy molded sheets of steel, approximating the volume of the animal's torso. Overall visual balance is achieved in this work because the outlines of the head and neck, silhouetted

3-11 WU JIDE. *River Dwellers* (1998). Multiblock woodcut printed with water-soluble ink. 16⅞" × 13⅝". Muban Foundation, London, England.

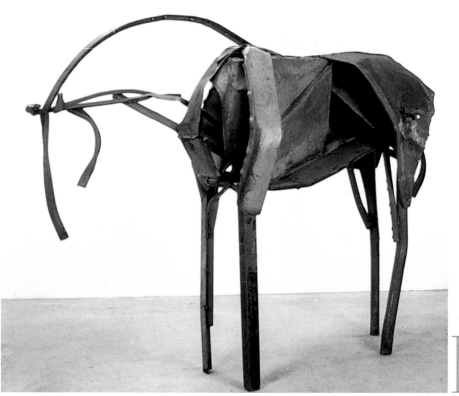

3-12 DEBORAH BUTTERFIELD. *Verde* (1990). Found steel. 79" × 108" × 31". Collection of the artist. Art © Deborah Butterfield/Licensed by VAGA, NY.

Käsebier's delicately textured photograph *Blessed Art Thou among Women* (Fig. **3-13**). Notice how the dark value of the girl's dress is balanced both by the dark wall to the left and by the woman's hair. Similarly, the stark light value of the vertical shaft of the doorway to the left and the light values of the right side of the composition are in equilibrium.

With **vertical balance**, the elements at the top and bottom of the composition are in balance. In Kay Sage's *I Saw Three Cities* (Fig. **3-14**), a firm horizon line separates a bleak landscape from a bleaker sky. Most of the visual weight in the composition occurs in the lower half, where geometric shapes casting long shadows lead your eye from the picture plane toward a kind of desolate futuristic city. The hard-edged structures that litter the landscape, however, are balanced in the upper reaches of the sky by a flowing column of drapery that billows up from the ground and across to the left, floating toward the source of the light on a strange breeze that breaks the stagnant gray air.

Artists employ **diagonal balance** by establishing equal visual weight to either side of a pictorial space that is divided

3-13 GERTRUDE KÄSEBIER. *Blessed Art Thou among Women* (c. 1898). Photograph. 9¼" × 5½".

against the white wall, pop out at the viewer. They become so prominent that they carry enough *visual weight* to balance the more densely compacted sheet metal of the animal's body.

Horizontal, Vertical, Diagonal, and Radial Balance

In works of art with **horizontal balance**, the elements at the left and right sides of the composition seem to be about equal in number or visual emphasis. The U.S. Capitol Building (Fig. 3-9) has horizontal balance. So too does Gertrude

3-14 KAY SAGE. *I Saw Three Cities* (1944). Oil on canvas. 36" × 27⅞". Princeton University Art Museum. Princeton, NJ.

1 ft.

1 in.

3-15 ADIL JAIN. *Two Heads* from the series *London Portraits*. (c. August 2004). Color C-Print. 16" × 16".

by means of a perceived diagonal. In Adil Jain's *Two Heads* (Fig. **3-15**), the photographer captures the juxtaposition of evocative images and, in the process, creates a striking compositional equilibrium. The elderly couple on a bench in the lower right are partially cut off by the frame of the camera's viewfinder. Yet they are pulled back into the work along an implied diagonal that visually connects them to the large blue square of the trash receptacle behind them. The diagonal positioning of the woman and her backward glance facilitate the connection. The spray-painted image of a bride and groom echoes their figures, balancing the composition and creating a symbolic connection. The viewer's eye moves from the couple to their graffiti counterparts and back along the perceived diagonal.

In the case of **radial balance**, the design elements radiate from a center point. Radial balance is familiar to us because nature offers us so many examples. From the petals of a daisy and the filaments of a spider's web to the sun's powerful rays, lines or shapes radiate from a central point and lead the viewer's eye in a circular pattern around the source.

Radial balance is frequently a major principle of design in art forms such as ceramics, jewelry, basketry, stained glass, and other crafts. The decorative tabletop from nineteenth-century Iran (Fig. **3-16**) is a classic example of radial balance. At the center of the piece is a large, round, intricately painted tile surrounded by a circular garland of flowers, birds, and clusters of grapes. Both the central tile and the garland are framed by narrow, decorative bands; diagonals fan outward from these bands toward the perimeter, dividing the remaining space into eight separate pictorial segments. Like the spokes of a wheel, the narrow framing device directs the gaze of the

1 ft.

3-16 ALI MUHAMMAD KASHIGAR ISFAHANI. Iranian tabletop (1887). Nine separate tiles. Table diameter 54½". Victoria and Albert Museum, London, England.

viewer both outward and inward and provides order to the content. The tiles are decorated with scenes inspired by the *Book of Kings*, an Iranian epic.

Imbalance

Balance affords a certain level of comfort. The viewer will usually try to impose balance on a work, even when there is asymmetry. But not all art is about comfort; not all art aims to be aesthetically pleasing. Some artists aim to shock the viewer or to play into a viewer's discomfort by creating works with **imbalance**.

Consider Robert Capa's photograph *Death of a Loyalist Soldier* (Fig. **3-17**), which was taken during the Spanish Civil War. The photographer has captured the soldier just as an enemy rifleman shot him. By allowing the composition to remain unbalanced, or weighted on the left, the drama of the moment is intensified. The long black shadow behind the soldier seems to pull the figure toward the ground, as he stumbles from the impact of the bullet. The photographer no doubt maintained the visual imbalance in the composition to correspond with the physical imbalance of the victim.

In Capa's photograph, there is a clear sense of movement. The soldier has been running down a grassy hill and suddenly falls backward. Imbalance in a work of art can be used to capture a sense of movement—the fourth dimension—in a two-dimensional or a three-dimensional work. Niki de Saint-Phalle's *Black Venus* (Fig. **3-18**) is a larger-than-life figure of a woman in a psychedelic bathing suit who is catching a beach ball. The placement of the legs and feet at the very least suggests a precariously balanced body. She seems to leap into the air to catch the ball, defying gravity and her own ponderousness. Despite, or because of, her mountainous appearance, the

3-18 NIKI DE SAINT-PHALLE. *Black Venus* (1967). Painted polyester. 110" × 35" × 24". Whitney Museum of American Art, NY. © 2011 Artists Rights Society (ARS), NY/ADAGP, Paris.

3-17 ROBERT CAPA. *Death of a Loyalist Soldier* (September 5, 1936). Gelatin silver print.

unbalanced position of her lower body gives the figure a contradictory sense of weightlessness. Niki de Saint-Phalle challenges the ideal of feminine beauty in the Western tradition with figures such as *Black Venus*. How does this spirited form stand apart from traditional Western nudes such as the *Venus of Urbino* (see Fig. 16-27)?

EMPHASIS AND FOCAL POINT

For the most part, we do not view a work of art as we read a page of text. The eye does not start in the upper left corner and then systematically work its way to the right in rows. Rather, some feature of the work usually commands our attention. Artists use the design principle of **emphasis** to focus the viewer's attention on one or more parts of a composition by accentuating certain shapes, intensifying value or color, featuring directional lines, or strategically placing the objects and images. Emphasis can be used to create **focal points** or specific parts of the work that seize and hold the viewer's interest.

As if the overwhelming presence of the face—that is, the *content*—in Chuck Close's *Lucas II* (Fig. **3-19**) is not enough to focus the viewer's attention on the center of the composition, the artist emphasizes or draws our eye to a single point—the focal point—between the subject's eyes by creating a target-like pattern of concentric circles around it. The circles are intersected by broken lines of color that radiate from the center, causing a sense of simultaneous movement outward from the center point and back inward.

Emphasis on a particular area or image in a composition can be effected when several of its components direct the viewer's gaze toward a focal point. *Welcome the World*

3-19 CHUCK CLOSE. *Lucas II* (1987). Oil on canvas. 36" × 30". Collection of John and Mary Shirley, NY.

3-20 THE LUO BROTHERS. *Welcome the World Famous Brand* (2000). Collage and lacquer on wood. 96⅞" × 49⅝" × 1³⁄₁₆". Ray Hughes Gallery, Sydney, Australia.

3-21 PABLO PICASSO. *Family of Saltimbanques* (1905). Oil on canvas. 83¾" × 90⅜". National Gallery of Art, Washington, D.C. © 2011 Estate of Pablo Picasso/ Artists Rights Society (ARS), NY.

1 ft.

Famous Brand (Fig. **3-20**) by the Luo Brothers features their signature emphasis on the convergence of consumerism and globalism. Mimicking the garish packaging of Chinese merchandise, their compositions are often overcrowded, intensely colored, and exuberant in mood. There is so much energy bound up in the imagery that it is almost impossible for the eyes to stop and focus. Emphasis through placement is an important device in this work, and to achieve it, once again, the Luo Brothers use mimicry. The "enthroned" baby raising a McDonald's sandwich in the center of the piece becomes the focal point. It is emphasized by the red and yellow bands of lines that look like divine rays emanating from behind the baby, who, in turn is bolstered on a floating rectangle by lesser, though no less jubilant, little ones. To the left and right are regimented stacks of burgers riding on chariots pulled by teams of lambs. Brightly colored peonies add to the outrageously festive atmosphere. This formula—enthroned central figure buoyed by devoted onlookers and flanked by symmetrical groups of regimented figures—is standard in religious altarpieces over centuries of art history. The Luo

Brothers appropriate this formula to sharpen their statement about what we "worship" in contemporary society.

In Pablo Picasso's *Family of Saltimbanques* (Fig. **3-21**), we see how artists use the principle of emphasis by isolation, in which they separate one object or figure from the many. Amidst a rather desolate landscape, figures of circus performers stand silent, seemingly frozen in their sculptural poses. The patterns, colors, and costume variety of the main figural group are, interestingly, less visually significant than the more delicately rendered figure of the woman seated apart from them in the lower right. Picasso has emphasized her aloneness by pulling her from the group. Her solitude draws us into her private musings; her inner world becomes the focus of our attention.

In *Bauhaus Stairway* (Fig. **3-22**), Oskar Schlemmer used powerful directional lines and a bright area of color to create the focal point in his composition. The diagonal thrusts of the staircase railing would meet in the center of the composition and would by themselves create the focal point. However, the focal point is further reinforced by the orange-red of point that despite other devices used to create focal points, the image will have the tendency to negate or override them. In Edgar Degas's *Woman Leaning near a Vase of Flowers* (Fig. **3-23**), the centerpiece—quite literally—of the composition is an enormous bouquet of chrysanthemums. It has almost everything one could ask of a focal point—central position, brilliant color, dominant texture. And yet our eyes are drawn to the woman who sits off to the side of the vase, daydreaming, gazing beyond the borders of the canvas. A viewer's gaze is seduced by the sight of a human face.

If you look at Francisco Goya's *The Third of May, 1808* (see Figure 19-6), you will see one of the best historical examples of the design principle of emphasis. Goya uses multiple strategies to focus the viewer's eyes and sympathies on a Spanish peasant who is about to be executed by riflemen under the authority of the French emperor Napoleon. The doomed man's bright white shirt, spotlighted by a cube-shaped lantern, immediately fixes our gaze. The bayonets read as strong, repeated, horizontal lines pointing directly at the victim; the soldiers lean determinedly into action along diagonals that also direct our eyes toward the group. Can you name other ways in which Goya has used emphasis in this painting?

3-22 OSKAR SCHLEMMER. *Bauhaus Stairway* (1932). Oil on canvas. 63⅞" × 45". The Museum of Modern Art, NY.

1 ft.

RHYTHM

The world would be a jumble of sights and sounds were it not for the **regular repetition** of sensory impressions. Natural **rhythms**, or orderly progressions, regulate events ranging from the orbits of the planets to the unfolding of the genetic code into flesh and blood. Artists can enhance or exaggerate individual elements in their compositions through minor and major variations in rhythm. And rhythm can move a viewer visually as well as emotionally. Repetitive patterns can be used to lead the eye over the landscape of the work and to evoke a psychological response in the viewer.

Rhythm can be present in a work of art even if there is a slight variation in repetition. Magdalena Abakanowicz's *Backs* (Fig. **3-24**), from a series of body works called *Alterations*, consists of 80 fiber sculptures representing human

a woman's sweater, while it partially obscures the meeting of the diagonals and leaps out against a backdrop of quiet blues and off-whites. Content helps too. The people in the foreground are in the act of climbing the stairs and, in so doing, ascending toward the focal point of the composition.

The power of content can sometimes overwhelm the power of shape, texture, and other elements of art to the

3-23 EDGAR DEGAS. *Woman Leaning near a Vase of Flowers* (Mme Paul Valpinçon; erroneously called *Woman with Chrysanthemums*) (1865). Oil on canvas. 29" × 36½". The Metropolitan Museum of Art, NY.

1 in.

backs. Although the individual forms look like hunched-over figures, they are without heads, legs, or arms. Even the fronts of the torsos have been hollowed out, leaving an actual and symbolic human shell. In this work, the artist, whose mother was mutilated by the Nazis in World War II, seems to bring to her work the memory of the dehumanization she witnessed. The potency of this message is largely attributable to the repetition of forms that have lost their individuality.

3-24 MAGDALENA ABAKANOWICZ. *Backs* (1976–1982). Burlap and glue. 80 pieces, 3 sizes: 24" × 19¹¹⁄₁₆" × 21¹¹⁄₁₆"; 27³⁄₁₆" × 22" × 26"; 28³⁄₈" × 23¼" × 27³⁄₁₆". Marlborough Gallery, NY.

Making art is about objectifying your experience of the world, transforming the flow of moments into something visual, or textual, or musical. Art creates a kind of commentary.
—Barbara Kruger

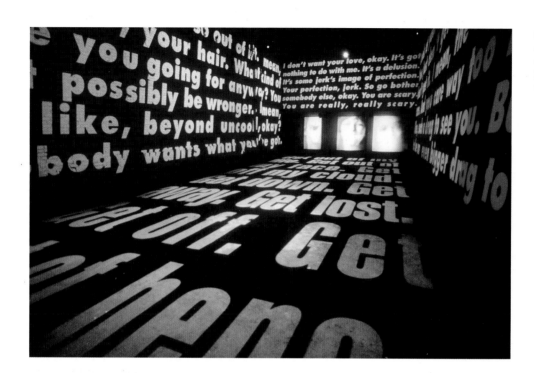

3-25 BARBARA KRUGER. *Power Pleasure Desire Disgust* (1997). Multimedia installation. © Barbara Kruger, Courtesy Mary Boone Gallery, NY.

SCALE

Scale refers to size—small, big, or in between. Scale is the relative size of an object compared with others of its kind, its setting, or human dimensions. The Great Pyramids at Gizeh (see Fig. 13-12) and the skyscrapers of New York are imposing because of their scale; that is, their size compared with the size of other buildings, their sites, and people. Their overall size is essential to their impact.

Barbara Kruger's multimedia installation *Power Pleasure Desire Disgust* (Fig. **3-25**) combines steadily changing video images of talking heads and projections of the artist's signature phrases and text all over the gallery floors and walls. The overwhelming scale of the work envelops us so completely and the slogans bombard us so relentlessly that it may seem as though the thoughts expressed in the environment have somehow originated in our own minds—phrases we may have once used to hurt others or that have been used to hurt us, comments that may have cut to the quick. But interspersed with the bitter are flashes of wit, even flirtatiousness, as the work touches on communication across boundaries of gender and social definition. Thoughts are compelling and haunting things, made all the more inescapable by the sheer size of their verbal and written articulation.

3-26 COUNT DE MONTIZON. *The Hippopotamus at the Zoological Gardens, Regent's Park* (1852). Salted-paper print.

In the Count de Montizon's photograph *The Hippopotamus at the Zoological Gardens, Regent's Park* (Fig. **3-26**), we see how artists communicate the scale of objects in their works by comparing them with other objects. In this photograph, a specimen record of the zoo's prized tenant, the photographer used *relative* size to communicate size. We see that it takes nine people standing shoulder to shoulder to match the length of one animal lazing in the sun. The photographer used the relationship between the familiar (the observers) and the unfamiliar (the hippopotamus) to communicate the size of the hippo to those who weren't there to witness it firsthand. At the time the picture was taken, 1852, the hippopotamus was not yet a familiar denizen of zoos in Europe and the United States. A gift from the pasha of Egypt to Queen Victoria, this hippo was the main attraction at the London Zoo.

Nineteenth-century London's hippopotamus was exotic, its size dramatic. In relation to the scale of ordinary human beings, it was extraordinary. In viewing the photograph, a person could pretty much grasp the magnitude of the animal. By contrast, in Magritte's *Personal Values* (Fig. **3-27**), it is impossible for the viewer to comprehend the dimensions of any of the objects within the work because their familiar size relationships are subverted. We don't know whether the objects—the comb and matchstick and glass—are blown out of proportion or whether the bed has shrunk. We cannot rely

3-28 VIOLA FREY. *Family Portrait* (1995). Glazed ceramic. 84" × 82⅝" × 34⅝". Collection of the Hirshhorn Museum and Sculpture Garden, Smithsonian Institution, Washington, D.C. Art © Artists' Legacy Foundation/Licensed by VAGA, NY.

on our experience of actual dimension to make sense of the content of the work, so our tendency to understand size in relation to other things fails us.

Hierarchical Scaling

Standing "ten feet tall" is a familiar idiom. We use it to describe heroes or to communicate a certain pride we feel in our own accomplishments. It describes our feelings about a deed that sets others or ourselves above the rest, even if for one fleeting moment. In the visual arts, this metaphor, this idiom, finds its analogy in **hierarchical scaling**, or the use of relative size to indicate the relative importance of the objects or people being depicted. The method has been used for thousands of years. In ancient Egyptian art, members of royalty and nobility are sized consistently larger than the underlings surrounding them, making very clear their social positions. In medieval manuscript illumination, artists often had their celestial figures, such as angels and saints, tower over humans.

In Viola Frey's *Family Portrait* (Fig. **3-28**), we interpret the positioning and relatively large scale of the central male figure as an

3-27 RENÉ MAGRITTE. *Personal Values* (1952). Oil on canvas. 31⅝" × 39½". San Francisco Museum of Modern Art, San Francisco, CA.

VAN EYCK'S *MADONNA IN THE CHURCH* WITH PANNINI'S *INTERIOR OF THE PANTHEON*

ARTISTS OVER THE GENERATIONS have used hierarchical scaling to assign relative importance to the subjects of their work. The Flemish artist Jan van Eyck dramatically increased the size or scale of his Madonna, depicted in a jewel-studded crown befitting her status as the Queen of Heaven, within the interior of a typical Gothic cathedral (Fig. **3-29**). He relies on the viewer's understanding of the vastness of such an interior to convey, through her relative size, her importance in Christian belief.

Van Eyck set himself the task of attempting to convey the notion of the Queen of Heaven. How can he signify such status within the realm of human experience? In order to

3-30 GIOVANNI PAOLO PANNINI. *Interior of the Pantheon* (c. 1740). Oil on canvas. 50½" × 39". National Gallery of Art, Washington, D.C.

find some measure of the vastness of the heavens relative to human experience, van Eyck went to the interior of a Gothic cathedral—the very height of which is intended to replicate the unreachable dome of heaven. By rendering the Madonna in such a large scale relative to the seemingly infinite height of the vaulted ceilings, the ordinary earthbound worshiper begins to comprehend her majesty.

Pannini's goal was quite different. The Pantheon is one of Rome's most awesome monuments. How to describe the feeling of overwhelming space that one experiences within the realm of the *Interior of the Pantheon* (Fig. **3-30**)? Pannini sprinkles his interior with figures rendered in a realistic scale relative to the architecture. They seem insectlike compared to the reaches of the dome and thus we get some idea of what it must feel like to stand beneath it. The relationship between these humans and the grandeur of this architecture makes it seem as if it must have been the work of giants.

What is the focus of each of these paintings? What is each of them about? Are they about architecture or about the figures within? In the van Eyck, the architecture is used to suggest the importance of the Madonna. In the Pannini, the people are used to show the grandeur of the architecture. ●

1 in.

3-29 JAN VAN EYCK. *Madonna in the Church* (c. 1437-1438). Oil on oak panel. 12¼" × 5½". Gemäldegalerie, Staatliche Museum, Berlin, Germany.

indicator of his status within the family. Frey includes only his head and shoulders, against which are measured the full-bodied figures of the other family members. The influence of the patriarch is sensed not only in his relative size, but also in the crowding of the group.

Distortion of Scale

Some artists distort or even subvert the realistic scale of objects to challenge the viewer to look at the familiar in a new way.

3-31 MARISOL. *Baby Girl* (1963). Wood and mixed media. 74" × 35" × 47". Albright-Knox Art Gallery, Buffalo, NY. Art © Marisol Escobar/Licensed by VAGA, NY.

Sometimes they are interested in providing a new perspective on the forms of things; sometimes on the relationships between things.

Altering the viewer's sense of scale partly creates the visual shock and sheer humor of Marisol's *Baby Girl* (Fig. **3-31**). A wooden doll with adjustable limbs and torso—the sort used for drawing exercises in art classes—sports a portrait of Marisol herself. It is perched on the stocky thigh of the baby, who neither looks at nor touches the "toy." The baby girl—by any other definition a subject that suggests delicacy and softness—is transformed into a cumbersome hunk of a figure. Only the shirring of her puffy sleeves and frilly gathers of her white dress soften the harshness of the overall form. Marisol's manipulation of scale and our perception of it are confirmed by the fact that in looking at the illustration of this work in your book (without sneaking a peek at the dimensions), you would have no real sense of how large or small the work actually is.

PROPORTION

"Everything is relative." That is, we tend to think of objects or of works of art as large or small according to their relationships to other things—often to ourselves. However, the objects depicted within works of art can also be large or small in relationship to one another and to the work as a whole. **Proportion**, then, is the comparative relationship, or ratio, of things to one another.

Artists through the ages have sought to determine the proper or most appealing ratios of parts of works to one another and the whole. They have used proportion to represent what they believed to be the ideal or the beautiful. They also have disregarded or subverted proportion to achieve special effects—often to compel viewers to take a new look at the familiar.

The Canon of Proportions

The ancient Greeks tied their vision of ideal beauty to what they considered the "proper" proportions of the human body. Polykleitos is credited with the derivation of a **canon of proportions**—a set of rules about body parts and their dimensions relative to one another that became the standard for creating the ideal figure. The physical manifestation of his canon was his *Doryphoros* (Fig. 3-7). Every part of the body is either a specific fraction or multiple of every other part. Ideally, for Polykleitos, the head is one-eighth of the total height of the body, and the width from shoulder to shoulder should not exceed one-fourth of the body's height.

3-32 ALICE NEEL. *The Family* (John Gruen, Jane Wilson, and Julia) (1970). Oil on canvas. 4′11⅞″ × 5′. The Museum of Fine Arts, Houston, TX.

Violating the Canon for Expressive Purposes

If the *Doryphoros* represents ideal form, Alice Neel's *The Family* (Fig. **3-32**) leaves the canon behind in what appears to be the pursuit of unidealized form. The enlarged heads, elongated fingers and calves, and outsized feet are glaring obstacles to realistic representation. And yet, somehow, there is an overarching realism despite these artistic liberties that emanates from the relationships among the family members.

The Golden Mean

Just as the Greeks developed a canon of proportions for representing the human figure in the ideal, they developed the concept of the **golden mean** or the **golden section** in order to create ideal proportions in architecture. The golden mean requires that a small part of a work should relate to a larger part of the work as the larger part relates to the whole. The line in Figure **3-33** is divided, or *sectioned*, at point B so that the ratio of the shorter segment (AB) is to the larger segment (BC) as the larger segment (BC) is to the whole line (AC). Segment BC is the golden mean.

The rectangle in Figure **3-34** is based on the golden mean and is termed a **golden rectangle**. Its width is 1.618 times its height. The golden rectangle was thought by the Greeks to be the most pleasing rectangle, and it became the basis for many temple designs.

3-33 The golden mean.
To create the golden mean, a line is divided ("sectioned") so that the ratio of the shorter segment (AB) is to the larger segment (BC) as the larger segment (BC) is to the whole (AC). Line segment BC is 1.618 times the length of segment AB. Segment BC is the "mean" in the sense that its length lies between the smaller segment (AB) and the entire line (AC). The Greeks considered segment BC to be "golden" in that its use created what they considered to be ideal proportions in architecture.

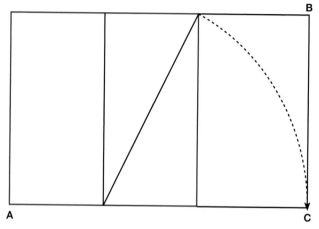

3-34 The golden rectangle.
The width of this rectangle is exactly 1.618 times its height. The triangle can be created by rotating the diagonal of the half square on the left (outlined in red) to the base on the right (point C). This "ideal" rectangle became the basis for the floor plans of Greek temples and represented the artistic embodiment of the Greek maxim "Moderation in all things."

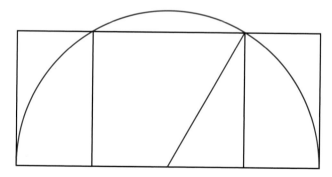

3-35 The root five rectangle.
One obtains a root five rectangle by rotating the diagonal of the square in Figure 3-34 in both directions. The rectangle obtains its name from the fact that its length is 2.236 (the square root of the number 5) times its width. The root five rectangle has frequently been used to define the frame for works of art, including buildings (Figure 3-36) and paintings (Figure 3.37).

A golden rectangle can be made either by measuring the lengths of the lines or by rotating the diagonal of the half square, as shown in Figure 3-34. We can also rotate the diagonal of the square in both directions, sort of like a windshield

3-36 The east facade of the Parthenon, superimposed with a root five rectangle. When we do not consider the gable (which is absent in this photograph), the facade of the Parthenon is a root five rectangle.

wiper. If we add the second smaller rectangle, we obtain a rectangle that is made up of a central square and two smaller rectangles (Fig. **3-35**). The entire rectangle is called a root five rectangle, because its length is 2.236 (the square root of 5) times its width.

The proportions of the root five rectangle have also served as the frame for various works of art and architecture. If you superimpose a diagram of a **root five rectangle** over a photograph of the east facade of the Parthenon (Fig. **3-36**), you can see the almost compulsive adherence to geometric order that the Greeks visited on their places of worship. The facade is constructed of eight columns. The four in the center fit within the central square of the root five rectangle. The portions of the facade occupying the flanking rectangles include the two end columns to either side as well as the outermost points defined by the steps leading to the temple platform.

Most viewers are unaware of the mathematical basis for the Parthenon's design, but they come away with an overall impression of harmony and order. The root five rectangle is also the foundation of some paintings that have harmonious compositions. Michelangelo's *The Fall of Man and the Expulsion from the Garden of Eden* (Fig. **3-37**), from the Sistine Chapel ceiling (see Figs. 16-21 and 16-22), maximizes the components of the root five rectangle. The central square contains the Tree of Knowledge from the book of Genesis, that all-important symbol of the temptation and fall of man. The Tree connects the imagery in the outer parts of the root five rectangle—the repetitive figures of Adam and Eve as separated by time and the serpent.

3-37 MICHELANGELO. *The Fall of Man and the Expulsion from the Garden of Eden* (1508–1512). Portion of the Sistine Chapel ceiling. Fresco. Vatican, Rome, Italy.

The duty of an artist is to strain against the bonds of the existing style.

—Philip Johnson

STYLE, FORM, AND CONTENT

4

Human languages combine words according to rules of grammar to express and communicate emotions and meanings. Artists use the language of art to combine the visual elements of art according to principles of design. The resultant works of art are said to have style and form and to express and communicate a certain content.

Despite individual differences—and despite wholesale revolutions!—through the ages several characteristic methods of expression have developed that we refer to as *style*. Works of art can also be said to have a certain *form*, which is the totality of what we see—the product of the composition of the visual elements according to (or in total violation of) principles of design. The *content* of a work includes not only its form but also its subject matter and its underlying meanings or themes. Some works of art can seem to be devoid of content other than the pencil marks or, perhaps, the swaths of paint we find on a sheet of paper or on a canvas. But many are filled with levels of content, more of which are perceived by some viewers than by others. The content of a work varies with the amount of information available to the viewer. For example, viewers who are aware of the symbolism of a particular work of art will find more content in it. Awareness of style, form, and content helps viewers understand and appreciate the visual arts more fully.

OSKAR KOKOSCHKA. *The Tempest* (1914). Oil on canvas. 71½" × 86½". Kunstmuseum, Basel, Switzerland.

STYLE

In the visual arts, **style** refers to a distinctive handling of elements and media associated with the work of an individual artist, a school or movement, or a specific culture or time period. Familiar subjects may come and go, but creativity, originality, and authenticity dwell in the style or unique handling of the artist.

One of the best ways to illustrate stylistic differences is to choose a group of works with a common theme (such as those illustrated in Figures 4-1 through 4-10) and challenge ourselves to articulate the similarities and differences among them. The first and seemingly obvious connection is that all of the works represent couples. Yet immediately we are struck by the differences among them, in terms of both the stories they imply and the styles in which they are rendered.

To begin with, the images demand that we get beyond the conventional definition of *couple*, for not all couples are composed of a male and a female. What is really striking, however, are the variations in *style*, sometimes linked to the use of different media and sometimes connected to diverse cultural contexts, but always indicative of the characteristic approach of the artist to the subject.

Art, Culture, and Context

The Mayan ceramic couple (Fig. **4-1**), for example, is an eighth- to tenth-century pre-Columbian sculpture, whose garments, hairstyles, and facial features link it to the life and times of the Yucatecan people before the onslaught of the Europeans. Similar telltale attributes connect Roy Lichtenstein's *Forget It! Forget Me!* (Fig. **4-2**) to the United States in the decade of the 1960s. Henri de Toulouse-Lautrec's *The Two Girlfriends* (Fig. **4-3**) transports us to the demimonde of

4-1 *Amorous Couple* (Mayan, Late Classic, 700–900 CE). Polychromed ceramic. H: 9¾". Detroit Institute of the Arts, Detroit, MI.

4-2 ROY LICHTENSTEIN. *Forget It! Forget Me!* (1962). Magna and oil on canvas. 79⅞" × 68". Rose Art Museum, Brandeis University, Waltham, MA.

4-3 HENRI DE TOULOUSE-LAUTREC. *The Two Girlfriends* (1894). Oil on cardboard. 18⅞" × 34⅝". Musée Toulouse-Lautrec, Albi, France.

1 in.

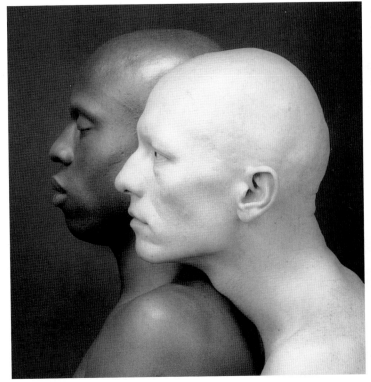

4-4 ROBERT MAPPLETHORPE. *Ken Moody and Robert Sherman* (1984). Photograph. 19½" × 19⅝". Solomon R. Guggenheim Museum, NY.

turn-of-the-century Paris where, as we were told in the film *Moulin Rouge*, the greatest thing is to love and be loved in return. The weather-worn faces and postcard-perfect surroundings in Grant Wood's *American Gothic* (Fig. 4-9) suggest the duality of rural life in modern America—hardship and serenity—whereas contemporary photographer Robert Mapplethorpe (Fig. **4-4**) drew the world's attention to what it was like to be gay and living in America at the end of the millennium. The tumult of Germany in the years leading up to World War I can be felt in the dark palette, whirling brushstrokes, and existentialist expressions in Oskar Kokoschka's

4-5 OSKAR
KOKOSCHKA. *The
Tempest* (1914). Oil on
canvas. 71½" × 86½".
Kunstmuseum, Basel,
Switzerland.

1 ft.

1 ft.

4-6 CONSTANTIN BRANCUSI. *The Kiss* (c. 1912). Limestone. 23" × 13" × 10". The Philadelphia Museum of Art, Philadelphia, PA. © 2011 Artists Rights Society (ARS), NY/ADAGP, Paris.

The Tempest (Fig. **4-5**). Donna Rosenthal's *He Said . . . She Said* (Fig. 4-10) seems to tap into some sort of collective unconscious ballroom in its unique yet universal ruminations. Constantin Brancusi's *The Kiss* (Fig. **4-6**) could be said to transcend context in the simple accessibility or readability of its subject.

In their abstraction, Jackson Pollock's *Male and Female* (Fig. **4-7**) and Barbara Hepworth's *Two Figures* (Fig. **4-8**) are more difficult to decipher. Pollock's painting was created while he was undergoing psychoanalytic therapy and ought to be read in that context. It reveals a complex scheme of images that he believed were derived from his collective unconscious mind. Hepworth, by contrast, aims to disconnect her work from context by reducing her figures to their most common denominators—organic vertical shapes punctuated by softly modeled voids. Yet curiously, when we view *Two Figures* in the context of this grouping of "couples," it seems to belong, even if eyes may resist making a connection.

Context has a profound influence on style. We can see this in the similarities among artists of a specific era, regardless of their individual "signature." Claude Monet and Auguste Renoir, for example—both Impressionist artists working in

1 ft.

4-7 JACKSON POLLOCK. *Male and Female* (1942). Oil on canvas. 73⅓" × 49". The Philadelphia Museum of Art, Philadelphia, PA. © 2011 Pollock-Krasner Foundation/Artists Rights Society (ARS), NY.

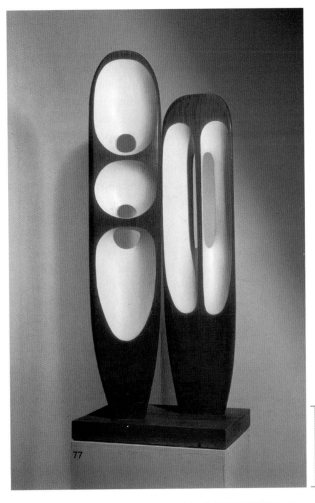

77

1 ft.

4-8 BARBARA HEPWORTH. *Two Figures (Menhirs)* (1954–1955). Teak. H: 54". The Art Institute of Chicago, Chicago, IL.

nineteenth-century France—are recognized for their distinct styles, but they have more in common with each other than they do with, say, Rembrandt. And although you probably wouldn't mistake one for the other, the works of both artists are very much a product of their culture at a moment in time.

Styles in art are numerous, ever changing, and ever new. The vocabulary we use to discuss style, on the other hand, has been fairly standard for a long time.

Realistic Art

Realism refers to the portrayal of people and things as they are seen by the eye or really thought to be, without ideal-ization, without distortion. Wood's painting (Fig. 4-9) is described as realistic in terms of style. The term, with a capital *R*, also defines a specific school of art that flowered during the mid-nineteenth century in France. Realism featured subjects culled from daily life and experience and developed a new respect for the real substance of the artist's materials.

Grant Wood's renowned *American Gothic* is a painstak-ingly realistic portrait of the staid virtues of the rural life in America. It is also one of our more commercialized works of art; images derived from it have adorned boxes of breakfast cereal, greeting cards, and numerous other products. Note the repetition of the pitchfork pattern in the man's shirtfront, the upper-story window of the house, and the plant on the porch.

He is very much tied to his environment. Were it not for the incongruously spry curl falling from the mistress's otherwise tucked-tight hairdo, we might view this composition—as well as the sitters therein—as solid, stolid, and monotonous.

We think of most photographs as realistic. The very nature of the technique—shooting, capturing, documenting—suggests candid truth, unadulterated reality. Although photographers in the twentieth century and beyond have pursued photography as an art form and strained against the bonds of representation, the impact of Mapplethorpe's photographs is largely a result of his unflinching realism (Fig. 4-4).

REALISTIC VERSUS REPRESENTATIONAL ART The Lichtenstein couple (Fig. 4-2) is portrayed in a style that departs from strict Realism, yet the observer clearly identifies the caricature-like renderings of the figures as that of a man and woman. This is **representational art**. It presents natural objects in recognizable, though not realistic, form. *Forget It! Forget Me!* is an example of Pop Art, which adopts the visual clichés of the comic strip. Donna Rosenthal's *He Said . . . She Said* (Fig. 4-10) also clearly depicts an interaction between a man and a woman, in this case capturing the verbal clichés of the human comedy. Both works can be described as representational.

The term *representational art*, often used synonymously with figurative art, is defined as art that portrays, however altered or distorted, things perceived in the visible world. The people in the Lichtenstein work may not be realistic, but they are clearly recognizable. The Mayan couple (Fig. 4-1) and Toulouse-Lautrec's *The Two Girlfriends* (Fig. 4-3) are similarly representational but not realistic.

Expressionistic Art

In expressionistic art, form and color are freely distorted by the artist in order to achieve a heightened emotional impact. Expressionism also refers to a modern art movement, but many earlier works are **expressionistic** in the broader sense of the term.

In *The Burial of Count Orgaz* (see Fig. 16-29), El Greco's expressionistic elongation of the heavenly figures seems to emphasize their ethereal spirituality. Postimpressionist Vincent van Gogh relied on both an expressionistic palette and brushwork to transfer emotion to his canvases. Kokoschka's expressionistic painting *The Tempest* (Fig. 4-5) is marked by frenzied brushstrokes that mirror the torment of his inner life as well as the impending darkness of war in Germany. Reclining figures occupy the center of a dark, imaginary landscape. Images of earth, water, and flesh merge in a common palette and bevy of strokes; little distinguishes one from another. All seem caught up in a churning sky, very much in danger of being swept away.

Abstract Art

The term **abstract** applies to art that departs significantly from the actual appearance of things. Such art may be completely **nonobjective**; that is, it may make no reference whatsoever to nature or reality. On the other hand, abstract art may be rooted in nature, even though the finished product bears little resemblance to the source that inspired it. Several aspects of the Brancusi sculpture (Fig. 4-6) are recognizable: One can discern an upper torso, arms, eyes, and hair. Yet the artist seems to have been more interested in the independent relationships of the shapes than in being true to the human form. For this reason, we would more likely characterize *The Kiss* as abstract rather than representational.

In *The Kiss*, the human torso is reduced to a simple block form. Twentieth-century proponents of **Cubism**, such as Pablo Picasso and Georges Braque (see Figs. 20-6 and 20-7) also transcribed natural forms into largely angular geometric equivalents. To some degree, despite their reduction to essential geometric components and line–shape relationships, the figures of Picasso and Braque remain somewhat decipherable. In any event, both artists—despite some brief dabbling in nonobjectivity—abstracted from reality.

Jackson Pollock's *Male and Female* (Fig. 4-7) "figures" are a great deal more difficult to discern than Brancusi's, but the totemic shapes bear some visual cues that suggest gender differences. At the time of the painting, Pollock was undergoing psychoanalysis, and he was quite convinced that the unconscious played a major role in his art. Using a method called **psychic automatism**, Pollock attempted to clear his mind of purpose and concerns so that inner conflicts and ideas could find expression through his work. The result in *Male and Female* is abstraction.

Although much of Barbara Hepworth's sculpture has been inspired by nature, it is not always derived from nature. That

WOOD'S *AMERICAN GOTHIC* WITH ROSENTHAL'S *HE SAID . . . SHE SAID*

THE STYLE OF A WORK OF ART refers to the characteristic ways in which artists express themselves and the times in which they live. In our consideration of the theme of couples, we were able to assess the way in which a full range of media, methods, and styles contributes to the uniqueness of each work. If we add to these the historical and cultural contexts of the works, we gain insight into the ways in which art reflects its place and time.

Consider Grant Wood's *American Gothic* and Donna Rosenthal's *He Said . . . She Said*. On a trip to Europe in the 1920s, Wood was influenced by the realistic works of fifteenth-century German and Flemish painters. His initial goal in *American Gothic* (Fig. **4-9**) was to render realistically the rural Iowan house in the background of the painting. He enlisted a local dentist along with his own sister to pose as models for the farmer and his wife. The realism of

their faces is so exacting and their expressions so intent that the viewer cannot but wonder what thoughts lie buried in their minds.

And then there is the expression "to wear one's heart on one's sleeve." In Rosenthal's *He Said . . . She Said* (Fig. **4-10**), thoughts and feelings are broadcast plainly, as the (implied) individuals quite literally wear their thoughts on their clothes—a suit and party dress made from the pages of discarded books and newspapers. We know exactly what's on their minds, verbalized through cultural stereotypes of the conflicting definitions of males and females perpetuated from childhood onward. A nursery rhyme that dates back to the nineteenth-century poses the questions "What are little girls made of?" ("Sugar and spice and all things nice") and "What are little boys made of?" ("Snips and snails and puppy-dogs' tails"). Rosenthal calls attention to the tendency for childhood gender expectations to frame gender discourse in adult relationships. Other works by the artist express man's desire for sex and woman's desire for security. Stereotypes are by definition extreme; they represent conventional notions and not individual conceptions. Yet Rosenthal succeeds in her communication with the viewer in large part because of the ubiquity of these phrases.

As the physical couple is absent from the work, we are left with the notion that the clothes make the individual. This is conceptual art; that is, the ideas being expressed by the artist have greater meaning than their physical expression. ●

4-9 GRANT WOOD. *American Gothic* (1930). Oil on beaverboard. 29⅞" × 24⅞". The Art Institute of Chicago, Chicago, IL.

4-10 DONNA ROSENTHAL. *He Said . . . She Said (Romance Comics)* (2007). Paper and mixed media. 25" × 16" × 10" each set.

is why we characterize work such as *Two Figures* (Fig. 4-8) as nonobjective; that is, it is not intended to make any reference to reality. On the other hand, titling the piece *Two Figures* places viewers in a quandary. It sends us searching for details that might represent the human form, even gender differences. Is the taller "figure" the male? Could the concave

1 ft.

4-11 JUDY PFAFF. *Voodoo* (1981). Contact paper collage on Mylar. 98" × 60" (framed). Albright-Knox Art Gallery, Buffalo, NY.

shapes in the shorter figure suggest femininity? Here the connection to reality may be fully in the eye of the beholder. Nonobjective artists do this type of thing quite a lot. Sometimes they label their paintings and sculptures *Untitled* partially as a way to discourage Rorschach-like readings of their work. At other times, they assign titles to their nonobjective works based on some association that is triggered by the work itself.

A case in point is Judy Pfaff's *Voodoo* (Fig. **4-11**), a nonobjective painting in which highly saturated colors and jagged shapes comprise the content and spirit of the work. Though the elements and technique are the "subject" of the work, the title suggests the presence of mysterious figures undulating in a Caribbean jungle undergrowth. One of the issues that many viewers have with nonobjective art is that they want it to make sense. They want to connect it with something familiar—even if the familiar in this case is as abstruse as the title, *Voodoo*. But nonobjective art is just that—nonobjective—and viewers may come closer to the intention of the artist by allowing themselves to focus on what's there rather than to go on scavenger hunts for what probably isn't.

FORM

The **form** of a work refers to its totality as a work of art. Form includes the elements, design principles, and composition of a work of art. A work's *form* may include, for example, the colors that are used, the textures and shapes, the illusion of three dimensions, the balance, rhythm, or unity of design. **Formalist criticism**, by extension, is an approach to art criticism that concentrates primarily on the elements and design of works of art rather than on historical factors or the biography of the artist.

CONTENT

The **content** of a work of art is everything that is contained in it. The content of a work refers not only to its lines or forms but also to its subject matter and its underlying meanings or themes.

The Levels of Content

We may think of works of art as containing three levels of content: (1) subject matter, (2) elements and composition, and (3) underlying or symbolic meanings or themes.

To give a body and a perfect form to your thought, this alone is what it is to be an artist.
—Jacques-Louis David

Consider a comparison between the subject matter of two visually similar paintings as a way of exploring these levels. In 1793, just a few years after the taking of the Bastille and the start of the French Revolution, Jacques-Louis David painted *Death of Marat* (Fig. **4-12**), a memorial to a political martyr. Almost 200 years later, Sandow Birk appropriated David's image for *Death of Manuel* (Fig. **4-13**), his graphic deposition on urban violence.

There is a macabre similarity between the two paintings in their elements and composition. David's Marat is found dead in his bath—murdered by a counterrevolutionary fanatic named Charlotte Corday. The artist brings the viewer face-to-face with the slaughtered hero, whose arm drops lifeless and whose sympathetic facial expression leans toward us yearningly. Birk's *Manuel* is rendered in the same pose, although

Marat's bath has been replaced with a Chevy Impala, riddled with bullets. Marat's left hand holds a false letter requesting a visit from the would-be murderer; Manuel's left hand grasps the steering wheel of his car. Marat's head is wrapped in a turban; Manuel's, in a brightly printed bandana. In both paintings, the figure is set in the extreme foreground, and the backgrounds are monochromatic and nondescript. The spatial depth is severely limited. This dramatic silhouette effect, coupled with the strong linear style used to render the figures, creates the feeling of a sculptural frieze.

The underlying themes or symbolism in these works may not bear the same relationship as do the elements and composition. Yet the choice of the David prototype suggests ideas of revolution, heroism as it is defined within a group or culture, and the cold-blooded murder of the unsuspecting victim. The

4-12 JACQUES-LOUIS DAVID. *Death of Marat* (1793). Oil on canvas. 63¾" × 49⅛". Musées Royaux des Beaux-Arts de Belgique, Brussels, Belgium.

1 ft.

4-13 SANDOW BIRK. *Death of Manuel* (1992). Oil on canvas. 33" × 25". Koplin Del Rio Gallery, Culver City, CA.

DAVID'S *THE OATH OF THE HORATII* WITH KRUGER'S *UNTITLED (WE DON'T NEED ANOTHER HERO)*

THE OATH OF THE HORATII (Fig. **4-14**), by Jacques-Louis David, is one of the most readily recognizable works of the nineteenth century—indeed, the whole of the history of art. It is a landmark composition—symbolically and pictorially. David worked for the king of France in the days before the French Revolution. Ironically, although the *Oath* was painted for Louis XVI, who along with his wife, Marie Antoinette, would lose his head to the guillotine, the painting became an almost instant symbol of the Revolution. The loyalty, courage, and sacrifice it portrayed were an inspiration to the downtrodden masses in their uprising against the French monarchy. David, because of his position, was imprisoned along with the members of the court and other French aristocracy, only to be—as it were—"bailed out" by another who could use his services

as a painter. Thus David, court painter to the French king, would become painter to Napoleon Bonaparte, who would eventually crown himself emperor.

Pictorially, the work is also groundbreaking. It compresses space and forces us to concentrate on the meticulously rendered figures in the foreground. This treatment of space would open the door to the flattening of space in Modernist paintings. The tradition of treating the picture frame as a window frame through which one peers into the infinite distance would be abandoned by many artists in favor of the two-dimensionality of the canvas.

Knowing something of the historical circumstances under which *The Oath of the Horatii* was created, and understanding what is new about it in terms of style and composition, helps us appreciate its significance. But our

1 ft.

4-14 JACQUES-LOUIS DAVID. *The Oath of the Horatii* (1784). Oil on canvas. 11' × 14'. Louvre, Paris, France.

full comprehension and appreciation of the work can occur only with our consideration and interpretation of the subject matter. The subject of David's *The Oath of the Horatii* is, on the face of things, fairly easy to read. Three brothers—the Horatii—swear their allegiance to Rome on swords held high by their father. They pledge to come back victorious or not come back at all. Their forward-thrusting and stable stances convey strength, commitment, and bravery. And there is something else—something that has been referred to by feminist critics and scholars as a *subtext*, or an additional level of content in the work. David's *Oath* is also a painting about the ideology of gender differences. The women in the painting collapse in the background, terrified at the prospect of the death of the brothers. To make matters worse, one of the Horatii sisters is engaged to be married to one of the enemy. She might lose her brother to the hands of her fiancé, or vice versa. The women's posture, in opposition to the men's, represents, according to historian Linda Nochlin, "the clear-cut opposition between masculine strength and feminine weakness offered by the ideological discourse of the period." Whatever else the content of this painting is about, it is also about the relationship of the sexes and gender-role stereotypes.

Several contemporary feminist artists have challenged the traditional discourse of gender ideology as damaging both to men and women. Barbara Kruger's *Untitled (We Don't Need Another Hero)* (Fig. **4-15**) can be interpreted as an "answer" to David's *Oath*. In appropriating a Norman Rockwell illustration to depict the "innocence" of gender ideology—in this case, the requisite fawning of a little girl over the budding muscles of her male counterpart—Kruger violates the innocuous vignette with a cautionary band blazing the words *We don't need another hero*. The representation of the opposition between strength and weakness—male and female—is confronted and replaced with the gender discourse of a more socially aware era.

The subject matter of these works is strangely related, oddly linked. Visually, the works could not be more dissimilar. In David's composition, the subtext of gender ideology exists simultaneously with the main narrative—that of the soldiers preparing for battle. In Kruger's work, by contrast, the main narrative *is* gender ideology—and how to counteract it. In both, however, the essential nature of evaluating the content, or subject matter of the works we view, is underscored. They are, after all, really about the same thing, aren't they? ●

1 ft.

4-15 BARBARA KRUGER. *Untitled (We Don't Need Another Hero)* (1987). Photographic silkscreen, vinyl. 109" × 210". Mary Boone Gallery, NY.

appropriation of the David image by Birk validates the historic significance of the eighteenth-century painting. Understanding the relationship between the two makes each more meaningful to the viewer.

Iconography

I prefer winter and fall, when you feel the bone structure in the landscape—the loneliness of it—the dread feeling of winter. Something waits beneath it—the whole story doesn't show.
—Andrew Wyeth

Winter is a perennial symbol of death and aloneness in the arts, and fall is a common symbol of either harvest or decline. Yet artists who paint the winter or the fall, or who write of them, may not directly speak of death or of the harvest. "The whole story" does not always show, but rather may lie beneath a work of art.

Iconography is the study of the themes and symbols in the visual arts—the figures and images that lend works their underlying meanings. Bronzino's sixteenth-century masterpiece *Venus, Cupid, Folly, and Time (The Exposure of Luxury)* (Fig. **4-16**) is a classic example of works in which there is much more than meets the eye. The painting weaves an intricate **allegory**, with many actors, many symbols. Venus, undraped by Time and spread in a languorous diagonal across the front plane, is fondled by her son Cupid. Folly prepares to cast roses on the couple, while Hatred and Inconstancy (with two left hands) lurk in the background. Masks, symbolizing falseness, and other objects, meanings known or unknown, complete the scene.

Works such as these offer an intricate iconographic puzzle. Is Bronzino saying that love in an environment of hatred and inconstancy is foolish or doomed? Is something being suggested about incest? self-love? Can one fully appreciate Bronzino's painting without being aware of its iconography? Is it sufficient to respond to the elements and composition, to the figure of a woman being openly fondled before an unlikely array of onlookers? No simple answer is possible, and a Mannerist artist such as Bronzino would have intended this ambiguity. Certainly one could appreciate the composition and the subject matter for their own sake, but awareness of the symbolism enriches the viewing experience.

4-16 BRONZINO. *Venus, Cupid, Folly, and Time (The Exposure of Luxury)* (c. 1546). Oil on wood. Approx. 61" × 56¾". National Gallery, London, England.

Whereas Bronzino's painting illustrates a complex allegory, the symbolism of which would seem relevant only to the initiated, Willie Bester's *Semekazi (Migrant Miseries)* (Fig. **4-17**) uses images and objects to communicate a tragic story to anyone who will listen. Bester is an artist who was classified as "colored" under South African apartheid rule and thus, as with most nonwhite artists, was deprived of opportunities for formal training in art. Collages such as *Semekazi* combine painting with found objects in a densely covered surface that seems, in its lack of space and air, to reflect the squalid living conditions among black Africans. The many images and objects serve as symbols of rampant oppression and deprivation affecting a whole people, while a single portrait of a worker in the center of the composition—peering from under bedsprings—serves as a single case study.

The paintings by Bronzino and Bester, as far apart in time, tenor, and experience as can be imagined, both supply the viewer with clear, familiar images intended to communicate certain underlying themes. But in some cases, the underlying themes may be at least in part the invention of the viewer. In Helen Frankenthaler's *Bay Side* (see Fig. 2-22), for example, we may interpret the juncture of the blue and tan fields as surf meeting sand. Did the artist intend this symbolism, however, or is it our own invention? Many of us love a puzzle and are willing to spend a great deal of time attempting to decipher the possible iconography of a work of art. In other cases, the subject matter of a work may be in the eye of the beholder.

Our exposition of the language of art is now complete. We have seen that artists use the visual elements of art in compositions that employ various principles of design. Their compositions are usually created within certain traditional and contemporary styles. The totality of the form of their works—everything that we see in them—also has certain subject matter or content, which may exist on several levels. Our understanding of these various levels of content helps us appreciate the works.

Several chapters follow that show how artists apply the language of art to works in two dimensions and three dimensions. Then we survey the history of art, where we see how artists through the ages and around the globe have spoken a similar language. Although it may take us adults years to become fluent in the spoken languages of other peoples in other times and other places, we may find ourselves capable of more readily understanding the language in their visual works.

4-17 WILLIE BESTER. *Semekazi (Migrant Miseries)* (1993). Oil, enamel paint, and mixed media on board. 49¼" × 49¼".

1 ft.

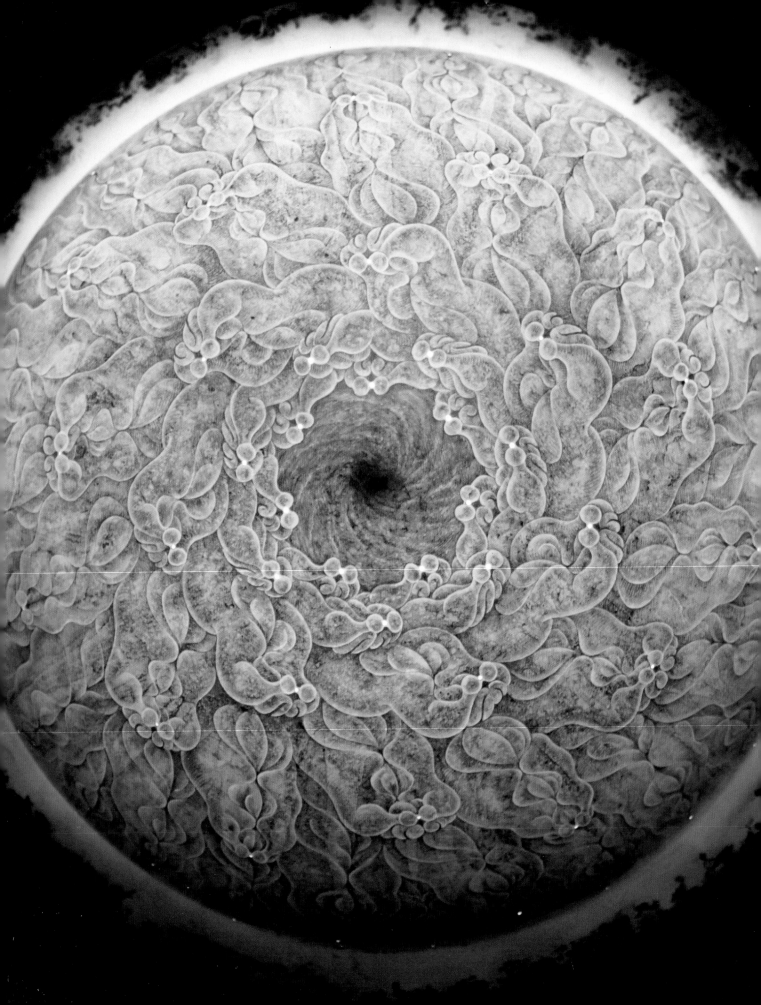

Drawing . . . is the necessary beginning of everything in art, and not having it, one has nothing.

—Giorgio Vasari

DRAWING

5

The first sketch was probably an accident. Perhaps some Stone Age human idly ran a twig through soft clay and was astounded to find an impression of this gesture in the ground. Perhaps this individual then made such impressions as signs for family members (as in an arrow pointing "that way") and to record experiences, such as the hunt for a beast or a gathering around a fire. Similarly, children may learn to trace a shell fragment through damp sand at the shore's edge and soon expand their shape vocabulary to include circles, triangles, animals, toys, and people. Artists engage in an essentially similar act when they sketch from life, from memory, from their imaginations.

Drawing is the most basic of two-dimensional art forms. In its broadest definition, **drawing** is the result of an implement running over a surface and leaving some trace of the gesture. But the art of drawing goes far beyond this simple description and its materials, forms, and functions vary widely.

The surface, or **support**, of a drawing is usually, although not always, two-dimensional. Most often the support is **monochromatic** paper or parchment, although drawings can be made on any number of surfaces. The implements and mediums can range from burned wood (charcoal) to burned paper, from bristle brushes dipped in ink to gunpowder ignited by a fuse. Most drawings, by virtue of the implements, consist of black and tones of gray. But many full-color drawings have also been created with colored chalks, pastels, and wax crayons.

CAROL PRUSA. *Whirl* (2010). Silverpoint, graphite, titanium white pigment with acrylic binder on acrylic hemisphere with fiber optics. 12" × 12" × 6". Bernice Steinbaum Gallery, Miami, FL.

Some drawings are predominantly **linear**; others are constructed solely by tonal contrasts. The quality of line and the nature of shading are affected by the texture of the support. Artists often capitalize on the idiosyncratic characteristics of the implements and support to create a specific effect in a drawing.

CATEGORIES OF DRAWING

Drawing is basic to the visual arts. For centuries, painters and sculptors have made countless preparatory sketches for their major projects, working out difficulties on paper before approaching the more permanent medium of paint or bronze. Architects proceed in the same fashion, outlining buildings in detail before breaking ground. Drawing has also served artists as a kind of shorthand method for recording ideas.

Artists carry sketchbooks everywhere, and perhaps no one is better known for his "little book of leaves" than Leonardo da Vinci (see the sketch by Leonardo on page 74), who advised artists to note everything, and when the book was "full, [to] keep it to serve [their] future plans, and take another and carry on with it." Leonardo's own work also served as inspiration for generations of artists who copied his masterpieces. Imitation has been said to be the sincerest form of flattery, and art-world luminaries and students alike have "gone to

1 in.

5-1 CHEYNEY THOMPSON. *Untitled* (2003). Ink on paper. 14" × 17". The Museum of Modern Art, NY.

school on" the works of the masters. As in Cheyney Thompson's untitled study (Fig. **5-1**), after Theodore Gericault's *The Raft of the Medusa* (see page 56), copying permits the artist to, in a sense, retrace another artist's steps—from conception to completion. Far from being an exercise in mere duplication, the effort can lead to an understanding and feeling of form, rhythm, and design. Many artists, over many generations, have traveled well beyond their cities of origin to meet the works of the masters and to unlock their secrets through the scrutiny of copying.

But drawing does not serve only a utilitarian purpose. Drawing can be the most direct way of bringing what is in the artist's mind to the artist's surface. Many artists enjoy the sheer spontaneity of drawing, tracing a pencil or piece of chalk across a sheet of paper to capture directly their thoughts or to record the slightest movement of their hand.

Yet a drawing can stand as complete work of art, an entity unto itself. Gary Kelley's sensual and rhythmic pastel drawing (Fig. **5-2**) possesses all of the detail, all of the finish of a work of art in a medium that might be considered more permanent. Its powerful zigzag composition contributes to the sense of life and movement, as do the contrasts between the harsh angularity of the male singer's zoot suit and the sinuous curves of the woman who writhes in response to his music. Kelley's drawing was commissioned as a promotional piece for the Mississippi Delta Blues Festival and was no doubt purposefully reminiscent of the Harlem jazz age as depicted by 1930s African American artists such as Archibald J. Motley Jr. (see Fig. 3-2).

Drawings may thus be said to fall into at least three categories:

1. Sketches that record an idea or provide information about something the artist has seen
2. Plans or preparatory studies for other projects, such as buildings, sculptures, crafts, paintings, plays, and films
3. Fully developed and autonomous works of art

1 in.

5-2 GARY KELLEY. Promotion for the Mississippi Delta Blues Festival (c. 1989). Pastel. 24" × 14".

DRAWING MATERIALS

Over the millennia, methods of drawing have become increasingly sophisticated and materials more varied and standardized. It would seem that we have come a long way from our prehistoric ancestors' use of twigs, hollow reeds, and lumps of clay. Conventional drawing materials are typically divided into two major groups: *dry mediums* and *fluid mediums*. But almost anything can be used to make a drawing, as we shall see.

Dry Mediums

The **dry mediums** used in drawing include silverpoint, pencil, charcoal, chalk, pastel, and wax crayon.

SILVERPOINT **Silverpoint** is one of the oldest drawing mediums and was used widely from the late Middle Ages to the early 1500s. Silverpoint drawings are created by dragging a silver-tipped implement over a surface that has been coated with a **ground**—a sort of base layer—of bone dust or chalk mixed with **gum**, water, and **pigment**. This ground is sufficiently coarse to allow small flecks of silver from the instrument to adhere to the prepared surface as it is drawn across. These bits of metal form the lines of the drawing; they are barely visible at the start but eventually oxidize, becoming tarnished or darkened. Each silverpoint line, a soft gray to begin with, mellows and darkens to a grayish brown hue.

If the artist desires to make one area of the drawing appear darker than others, it is necessary to build up a series of close, parallel, or cross-hatched lines in that area to give the impression of deepened tone. Because they lack sharp tonal contrasts, the resultant drawings are often extremely delicate in appearance.

The technique of working in silverpoint is itself delicate. The medium allows for little or no correction. Thus, the artist is not in a position to experiment while working. The artist must have a fairly concrete notion of what the final product will look like, and the lines must be accurate and confidently drawn. Although this challenging medium is most closely associated with drawings of the past, its signature effect has been explored by contemporary artist Carol Prusa in works such as *Whirl* (Fig. **5-3**). Complex, intertwining and repetitive patterns of silverpoint, graphite, and white acrylic paint pulse across its acrylic domed surface.

The bright spots of light that coalesce at the work's center are emitted through pinpoint holes in the dome and illuminated from within using fiber optics. Her works, painstakingly rendered, are flawless in execution, their finish exquisite and polished. This technique is not for the fainthearted. Anyone working in silverpoint is likely to create detailed preliminary sketches before launching into this more permanent and less forgiving medium.

PENCIL Silverpoint was largely replaced by the lead **pencil**, which came into use during the 1500s. Medieval monks, like the ancient Egyptians, ruled lines with metallic lead but pencils, as we know them, began to be mass-produced only in the late eighteenth century. A pencil consists of a thin rod of **graphite** encased within wood or paper. The graphite is composed of ground dust mixed with clay that is baked until hardened. The relative hardness or softness of a pencil's lead depends on the quantity of clay in the mixture. The more clay, the harder the pencil.

Pencil produces a wide range of effects. Lines drawn with hard pencil can be thin and light in tone; those rendered in soft lead can be thick and dark. The sharp point of the pencil will create a firm, fine line suitable for meticulous detail. Softer areas of tone or shading can be achieved through a buildup of parallel lines, smudging, or dragging the side of a lead tip across a surface.

As seen in the contrasting works of George Condo and Marc Brandenburg, pencil can be manipulated to achieve dramatically different effects that complement the subject. The juxtaposition of fine cross-hatching, compact wavy and curly lines, and quick, zigzag scribbles work in tandem with the multiple perspectives that comprise the facial features in Condo's *Study for The Jester* (Fig. **5-4**).

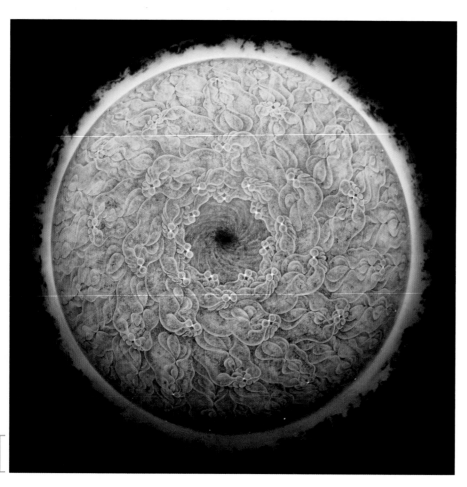

1 in.

5-3 CAROL PRUSA. *Whirl* (2010). Silverpoint, graphite, titanium white pigment with acrylic binder on acrylic hemisphere with fiber optics. 12" × 12" × 6". Bernice Steinbaum Gallery, Miami, FL.

Brandenburg's drawing (Fig. **5-5**), on the other hand, emulates a photographic negative in its meticulous execution and sharp tonal contrasts. The artist creates a visual correlate to paparazzi's candid photos of unsuspecting celebrities. In this drawing, Brandenburg highlights the instantly recognizable attributes of the pop star Michael Jackson, reduced to binary lights and darks. The convincing suggestion of another medium altogether is a consequence of the exacting detail that is possible with a tightly controlled use of pencil.

The exercise of drawing from life has been integral to the art academy experience for hundreds of years, a method by which the human form might be painstakingly analyzed and recorded. Perhaps this is why, in part, Adrian Piper chose the medium of drawing to render her dramatic *Self-Portrait Exaggerating My Negroid Features* (Fig. **5-6**). With it, Piper invites the spectator to focus on those aspects of her physical genetic composition that reveal her mixed black and white parentage. The portrait gives us an unflinching record of Piper's countenance, but perhaps more important, the image challenges us to confront our prejudices about the physical differences between the races.

1 in.

5-5 MARC BRANDENBURG. *Untitled* (2004). Pencil on paper. 8¼" × 8⅜". The Museum of Modern Art, NY.

1 in.

5-4 GEORGE CONDO. *Study for The Jester* (2003). Pencil on paper. 11¾" × 10⅞". The Museum of Modern Art, NY.

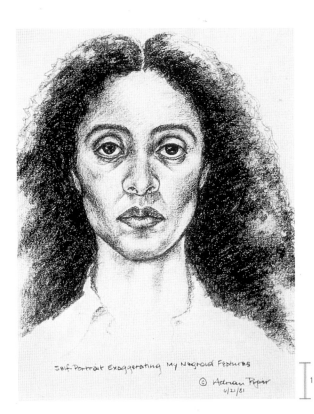

Self-Portrait Exaggerating My Negroid Features

© Adrian Piper
6/21/81

1 in.

5-6 ADRIAN PIPER. *Self-Portrait Exaggerating My Negroid Features* (1981). Pencil on paper. 10" × 8".

Adrian Piper has authored "calling cards" to hand out to people whom she overhears making racist remarks: "I regret any discomfort my presence is causing you, just as I am sure you regret the discomfort your racism is causing me."

COLORED PENCIL Colored pencils consist of waxlike cores mixed with pigment and other substances surrounded, as with graphite pencils, by wood or paper. Like graphite pencils, which can be sharpened to a point, colored pencils can render fine lines, as in Elizabeth Peyton's drawing *Marc (April)* (Fig. **5-7**). The young man's hair is composed of myriad nesting lines that create an expressive counterpoint to the more tightly controlled, finely modeled, and realistic drawing of his face. The movement suggested in his wispy, tousled locks is echoed in the sketchy rendering of his tailored shirt.

5-8 KÄTHE KOLLWITZ. *Self-Portrait* (1924). Charcoal. 18¾" × 25". National Gallery of Art, Washington, D.C. © 2011 Artists Rights Society (ARS), NY/VG Bild-Kunst, Bonn.

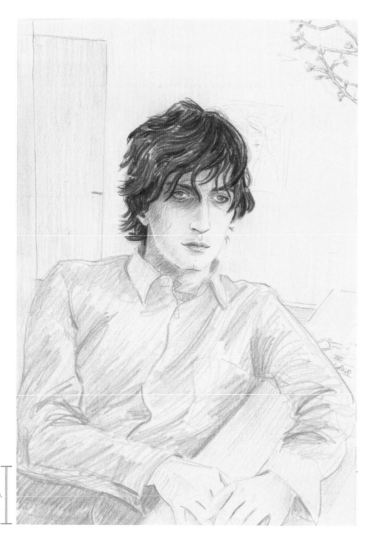

5-7 ELIZABETH PEYTON. *Marc (April)* (2003). Colored pencil on paper. 8⅝" × 6". The Judith Rothschild Foundation Contemporary Drawings Collection Gift. Digital Image © The Museum of Modern Art/Licensed by SCALA/Art Resource, NY/The Museum of Modern Art, NY.

1 in.

CHARCOAL **Charcoal**, like pencil, has a long history as a drawing implement. Used by our primitive ancestors to create images on cave walls, these initially crumbly pieces of burnt wood or bone now take the form of prepared sticks that are formed by the controlled charring of special hardwoods. Charcoal sticks are available in textures that vary from hard to soft. The sticks may be sharpened with sandpaper to form fine and clear lines or may be dragged flat across the surface to form diffuse areas of varied tone. Like pencil, charcoal may also be smudged or rubbed to create a hazy effect.

When charcoal is dragged across a surface, bits of the material adhere to that surface, just as in the case of silverpoint and pencil. But charcoal particles rub off more easily, and thus the completed drawings must be sprayed with a solution of thinned varnish to keep them affixed. Also, because of the way in which the charcoal is dispersed over a surface, the nature of the support is evident in each stroke. Coarsely textured paper will yield a grainy image, whereas smooth paper will provide a clear, almost pencil-like line.

A self-portrait of the German Expressionist Käthe Kollwitz (Fig. **5-8**) reveals one aspect of the character of the charcoal medium. Delicate lines of sharpened charcoal drawn over broader areas of subtle shading enunciate the two main points of interest: the artist's face and her hand. Between these two points—that of intellect and that of skill—runs a surge of energy described by aggressive, jagged strokes overlaying the lightly sketched contour of her forearm.

Values in the drawing range from hints of white at the artist's knuckles, cheekbone, and hair to the deepest blacks of the palm of her hand, eyes, and mouth. The finer lines override the texture of the paper, whereas the shaded areas,

Chalks are available in many colors, some of which occur in nature. **Ocher**, for example, derives its dark yellow tint from iron oxide in some clay. **Umber** acquires its characteristic yellowish or reddish brown color from earth containing oxides of manganese and iron. Other popular "organic" or "earth" colors include white, black, and a red called **sanguine**.

Michelangelo used red chalk in a sketch for the Sistine Chapel (see Chapter 16), in which he attempted to work out certain aspects of the figure of the Libyan Sibyl (Fig. **5-10**). Quick, sketchy notations of the model's profile, feet, and toes lead to a detailed torso rendered with confident lines and precisely defined tonal areas built up from hatching. The exactness of muscular detail and emphasis on the edges of the body provide insight into the concerns of an artist whose forte was sculpture.

Pastels consist of ground chalk mixed with powdered pigments and a binder. Whereas chalk drawings can be traced to prehistoric times, pastels did not come into wide use until the 1400s. They were introduced to France only in the 1700s,

5-9 CLAUDIO BRAVO. *Package* (1969). Charcoal, pastel, and sanguine. 30⅞" × 22½".

particularly around the neck and chest area, reveal the faint white lines and tiny flecks of pulp that are visual remnants of the papermaking process.

Charcoal can be expressive or descriptive, depending on its method of application. Claudio Bravo's *Package* (Fig. **5-9**) is a finely rendered, trompe l'oeil drawing that bears almost no trace of the artist's gesture and almost no indication of the "dusty" quality of the media—primarily charcoal and pastel. The illusion of the smooth sheen and crinkled indentations of the wrapping paper, attributed to painstaking gradations in value, is so convincing that the implied texture of the package completely overrides the actual texture of the drawing materials. The viewer is enticed to touch the forbidden surfaces, just to test whether they are real.

CHALK AND PASTEL The effects of charcoal, **chalk**, and **pastel** as they are dragged across a surface are very similar, although the mediums differ in terms of their composition. Chalk and pastel consist of pigment and a **binder**, such as **gum arabic**, shaped into workable sticks.

5-10 MICHELANGELO. *Studies for The Libyan Sybil* (1510–1511). Red chalk. 11⅜" × 8⅜". The Metropolitan Museum of Art, NY.

create a glowing, almost iridescent effect, whereas Severini's rigorous technique and more reserved palette mirror the cool and exacting movements of his dancer.

CRAYON Strictly defined, the term **crayon** includes any drawing material in stick form. Thus, charcoal, chalk, and pastels are crayons, as are the familiar Crayolas you used on walls, floors, and occasionally coloring books when you were a child. Wax crayons, like pastels, combine ground pigment with a binder—in this case, wax. Wax crayon moves easily over a surface, creating lines that have a characteristic sheen. These lines are less apt to smudge than charcoal, chalk, and pastels.

One of the most popular commercially manufactured crayons for artists is the **conté crayon**, a square stick of

1 in.

5-11 LUCAS SAMARAS. *Head #12* (1981). Pastel on black paper. 17¾" × 11½". The Museum of Modern Art, NY.

5-12 GINO SEVERINI. *Dancer* (1912). Pastel on paper. 19¼" × 12½". The Riklis Collection of McCrory Corporation.

but within a century, pastels captured the imagination of many important painters. Their wide range of brilliant colors offered a painter's palette for use in the more spontaneous medium of drawing.

Pastels are manipulated in countless ways to create different effects. At times, colors are left pure and intense, as in *Head #12* (Fig. **5-11**) by Lucas Samaras. At other times subtle harmonies can be created through blending or smudging. As with pencil and other dry mediums, pastel can be used to render precise drawings like Gino Severini's *Dancer* (Fig. **5-12**), in which clean contours and discreet shapes evoke fragmented glimpses of a dancer whirling in space. Samaras's coarse splotches of vibrant color contrast with black paper to

SOME YEARS AGO, AFRICAN AMERICAN SCULPTOR Beverly Buchanan came to know Ms. Mary Lou Furcron. They were both artists, one might say. Both the builders of structures. Both nurturing, creative, and colorful. Ever since this meeting, Buchanan's life and art have revolved around the art and life of the Southern shack dweller.

This way of living is an existence unto itself, as the photographs indicate (Fig. 5-13). Ms. Furcron's shack reflects her life, and her life reflects the shack in which she lived. She devoted a part of each day to maintaining the structure, replacing rotted posts with new logs; using bark, lathing, and other odd materials to repair the siding. The shack stood as an organic and ever-evolving structure—an extension of Ms. Furcron herself. Because the shack required her constant attention for its survival, her move to a nursing home brought its rapid disrepair. Just one month after Ms. Furcron's departure, the shack was unrecognizable as its former self.

Buchanan's art, in sculpture, and especially in drawing, reflects a structural approach to the creation of the shack image. As Ms. Furcron built with the recycled remnants of nature and human existence, so does Beverly Buchanan. Her mixed-media shacks are created from old pieces of wood, metal, and found objects, such as in *Hometown—Shotgun Shack* (Fig. 5-14). Her oil pastel drawing *Henriette's Yard* (Fig. 5-15) is vigorously and lovingly constructed of a myriad of vibrant strokes. These strokes at once serve as the building blocks of the shack image and the very stuff that reduces the structure to an almost indecipherable explosion of color. The precarious balance of the shacks in relation to one another and the uncertain ground on which they stand further symbolize the precious and fragile nature of the shack dwelling, and human existence. ●

A

B

5-13 Photographs of Ms. Mary Lou Furcron's home.
Photo A shows the shack while Ms. Furcron was living in it and tending to it. Photo B shows the shack just one month after her placement in a nursing home.

5-14 BEVERLY BUCHANAN. *Hometown—Shotgun Shack* (1992). Wood, mixed media. 12" × 9¼" × 15".

1 ft.

5-15 BEVERLY BUCHANAN. *Henriette's Yard* (1995). Oil pastel on paper. 60" × 60".

compressed graphite or charcoal mixed with wax or clay. Like pencils, conté crayons are available in different degrees of hardness and can be manipulated to create different effects. Artists working with conté crayons often use rough paper so that bits of crayon will adhere to the surface as it is dragged across, creating an overall texture that can be a prominent feature of the drawing.

The conté crayon was invented in the late eighteenth century by Nicola-Jacques Conté out of necessity: there was a shortage of graphite in France due to a blockade during the Napoleonic Wars with England. A century or so later, conté crayon became one of the favorite mediums of the French painter Georges Seurat. *At the Concert Européen* (Fig. 5-16) is built up almost solely through contrasts of tone. Deep, velvety blacks absorb the almost invisible heads of the musicians in the orchestra pit, while a glaring strip of untouched white paper seems to illuminate the stage. The even appli-

cation of crayon to coarse paper creates a diffuse light that accurately conveys the atmosphere of a small café. By working the crayon over a highly textured surface he was able to emulate the fine points of paint that comprised his signature technique in his large canvas works (see Fig. 19-25).

Fluid Mediums

The primary **fluid medium** used to make a drawing is ink. The traditional instruments used to carry ink are pen and brush, but, as evident in Rosemary Trockel's untitled drawing (Fig. **5-17**) or Gabriel Orozco's handprint piece (Fig. **5-18**), ink can be applied to paper or any other surface in any number of ways. Ink has a history that stretches back thousands of years, appearing in Egyptian **papyrus** drawings and ancient Chinese scrolls. Some ancient peoples made ink from the dyes of plants, squid, and octopus. By the second century CE, blue-black inks were being derived from galls—growths found on oak trees that are rich in resin and tannic acid. The oldest-known ink is India or China ink, composed of a solution of carbon black (tar mixed with oil) and water. It is a permanent, rich, black ink that is used in Asian **calligraphy** to this day.

As with the dry mediums, dramatically different effects can be achieved with fluid mediums through a variety of tech-

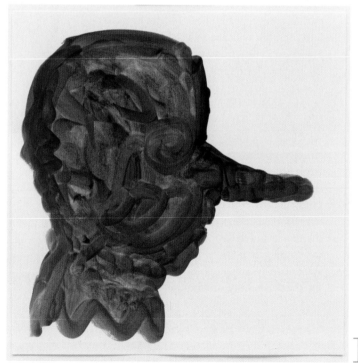

will vary in width according to the amount of downward pressure exerted on the tip.

Jean Dubuffet all but filled his *Garden* (Fig. **5-19**) with pen-and-ink scribbles of varying thicknesses outlining mostly organic shapes. Just as a garden's plant life may give the eye a variegated experience of texture as well as color, Dubuffet's lines vary in length and thickness, sometimes culminating in little pools of ink. Here and there more angular, even craggy shapes suggest a path or an outcropping of rock, but realism was not the artist's aim. Rather, the high horizon line and the endless intertwining of lines and shapes convey the feeling or memory of a lush bed of flowers and plants in which the eye can wander and get lost.

5-18 GABRIEL OROZCO. *Untitled* (handprints) (2000). Ink and gouache on paper. 12" × 9". The Museum of Modern Art, NY. © 2011 Artists Rights Society (ARS), NY/SOMAAP, Mexico City.

5-19 JEAN DUBUFFET. *Garden* (1952). Pen and carbon ink on glazed white wove paper. 18¾" × 23¾". Harriott A. Fox Fund, 1952.1144, The Art Institute of Chicago, Chicago, IL. © 2011 Artists Rights Society (ARS), NY/ADAGP, Paris.

niques. The ratios of water to ink can be altered to achieve lighter or darker tones, and a wide variety of brushes and pen points can be used to render lines of different character.

PEN AND INK Pens also have been used since ancient times. The earliest ones were hollow reeds that were slit at the ends to allow a controlled flow of ink. **Quills** plucked from live birds became popular writing instruments during the Middle Ages. These were replaced in the nineteenth century by the mass-produced metal **nib**, which is slipped into a wooden **stylus**.

Pen and ink are used to create drawings that are essentially linear, although the nature of the line can vary considerably according to the type of instrument employed. A fine, rigid nib will provide a clear, precise line that is uniform in thickness. Lines created by a more flexible quill tip, by contrast,

BRUSH AND INK Brushes are extremely versatile drawing implements. They are available in a wide variety of materials, textures, widths, and shapes that produce many different effects. The quality of line in brush and ink drawing will depend on whether the brush is bristle or nylon, thin or thick, pointed or flat tipped. Likewise, characteristics of the drawing surface, such as texture or absorbency, will affect the character of the completed drawing. Brush and ink touched to silk leaves an impression quite different from that produced by brush and ink touched to paper.

It is only by much drawing, drawing everything, drawing unceasingly that one fine day one is very surprised to find it possible to express something in its true spirit.
—Camille Pissarro

5-20 KATSUSHIKA HOKUSAI. *Boy Playing Flute* (c. 1800). Ink and brush on paper. 4½" × 6¼". Freer Gallery of Art, Smithsonian Institution, Washington, D.C.

5-21 GIOVANNI BATTISTA TIEPOLO. *Hagar and Ishmael in the Wilderness* (c. 1725–1735). Pen, brush and brown ink, and wash, over sketch in black chalk. 16½" × 11⅛". Sterling and Francine Clark Art Institute, Williamstown, MA.

Japanese artists are masters of the brush-and-ink medium. They have used it for centuries for every type of calligraphy, ranging from works of art to everyday writing. Their facility with the technique is most evident in seemingly casual sketches, such as those done in the late eighteenth and early nineteenth centuries by Japanese artist Katsushika Hokusai (Fig. **5-20**). Longer, flowing lines range from thick and dark to thin and faint, capturing, respectively, the heavy folds of the boy's clothing and the pale flesh of his youthful limbs. Short, brisk strokes define the youngster's disheveled hair and are echoed in the pattern of the woven hemp basket. There is an extraordinary simplicity to the drawing attributable to the surety and ease with which Hokusai handles his medium.

WASH Wash is diluted ink that typically is applied with a brush. It can be used exclusively or can be combined, as in Giovanni Tiepolo's eighteenth-century drawing (Fig. **5-21**), with fine, clear, pen-and-ink lines. If you compare this drawing with Dubuffet's *Garden*, you will see what a difference it makes to add areas of subtly washed tone. The contours of the biblical figures of Hagar, Ishmael, and the angel are described in pen and ink, but their volume derives from the application of wash. The gestural vitality of the pen lines and the generous swaths of watery ink surrounding areas of untouched white paper combine to create an illusion of three-dimensionality and a sense of dynamic movement.

The medium of brush and wash is even more versatile. It can duplicate the linearity of brush-and-ink drawings or be used to create images solely through tonal contrasts. The remarkable illusion of deep space in Fang Lijun's drawing (Fig. **5-22**) is achieved through the distribution of zones of grey wash rendered in a variety of grayscale tones. They originate at the feet of an old man on a bluff and meander, like irregular stepping-stones, toward a large sun disk on the horizon. The glowing sphere, ringed in light (unwashed areas of paper), creates a halo effect at the edges of the man's clothing and encircles the pebblelike concentrations of wash. The detail in the drawing—from fine to fluid—is a result of the artist's control of his brush as well as the ratio of ink to water. The ink can be diluted to varying degrees to provide a wide tonal range. Different effects can be achieved either by adding water directly to the ink or by moistening the surface before drawing.

CARTOONS

The word **cartoon** derives from the Italian *cartone*, meaning "paper." Originally, cartoons were full-scale preliminary drawings done on paper for projects such as fresco paintings, stained glass, or tapestries. The meaning of *cartoon* was expanded to include humorous and satirical drawings when a parody of fresco cartoons submitted for decoration of the Houses of Parliament appeared in an English magazine in 1843. Modern cartoons rely on *caricature*, the gross exaggeration and distortion of natural features. While students today may be more familiar with cartoons created for animated films (see Fig. 8-28), video games, action comics, anime (Japanese animation), or manga (Japanese print cartoons, Fig. **5-23**), the art of the cartoon has deep historical roots.

Honoré Daumier is perhaps the only famous painter to devote so great a part of his production—some 4,000 works—to cartoons. Known for his riveting images of social and moral

5-22 FANG LIJUN. *Ink-and-Wash-Painting No. 3* (2004). Ink on paper, 54½" × 28½". The Museum of Modern Art, NY.

5-23 Example of manga artwork.

5-24 HONORÉ DAUMIER. *Counsel for the Defense (the Advocate)* (1862–1865). Pen and ink, charcoal, crayon, gouache, and watercolor. 20⅜" × 23¾". The Corcoran Gallery of Art, Washington, D.C.

injustices in nineteenth-century France, he also created caricatures in which he displayed a sharp, sardonic wit. Daumier's *Counsel for the Defense (the Advocate)* (Fig. **5-24**) is a taunting illustration of the theatrics employed by a defense attorney to win sympathy for his client. The crocodile tears streaming down his face along with his melodramatic gestures are in stark contrast with the composure of the defendant. Yet her inscrutable smile suggests that she may not be quite as innocent as the lawyer pretends.

Cartoons have a long history of social commentary, consciousness raising, and political activism. We are all familiar with the children's books of Dr. Seuss, but few of us are aware of Theodor Seuss Geisel's political cartoons (Fig. **5-25**). For two years during World War II, Dr. Seuss was the chief editorial cartoonist for the New York tabloid newspaper *PM*. During that time, he drew more than 400 cartoons, many of which pertained to the war effort. It's fascinating to see Dr. Seuss's legendary, signature style (and creatures) called into service for an altogether different purpose.

5-25 DR. SEUSS. *Cages Cost Money! Buy More U.S. Savings Bonds and Stamps!* From Dr. Seuss Collection, the Mandeville Special Collections Library, University of California, San Diego, CA.

NEW APPROACHES TO DRAWING

Drawings display endless versatility in terms of their intended purposes, their mediums, and their techniques. It is not unusual to find drawings that are not "drawn" at all on materials that are far removed from traditional paper. You'd be right to ask, "What *is* a drawing, after all?"

Chinese artist Cai Guo-Qiang is renowned for his works of ephemeral art, a contemporary genre in which works of art are transitory, impermanent, not intended to last (except in documentation) beyond the experience of a moment. His carefully calibrated fireworks displays (see Fig. 10-13) are among his most famous pieces, and Figure **5-26** is a drawing for one titled *Transient Rainbow*. The circular image emerges from a concentration of pinpoints of blackened paper, created through the discharge of gunpowder on two sheets of paper. As insubstantial as this work may first appear, it has more material substance—and potential longevity—than the monumental ephemeral work it inspired.

5-26 CAI GUO-QIANG. *Drawing for Transient Rainbow* (2003). Gunpowder on two sheets of paper. 179" × 159½" (overall).

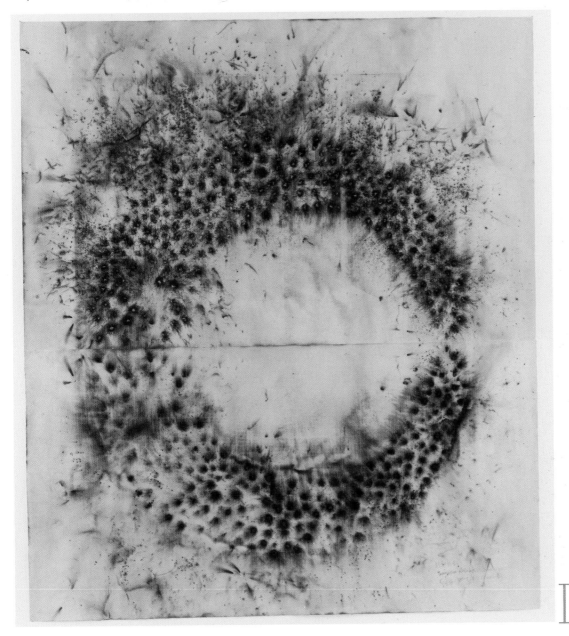

1 ft.

PAINTING

6

A painting is a work in which the primary aspect is liquid material applied to a surface with an implement. By that definition, Michelangelo's *Sistine Ceiling* and the finger paintings on newsprint that you once brought home to hang on the refrigerator fall into the same category. Granted, the latter might not be defined as a work of fine art, but the technical components of your doodles remind us that the parameters of painting are indeed broad. In a traditional painting, the liquid material that is applied is pigment, the surface is two-dimensional, and the implement is a brush. More recently, the medium has come to include a wide variety of sometimes unorthodox materials (fabric dyes, synthetic polymers, glitter, resin, animal dung), tools (sticks, trowels, spray cans, and, yes, fingers), and surfaces (shaped canvas, cutout steel reliefs, ceramic slabs, Plexiglas, found objects).

As with drawing, there are almost no limits when it comes to the materials and processes that will constitute a painting. Nor is the use of paint, throughout art history, exclusive to what we would define as a painting per se. Paint has been used to decorate pottery, enhance sculpture, embellish architecture, and more.

GILBERT STUART. *George Washington* (1796). Oil on canvas. 39⅝" × 34½" (entire work). National Portrait Gallery, Smithsonian Institution, Washington D.C.

PAINT

To most of us, paint is synonymous with color. The color in paint derives from its pigment. The pigment in powdered form is mixed with a binding agent, or **vehicle**, and a solvent, or **medium**, to form **paint**—the liquid material that imparts color to a surface. Pigments are available in a wide chromatic range. Their color is derived from chemicals and minerals found in plant and animal life, clay, soil, and sand.

Different vehicles are employed in different painting mediums. The main criterion for a successful vehicle is that it holds the pigments together. Lime plaster, wax, egg, oil, acrylic plastic, water, and gum arabic are commonly used vehicles. Unfortunately, most vehicles are subject to long-term problems, such as cracking, yellowing, or discoloration.

The task of a medium is to provide fluency to the paint so that the color may be readily dispersed over the surface. Water or turpentine is frequently used as a thinning agent for this purpose.

TYPES OF PAINTING

A variety of paints, surfaces, and tools have been used throughout the history of art to create paintings. In Chapter 13, you will see some of the first—Paleolithic paintings of animals on cave walls created with black pigment and red ocher that date back over 30,000 years. The ancient Egyptians painted on walls (**murals**), sheets of papyrus, and linen. The Greeks were renowned for their vase painting, which gives us an idea of what their other paintings must have looked like. Although no paintings on wood panels survive from ancient Greece, we know from writings that it was a highly developed art form associated with artists who were famous for their techniques. The historian Pliny the Elder, for example, remarked that the painter Zeuxis was so skilled that birds tried to eat the painted grapes in one of his works. Roman artists, who were very much influenced by the Greeks, nonetheless surpassed their predecessors in their painting innovations. Much of what we know about Roman painting comes from the ruins of the great sites of Pompeii and Herculaneum, preserved amid the ash of the historic eruption of Mount Vesuvius. Most medieval murals were destroyed, but brilliant painted (illuminated) manuscripts survive and offer stylistic parallels to other painting of the era.

Painting, as we typically define it, came into its own during the Renaissance—the so-called Golden Age of painting. Although artists continued to paint murals, paintings on wood panels and on canvas exploded in popularity, freeing the medium from its relationship to architecture. Paint-

1 ft.

6-1 GIOTTO. *Lamentation* (c. 1305). Fresco. 7'7" × 7'9". Capella Scrovegni, Arena Chapel, Padua, Italy.

ings could be hung anywhere and moved anywhere, were much less expensive and time-consuming to produce, and could be bought and sold to a wide variety of patrons and clients.

Fresco

Fresco is the art of painting on plaster. **Buon fresco**, or true fresco, is executed on damp, lime plaster; **fresco secco** is painting on dry plaster. In buon fresco, the pigments are mixed only with water, and the lime of the plaster wall acts as a binder. As the wall dries, the painted image on it becomes permanent. In fresco secco—a less permanent method—pigments are combined with a vehicle of glue that affixes the color to the dry wall.

Fresco painters encounter several challenges: Because in true fresco the paint must be applied to fresh, damp plaster, artists cannot bite off more than they can chew—or paint—in one day. For this reason, large fresco paintings are composed of small sections, each of which has been painted in a day. The artist tries to arrange the sections so that the joints will not be obvious, but sometimes it is not possible to do so. In a fourteenth-century fresco painting by the Italian master Giotto (Fig. **6-1**), these joints are clearly evident, particularly in the sky, where the artist was not able to complete the vast expanse of blue all at once. In spite of this limitation, or because of it, fresco painting is often noted for its freshness and directness of expression. The sixteenth-century art historian Giorgio Vasari wrote that of all the methods painters employ, fresco painting "is the most masterly and beautiful, because it consists in doing in a single day that which, in other methods, may be retouched day after day, over the work already done." Another challenge concerns chemistry. Although fresco paintings can be brilliant in color, some pigments will not form chemical bonds with lime. Thus, these pigments are not suitable for the medium. Artists in Giotto's era, for example, encountered a great deal of difficulty with the color blue. Such lime resistance limits the artist's palette and can make tonal transitions difficult.

Leonardo da Vinci, in his famous *The Last Supper* (see Fig. 16-17), attempted to meet these nuisances head-on, only to suffer disastrous consequences. The experimental materials and methods he employed to achieve superior results were unsuccessful. He lived to see his masterpiece disintegrate beyond repair, at least until modern conservation and restoration techniques preserved what remained by his hand.

Despite these problems, fresco painting enjoyed immense popularity from its origins until its full flowering in the Renaissance. Although it fell out of favor for several centuries thereafter, Mexican muralists revived the art of fresco after World War I.

Encaustic

One of the earliest methods of applying color to a surface was **encaustic**. It consists of pigment in a wax vehicle that has been heated to a liquid state. The ancient Egyptians and Greeks tinted their sculptures with encaustic to grant them a lifelike appearance. The Romans applied encaustic to walls, using hot irons. Often, as in the Egyptian mummy portrait of a priest of Serapis (Fig. **6-2**) dating back to the second century CE, the medium

1 in.

6-2 Mummy portrait of a priest of Serapis, from Hawara, Egypt (c. 140-160 CE); Egypto-Roman, Faiyum (c. 160-179 CE). Encaustic on wood. 14" × 8". The British Museum, London, England.

was applied to small, portable wooden panels covered with cloth. As evidenced by the startling realism and freshness of the portrait, encaustic is an extremely durable medium whose colors remain vibrant and whose surface maintains a hard luster. But encaustic is a difficult medium to manipulate: one must keep the molten wax at a constant temperature. For this reason, it has been used by only a handful of contemporary artists.

Native American painter Kay Walkingstick derives a certain plasticity from her very different use of acrylic and wax on canvas (Fig. **6-3**). In *Solstice*, two flattened arcs of sharply contrasting hues are about to merge in a viscous sea of mauve and purple. The canoelike image, although common to Native American symbolism, can also be viewed as an abstraction signifying the shifting of seasons from autumn to winter—a kind of quiet cosmological passage. Walkingstick builds her textural surface through successive layers of colored wax, gouging the field here and there with lines that reveal the palette of the lower layers. It is at once an image of power and of solitude.

1 ft.

6-3 KAY WALKINGSTICK. *Solstice* (1982). Acrylic and wax on canvas. 48" × 48" × 3½". Collection of the artist.

6-4 GENTILE DA FABRIANO. *Adoration of the Magi* (1423). Tempera on wood panel. 9'10⅛" × 9'3". Galleria degli Uffizi, Florence, Italy.

1 ft.

Tempera

Tempera, like encaustic, was popular for centuries, but its traditional composition—ground pigments mixed with a vehicle of egg yolk or whole eggs thinned with water—is rarely used today. Tempera now describes a medium in which pigment can be mixed with an emulsion of milk, different types of glues or gums, and even the juices and saps of plants and trees. The use of tempera dates back to the Greeks and Romans. Tempera was the exclusive painting medium of artists during the Middle Ages. Not until the invention of oil paint in northern Europe in the 1300s did tempera fall out of favor.

Tempera offered many advantages. It was an extremely durable medium if applied to a properly prepared surface. Pure and brilliant colors were attainable. Colors did not become compromised by gradual oxidation. Also, the consistency and fluidity of the mixture allowed for a great deal of precision. Tempera, unlike oil paint, however, dries quickly and is difficult to rework. Also, unlike oils, it cannot provide subtle gradations of tone.

Tempera can be applied to wood or canvas panels, although the latter did not come into wide use until the 1500s. Both types of supports were prepared by covering the surface with a ground. The ground was generally a combination of powdered chalk or plaster and animal glue called **gesso**. The gesso ground provided a smooth, glistening white surface on which to apply color.

All that is desirable in the tempera medium can be found in Figure **6-4**, the panel painting by the fifteenth-century Italian artist Gentile da Fabriano. Combined with the technique of **gilding**—the application of thinly hammered sheets of gold to the panel surface—the luminous reds and blues and pearly grays of the tempera paint provide a sumptuous display. The fine details of the ornate costumes testify to the precision made possible by **egg tempera**.

Several contemporary artists, such as the Swiss Photorealist painter Franz Gertsch, have also been enticed by the exactness and intricacies made possible by tempera. Suited to a methodical and painstaking approach to painting, this medium of the old masters yields unparalleled displays of contrasting textures and sharp-focused realism, as shown in Gertsch's large-scale portrait of *Silvia* (Fig. **6-5**).

1 ft.

6-5 FRANZ GERTSCH. *Silvia* (1998). Tempera on unprimed canvas. 9'6½" × 9'2¼". Museum Franz Gertsch, Burgdorf, Switzerland.

Oil

The transition from egg tempera to **oil paint** was gradual. For many years following the introduction of the oil medium, artists used it only to apply a finishing coat—a **glaze**—over a tempera painting. Glazes are thin, transparent or semitransparent layers of oil tinted with color that impart a warm atmosphere not possible with tempera alone. From the fifteenth century onward, the medium of oil painting became standard, and artists continued to use the glazing technique to create subtle tonal variations in their work. Venetian artists of the Renaissance, like Titian (Fig. 16-27), achieved a remarkable sense of realism in subtly modeled flesh made possible through glazing.

Oil paint consists of ground pigments combined with a linseed oil vehicle and turpentine medium or thinner. Oil paint is naturally slow drying, but this property can be accelerated by the addition of various agents to the basic mixture.

Oil painting's broad capability accounts for its popularity. Colors can be blended easily, offering a palette of almost limitless range. Slow drying facilitates the reworking of problem areas. It can be applied with any number of brushes or knives that yield different effects. When applied with smooth, fine-tipped brushes, oil paint can capture the most intricate detail and render a glasslike surface in which brushstrokes are barely evident (see Fig. 19-7). When considerably thinned and broadly brushed—or even poured (see Fig. 21-9) it can be used to create diaphanous fields of pulsating color.

6-6 GILBERT STUART. *George Washington* (1796) (detail). Oil on canvas. 39⅝" × 34½" (entire work). National Portrait Gallery, Smithsonian Institution, Washington D.C.

imparted a sense of roundness to Stuart's figure is replaced by stylized shadows that sit flatly on the canvas. Lichtenstein forsakes the psychological portrait in favor of billboard advertising. Washington has been translated into a commodity. Unlike Stuart's Washington, the physical characteristics suggest nothing of the human being to whom they refer.

Oil paint, precisely handled, can be used to create implied texture. Stuart creates the illusion of soft ruddy flesh and wispy grey hair through carefully wrought strokes that do not have a dominant physical presence. Oil paint can also be used to create actual texture—a surface that has its own tangible property and, by contrast, a dominant physical presence. In a work like the *Head of St. Matthew* (Fig. **6-8**), the brushstrokes are thick and brusquely applied, as if the head had been modeled in clay with the artist's fingers. Glints of white and lighter tints of gold, red-orange, and brown visually pull the man out of the shadows and give him literal substance. The broken patches of pigment suggest movement and a departure from the typical "frozen moment." The artist does

It can be applied with a palette knife or square-tipped, rough-bristled brush in thick layers or strokes (**impasto**) that assert the physical aspect of the material as well as the physical process of the act of painting (see Fig. 6-8 and 21-2).

The versatility of oil paint is illustrated in portraits of George Washington by American artists who worked centuries apart. Gilbert Stuart's iconic eighteenth-century portrait (Fig. **6-6**)—the one on the U.S. dollar bill—is actually an unfinished work. Stuart created a realistic likeness through a fairly taut handling of the medium and the manipulation of light and shade to create a three-dimensional effect. His delicate treatment of Washington's pensive eyes and the firm outline of his determined jaw speak volumes about the personality traits of the wise and aging leader.

Roy Lichtenstein's contemporary portrait (Fig. **6-7**), by contrast, is an image of glamour and success. Lichtenstein capitalized on oil paint's clarity and precision, constructing the image from sharp contrasts of black and white and discrete lines and shapes. The only departure from the stark palette consists of occasional fields of gray with patterning that mimics the Benday dots found in comic strips. A younger, debonair Washington is presented as if on a campaign poster, or as a Marvel Comics hero with a chiseled profile akin to Dick Tracy's. His eyes are alert and enthralling; his chin is jaunty and confident. The mechanical quality of the portrait (no sense of the artist's touch in these brushstrokes) deprives it of any subtlety or atmosphere, and deliberately so. The rich modeling that

6-7 ROY LICHTENSTEIN. *George Washington* (1962). Oil on canvas. 51" × 38".

1 in.

not use his technique to create a grand illusion of reality but instead concentrates our attention on another reality—that of the painted surface.

The first oil paintings were done on wood panels, followed by a gradual shift to canvas supports. As for wood panels, the canvas surface is covered with a gesso ground prior to painting. The pliability of fabric stretched over a wooden frame renders the working surface more receptive to the pressure of the artist's implement. The lighter weight of canvas also allows for larger compositions than were possible on wooden panels.

Acrylic

Acrylic paint offers many of the advantages of oil paint, but "without the mess." Acrylic paint is a mixture of pigment and a plastic vehicle that can be thinned (and washed off brushes and hands) with water. Unlike linseed oil, the synthetic resin of the binder dries colorless and does not gradually compromise the brilliance of the colors. Also, unlike oil paint, acrylic can be used on a variety of surfaces that need no special preparation. Acrylic paint is flexible and fast drying, and, as it is water soluble, it requires no flammable substances for use or cleanup.

NOLAND'S *GRADED EXPOSURE* WITH DAVIE'S *BETWEEN MY EYE AND HEART*

OIL AND ACRYLIC PAINTS often mimic each other in effects, but their idiosyncratic properties account for why one material may be chosen over the other for a specific painting. Why did Kenneth Noland use acrylic for his *Graded Exposure* (Fig. 6-9) and why did Karin Davie choose oil paint for *Between My Eye and Heart* (Fig. 6-10)?

Oil painting produces rich colors, but the pigment often fades and cracks over time. The drying time for oil paint is much longer than that of acrylic paint, producing both advantages and disadvantages. A longer drying time means that artists can rework surfaces, blend colors, and apply glazes more smoothly. Also, even after oil paint is dry, it can be resuscitated with subsequent applications of turpentine mixtures. Acrylic, on the other hand, is a medium that dries quickly. The artist must work rapidly and, once the paint is dry, it cannot be resolubilized. Because of its drying time, acrylic is not conducive to color blending, but the upside is that sharply distinct zones of color can be created without the threat of colors blurring or running into each other.

Kenneth Noland was one of the pioneers of hard-edge Color Field painting in the 1960s. His *Graded Exposure* is composed of precisely delineated stripes or fields that represent abrupt transitions between variations on the color spectrum. Razor-sharp edges are achieved using tape lines and adjusting the acrylic medium so that each application dries quickly and will not leach into crevices between the tape and the canvas. The meticulous, glasslike, unbroken surface is free of gestural brushwork. The overall feeling is one of flatness, consistency, and control.

Karin Davie's oil-on-canvas painting, *Between My Eye and Heart*, appears the polar opposite of Noland's work. Lines loop around and over each other, nesting in the shallow pictorial space and pressing against the edges of the canvas. The artist's gesture is everywhere evident, though

6-10 KARIN DAVIE. *Between My Eye and Heart No. 12* (2005). Oil on canvas. 5'6" × 7'. Margulies Warehouse Collection, Miami, FL.

also precise in its parameters. A single brush of a specific width is used to produce all of the lines and the palette is pretty much confined to red, yellow, and blue with some touches of white. The artist allows oil paint to do what it does best: blend. And it is the blending that adds dimension or volume to the lines. They aren't flat. They look more like tangled spaghetti. Variations in the overlapping hues also create a sense of space, with warm colors advancing and dark colors mostly receding.

Hard-edge painting can be done in oil and color-blending certainly is seen in acrylic works. But Noland and Davie offer us excellent case studies in the specific capabilities of each medium. ●

1 ft.

6-9 KENNETH NOLAND. *Graded Exposure* (1967). Acrylic on canvas. 7'4¾" × 19'1". Collection Mrs. Samuel G. Rautbord, Chicago, IL. Art © Estate of Kenneth Noland/Licensed by VAGA, NY.

6-11 HELEN OJI. *Mount St. Helens* (1980). Acrylic, Rhoplex, glitter on paper. 60" × 72". Collection of Home Insurance Company, NY.

One of the few effects of oil paint that cannot be duplicated in acrylic is delicate nuance of colors. Like oil, however, acrylic paint can be used thinly or thickly; it can be applied in transparent films or opaque impastos, as in Helen Oji's *Mount St. Helens* (Fig. 6-11). The artist fills the shaped canvas with an explosion of color and texture that simulates the unbridled power of one of the world's few active volcanoes. This image, which gave rise to a whole series on these natural wonders, serves, from another perspective, as "textile" ornamentation for a Japanese kimono. Canvases shaped in this garment design first preoccupied Oji in an earlier series, and here the reference to her Japanese heritage (her parents were interned during World War II, while she grew up in California) and the volcano image may symbolize a convergence of cultures from both sides of the Pacific.

Watercolor

The term **watercolor** originally defined any painting medium that employed water as a solvent. Thus, fresco and egg tempera have been called watercolor processes. But today watercolor refers to a specific technique called **aquarelle**, in which transparent films of paint are applied to a white, absorbent surface. Contemporary watercolors are composed of pigments and a gum arabic vehicle, thinned, of course, with a medium of water.

Variations of the watercolor medium have been employed for centuries. Ancient Egyptian artists used a form of watercolor in their paintings. Watercolor was also used extensively for manuscript illumination during the Middle Ages, as we shall see in Chapter 15. **Gouache**, or watercolor mixed with a high concentration of vehicle and an opaque ingredient such as chalk, was the principal painting medium during the Byzantine and Romanesque eras of Christian art. This variation has enjoyed popularity across time and a myriad of styles and is used to great effect by many contemporary artists, such as David Hockney (Fig. **6-12**).

Transparent watercolor, however, did not appear until the fifteenth century. It is a difficult medium to manipulate, despite its simple components. Tints are achieved by diluting the colors with various quantities of water. White, then, does not exist; white must be derived by allowing the white of the paper to "shine" through the color of the composition or by leaving areas of the paper exposed. To achieve the latter effect, all areas of whiteness must be mapped out with precision before the first stroke of color is applied.

With oil paint and acrylic, the artist sometimes overpaints areas of the canvas in order to make corrections or to blend colors. With transparent watercolors, overpainting obscures the underlying layers of color. For this reason, corrections are virtually impossible, so the artist must have the ability to

1 in.

6-12 DAVID HOCKNEY. *Punchinello with Block,* for "Parade Triple Bill" (1980). Gouache on paper. 14" × 17".

THE ACRYLIC PAINTINGS OF JAPANESE AMERICAN Roger Shimomura blend Western Pop Art with traditional Japanese imagery as found in *ukiyo-e* prints. As a child during World War II, Shimomura was interned with his parents and grandparents in Idaho. At the same time, ironically, his uncle served with the valiant 442nd division of Japanese Americans. Shimomura remembers statements made by white Americans about Japanese Americans during this deeply disturbing period. For example, Idaho's attorney general remarked, "We want to keep this a white man's country."

Shimomura's *Untitled* (Fig. **6-13**) is at first glance an amusing clash of American and Japanese pop cultures. American cartoon characters, Donald Duck, Pinocchio, Dick Tracy, and the combination Batman-Superman vie for space on the crowded canvas with Japanese samurai warriors and a contemporary Japanese portrait. The battle of East and West imagery may reflect the tensions within the artist regarding his ancestral roots and his chosen country. This is succinctly symbolized in the inclusion of Shimomura's self-portrait-as-Statue-of-Liberty in the extreme upper left. In this painting, conflicts between people and cultures are safely if not satirically played out among their stereotypes and myths. ●

1 ft.

6-13 ROGER SHIMOMURA. *Untitled* (1984). Acrylic on canvas. 60" × 72".

6-14 RALPH GOINGS. *Rock Ola* (1992). Watercolor on paper. 14" × 20¾".

1 in.

plan ahead, as well as a sure hand and a stout heart. When used skillfully, watercolor has an unparalleled freshness and delicacy. The colors are pure and brilliant, and the range of effects surprisingly broad.

Contemporary painter Ralph Goings—one of the driving forces behind and consistent contributors to the school of **Photorealism**—uses transparent watercolor ingeniously. His virtuoso handling of the medium can be seen in works such as *Rock Ola* (Fig. **6-14**), which belie the difficulties of the medium. Confident strokes of color precisely define the gleaming "retro" chrome surfaces of a diner interior—the classic backdrop for the countertop jukebox and standard "still life with ketchup bottle and ashtray." Washes are kept to a minimum, as the painting emphasizes form over color, line over tonal patterns.

The broader appeal of watercolor, however, is not to be found in its capability of rendering meticulous detail. When the medium came into wide use during the sixteenth century, it was seen as having other, very different advantages. The fluidity of watercolor was conducive to rapid sketches and preparatory studies. Simple materials allowed for portability. Artists were able to cart their materials to any location, indoors or outdoors, and to register spontaneously their impressions of a host of subjects. Of course, watercolor is also used for paintings that stand as completed statements. German Expressionist Emil Nolde (Fig. **6-15**), who turned to watercolor when he was forbidden to paint by the Nazis during World War II (it doesn't smell like oil paint so

1 in.

6-15 EMIL NOLDE. *Still Life, Tulips* (c. 1930). Watercolor on paper. 18½" × 13½". North Carolina Museum of Art, Raleigh, NC.

he could work in secrecy), was enticed by the transparency of tinted washes. Such washes permitted a delicate fusion of colors. As with the drawing medium of brush and wash, the effect is atmospheric. The edges of the forms are softened; they seem to diffuse into one another or the surrounding field. Nolde created his explosions of blossoms through delicately balanced patches of bold color and diaphanous washes. The composition is brightened by the white of the paper, which is brought forward to create forms as assertive as those in color.

Spray Paint

One can consider that spray painting has had a rather long history. The subtle coloration marking different species of animals on the walls of Paleolithic caves was probably achieved by blowing pigments onto a surface through hollowed-out reeds. Why are they there: decoration? ritual? history? Oddly enough, these questions can be asked of the contemporary graffiti artist and the thousands upon thousands of writings that range in definition from "tags" to "masterworks." Why do they do it? Is it art? urban ritual? Will it speak in history to the trials of inner-city living?

Everyone has seen graffiti, but the complexity of the work and the social atmosphere from which it is derived may not be common knowledge. Stylized signatures, or "tags," can be seen everywhere; it seems as though no urban surface—interior or exterior—is immune. Some are more likely to call this defacing public property than creating works of art, but how do we describe the elaborate urban "landscapes" that might cover the outside of an entire subway car, filling the space with a masterful composition of shapes, lines, textures, and colors? On the street, they are called masterworks, and their artists are indeed legendary.

Some graffiti writers have "ascended" to the art **gallery** scene, exchanging their steel "canvases" for some of fabric and their high-speed exhibition spaces for highbrow gallery walls. One such artist, Crash (or John Matos), created a parody of his own subway style in a complex canvas work called *Arcadia Revisited* (Fig. **6-16**). All of the tools and techniques of his trade—commercial cans of spray paint, the Benday dots of comic-strip fame, the sharp lines of the tag writer's logos, the diffuse spray technique that adds dimensionality to an array of otherwise flat objects—are used to describe a violent clash of cultural icons that are fragmented, superimposed, and barely contained within the confines of the canvas.

1 ft.

6-16 CRASH (JOHN MATOS). *Arcadia Revisited* (1988). Spray paint on canvas. 96¼" × 68".

MIXED MEDIA

Contemporary painters have in many cases combined traditional painting techniques with other materials, or they have painted on nontraditional supports, stretching the definition of what has usually been considered painting. For example, in *The Bed* (see Fig. 21-11), Pop artist Robert Rauschenberg splashed and brushed paint onto a quilt and pillow, which he then hung on a wall like a canvas work and labeled a "combine painting." The Synthetic Cubists of the early twentieth century, Picasso and Braque, were the first to incorporate pieces of newsprint, wallpaper, labels from wine bottles, and oilcloth into their paintings. These works were called *papiers collés* and have come to be called **collages**.

The base mediums for Howardena Pindell's *Autobiography: Water / Ancestors, Middle Passage / Family Ghosts* (Fig. **6-17**) are tempera and acrylic, but the work, on sewn canvas, also incorporates an array of techniques and substances—markers, oil stick, paper, photo-transfer, and vinyl tape. The detail achieved is quite remarkable. The artist seems to float

Painting is self-discovery. Every good artist paints what he is.
—Jackson Pollock

in a shimmering pool of shallow water, while all around her images and objects of memory seem to enter and exit her consciousness. Included among them are the prominent white shape of an African slave ship, a reference to Pindell's African ancestry, and the whitened face of the artist's portrait that may have been influenced by Michael Jackson's "Thriller" makeup. The work resembles as much a weaving as a painting, further reflecting the tapestry-like nature of human recollection.

Miriam Schapiro is best known for her paint and fabric constructions, which she has labeled "femmage," to express

6-18 MIRIAM SCHAPIRO. *Maid of Honour* (1984). Acrylic and fabric on canvas. 60" × 50".

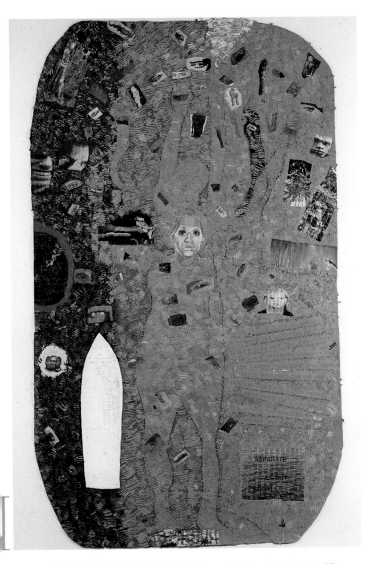

6-17 HOWARDENA PINDELL. *Autobiography: Water / Ancestors, Middle Passage / Family Ghosts* (1988). Acrylic, tempera, cattle markers, oil stick, paper, polymer photo-transfer, and vinyl tape on sewn canvas. 118" × 71". The Wadsworth Atheneum, Hartford, CT.

what she sees as their unification of feminine imagery and materials with the medium of collage. In *Maid of Honour* (Fig. 6-18), Schapiro combines bits of intricately patterned fabric with acrylic pigments on a traditional canvas support to construct a highly decorative garment that is presented as a work of art. The painting is a celebration of women's experiences with sewing, quilting, needlework, and decoration.

The two-dimensional mediums we have discussed in Chapter 5 and in this chapter, drawing and painting, create unique works whose availability to the general public is usually limited to photographic renditions in books such as this. Even the intrepid museumgoer usually visits only a small number of collections. So let us now turn our attention to the two-dimensional medium that has allowed millions of people to own original works by masters—printmaking.

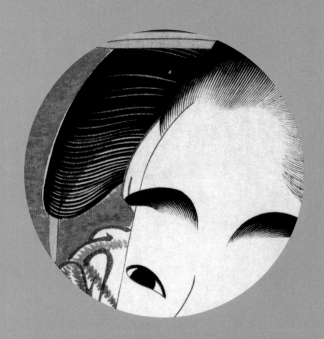

PRINTMAKING

7

The value of drawings and paintings lies, in part, in their uniqueness. Hours, weeks, sometimes years are expended in the creation of these one-of-a-kind works. Printmaking permits the reproduction of these coveted works as well as the production of multiple copies of original prints. Printmaking is an important artistic medium for at least two reasons. First, it allows people to study great works of art from a distance. Second, because prints are less expensive than unique works by the same artist, they make it possible for the general public, not just the wealthy few, to own original works. With prints, art has become accessible. Like some drawings, however, prints not only serve a functional purpose but may also be considered works of art in themselves.

Ukiyo-e color woodblock print (1798). Private collection.

METHODS OF PRINTMAKING

The printmaking process begins with a design or image made in or on a surface by hitting or pressing with a tool. The image is then transferred to paper or a similar material. The transferred image is called the **print**. The working surface, or **matrix**, varies according to the printmaking technique. Matrices include wood blocks, metal plates, stone slabs, and silkscreens. There are special tools for working with each kind of matrix, but the images in printmaking are usually rendered in ink.

Printmaking processes are divided into four major categories: relief, intaglio, lithography, and serigraphy (Fig. **7-1**). We shall examine a variety of techniques within each of these processes. Finally, we will consider the monotype and the combining of printmaking mediums with other mediums.

RELIEF

In **relief printing**, the matrix is carved with knives or gouges. Areas that are not meant to be printed are cut below the surface of the matrix (Fig. 7-1A), and areas that form the image and are meant to be printed are left raised. Ink is then applied to the raised surfaces, often from a roller. The matrix is pressed against a sheet of paper, and the image is transferred. The transferred image is the print. Relief printing includes woodcut and wood engraving.

Woodcut

Woodcut is the oldest form of printmaking. The ancient Chinese stamped patterns onto textiles and paper using carved wood blocks. The Romans used woodcuts to stamp symbols or letters on surfaces for purposes of identification. During the 1400s in Europe, woodcuts provided multiple copies of religious images for worshippers. After the invention of the printing press, woodcut assumed an important role in book illustration.

Woodcuts are made by cutting along the grain of the flat surface of a wooden board with a knife. Different types of wood and different gouging

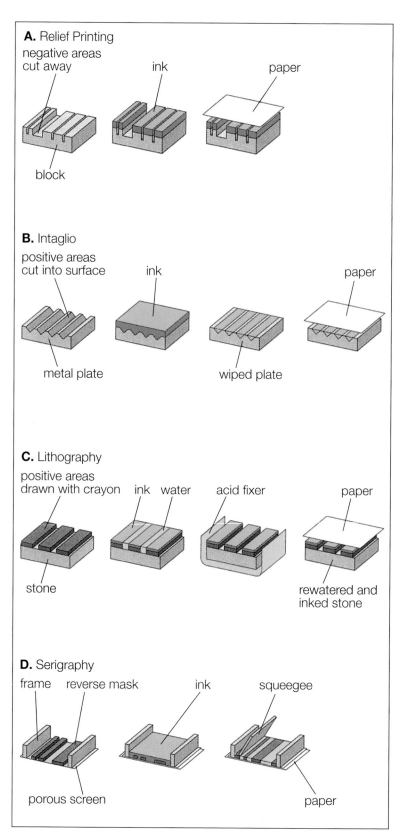

A. Relief Printing
negative areas cut away   ink   paper

block

B. Intaglio
positive areas cut into surface   ink   paper

metal plate   wiped plate

C. Lithography
positive areas drawn with crayon   ink   water   acid fixer   paper

stone   rewatered and inked stone

D. Serigraphy
frame   reverse mask   ink   squeegee

porous screen   paper

7-1 Printmaking technologies.

HIROSHIGE'S *RAIN SHOWER ON OHASHI BRIDGE* WITH XIAOMO'S *FAMILY BY THE LOTUS POND*

7-2 ANDO HIROSHIGE. *Sudden Rain at Atake and Ohashi* (1857). Color woodblock print. 13⅞" × 9⅛". The Cleveland Museum of Art, Cleveland, OH. Gift from J. H. Wade 1921.318.

ANDO HIROSHIGE, a nineteenth-century Japanese artist, achieved the finest detail in his works by choosing a close-grained wood and by tightly controlling the movement of his carving tools. Clean-cut, uniform lines define the steady rain and the individuals who tread huddled against

the downpour across a wooden footbridge (Fig. **7-2**). These fine lines provide a delicate counterpoint to bold shapes and broad areas of color and create the illusion of a drawing.

The meticulous process by which Hiroshige achieved his sharply defined images is used to a very different effect in Zhao Xiaomo's *Family by the Lotus Pond* (Fig. **7-3**). This contemporary Chinese printmaker uses a range of wood-block techniques to create complex, energetic compositions that often simulate oil paintings. Inspired by Chinese peasant paintings, as they are not bound by "academic rules," Xiaomo creates mosaic-like surfaces with bold, two-dimensional patterns.

How does the visual impact of these two works differ? Consider the use of line, shape, and color. ●

7-3 ZHAO XIAOMO. *Family by the Lotus Pond* (1998). Multiblock woodcut printed with water-soluble ink. 16¾" × 16½". The Art Institute of Chicago, Chicago, IL.

1 in.

7-4 CHEN XUHAI. *Golden Autumn* (1998). Woodcut, printed with oil-based ink. 25¼" × 24". The Art Institute of Chicago, Chicago, IL.

The razor-sharp tips of engraving implements and the hardness of the end-grain blocks make possible the exacting precision found in wood engravings such as that by Paul Landacre (Fig. 7-6), a well-known twentieth-century American printmaker. Tight, threadlike, parallel, and cross-hatched lines compose the tonal areas that define the form. The rhythmic, flowing lines of the seedling's unfurling leaves contrast dramatically with the fine, prickly lines that emanate like rays from the young corn plant. The print is a display of technical prowess in a most demanding and painstaking medium.

tools yield various effects. *Golden Autumn* (Fig. 7-4) by Chen Xuhai is a masterfully complex woodcut in which pockets of short lines of varying direction combine with long, velvet black crevices to create the signature landscape of an aging face.

Wood Engraving

The technique of **wood engraving** and its effects differ significantly from those of woodcuts. Whereas in woodcuts the flat surface of boards is used, in wood engraving many thin layers of wood are **laminated**. Then the ends of these sections are planed flat, yielding a hard, nondirectional surface. In contrast to the softer matrix used for the woodcut, the matrix for the wood engraving makes it relatively easy to work lines in varying directions. These lines are **incised** or engraved with tools such as a **burin** or **graver** (Fig. 7-5), instead of being cut with knives and gouges. The lines can be extremely fine and are often used in close alignment to give the illusion of tonal gradations. This process was used to illustrate newspapers, such as *Harper's Weekly*, during the nineteenth century.

INTAGLIO

The popularity of relief printing declined with the introduction of the **intaglio** process. Intaglio prints are created by using metal plates into which lines have been incised. The plates are covered with ink, which is forced into the linear depressions, and then the surface is carefully wiped. The cut depressions retain the ink, whereas the flat surfaces are clean. Paper is laid atop the plate, and then paper and plate are passed through a printing press, forcing the paper into the incised lines to pick up the ink, thereby accepting the image. In a reversal of the

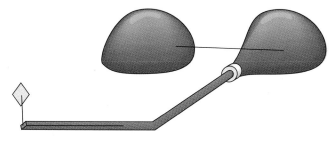

7-5 Burin.

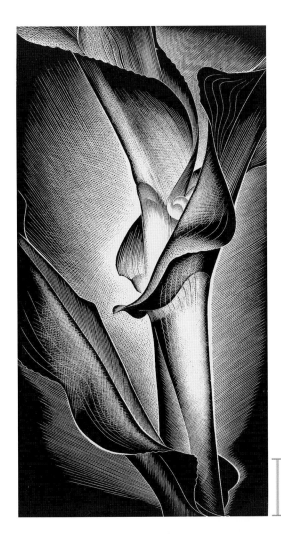

relief process, then, intaglio prints are derived from designs or images that lie *below* the surface of the matrix (Fig. 7-1B).

Intaglio printing encompasses many different mediums, the most common of which are engraving, drypoint, etching, and mezzotint and aquatint. Some artists have used these techniques recently in interesting variations or combinations and have pioneered approaches using modern equipment such as the camera and computer.

Engraving

Although **engraving** has been used to decorate metal surfaces such as bronze mirrors or gold and silver drinking vessels since ancient times, the earliest engravings printed on paper did not appear until the fifteenth century. In engraving, the artist creates clean-cut lines on a plate of copper, zinc, or steel, forcing the sharpened point of a burin across the surface with the heel of the hand. Because the lines are transferred to paper under very high pressure, they not only reveal the ink from the grooves but have a ridgelike texture that can be felt by running a finger across the print.

An early, famous engraving came from the hand of the fifteenth-century Italian painter Antonio Pollaiuolo (Fig. **7-7**). Deep lines that hold a greater amount of ink define the contours of the ten fighting figures. As Landacre did, Pollaiuolo used parallel groupings of thinner and thus lighter lines to render the tonal gradations that define the exaggerated musculature. The detail of the print is described with the utmost precision, revealing the artist's painstaking mastery of the burin.

7-6 PAUL LANDACRE. *Growing Corn* (1940). Wood engraving. 8½" × 4¼".

7-7 ANTONIO POLLAIUOLO. *Battle of Ten Naked Men* (c. 1465–1470). Engraving. 15½" × 23³⁄₁₆". The Metropolitan Museum of Art, NY.

Intaglio **139**

1 in.

7-8 REMBRANDT VAN RIJN. *Christ Crucified between the Two Thieves* (1653). Drypoint, 4th state. 15" × 17½". Museum of Fine Arts, Boston, MA.

Drypoint

Drypoint is engraving with a simple twist. In drypoint, a needle is dragged across the surface, and a metal burr, or rough edge, is left in its wake to one side of the furrow. The burr retains particles of ink, creating a softened rather than crisp line when printed. The burr sits above the surface of the matrix and therefore is fragile. After many printings, it will break down, resulting in a line that simply looks engraved.

The characteristic velvety appearance of drypoint lines is seen in Rembrandt's *Christ Crucified between the Two Thieves* (Fig. **7-8**). The more distinct lines were rendered with a burin, whereas the softer lines were created with a drypoint needle. Rembrandt used the blurriness of the drypoint line to enhance the sense of chaos attending the Crucifixion and the darkness of the encroaching storm. Lines fall like black curtains enshrouding the crowd, and rays of bright light illuminate the figure of Jesus and splash down onto the spectators.

Etching

Although they are both intaglio processes, **etching** differs from engraving in the way the lines are cut into the matrix. With engraving, the depth of the line corresponds to the amount of force used to push or draw an implement over the surface. With etching, minimal pressure is exerted to determine the depth of line. A chemical process does the work.

In etching, the metal plate is covered with a liquid, acid-resistant ground consisting of wax or resin. When the ground has hardened, the image is drawn upon it with a fine needle. Little pressure is exerted to expose the ground; the plate itself is not scratched. When the drawing is completed, the matrix is slipped into an acid bath, which immediately begins to eat away, or etch, the exposed areas of the plate. This etching process yields the sunken line that holds the ink. The artist leaves the plate in the acid solution just long enough to achieve the desired depth of line. If a variety of tones is desired, the artist may pull the plate out of the acid solution after a while, cover lines of sufficient depth with the acid-resistant ground, and replace the plate in the bath for further etching of the remaining exposed lines. The longer the plate remains in the

7-10 GIOVANNI DOMENICO TIEPOLO. *A Negro* (1770). Etching, 2nd state. 5⅝" × 4⁹⁄₁₆". Museum of Fine Arts, Boston, MA.

acid solution, the deeper the etching. Deeper crevices hold more ink, and for this reason they print darker lines.

Etching is a versatile medium, capable of many types of lines and effects. The modern French painter Henri Matisse used but a few dozen uniformly etched lines to describe the essential features of a woman, *Loulou Distracted* (Fig. 7-9). The extraordinarily simple yet complete image attests to the delicacy that can be achieved with etching.

Whereas Matisse's figure takes shape through the careful placement of line, the subject of the etching by Giovanni Domenico Tiepolo (who was the son of Giovanni Battista Tiepolo) exists by virtue of textural and tonal contrasts (Fig. 7-10). This eighteenth-century Italian artist used a variety of wavy and curving lines to differentiate skin from cloth, fur from hair, figure from ground. Lines are spaced to provide a range of tones from the sharp white of the paper to the rich black of the man's clothing. The overall texture creates a hazy atmosphere that caresses the pensive figure.

7-9 HENRI MATISSE. *Loulou Distracted* (1914). Etching, printed in black. 7¹⁄₁₆" × 5". Archives Matisse, Paris, France. © 2011 Succession H. Matisse/ Artists Rights Society (ARS), NY.

IN MANY WAYS, HUNG LIU epitomizes the concerns and preoccupations of the Chinese artist whose life experiences during that country's Cultural Revolution have shaped their art—indeed, their very existence. In 1984, Hung Liu arrived in the United States. In her words, with her "Five-thousand-year-old culture on my back. Late-twentieth-century world in my face. . . . My Alien number is 28333359." For four years in her country of origin, she was forced to work in the fields. In her chosen country, she is now a professor at Mills College and has had one-woman shows in New York, San Francisco, Texas, and Miami. Her art focuses on what she has called "the peculiar ironies which result when ancient Chinese images are 'reprocessed' within contemporary Western materials, processes, and modes of display."

Figure 7-11 shows an untitled mixed-media print, whose main image consists of a photo-etching onto which are affixed small rectangular wooden blocks—mahjong pieces—bearing the "high-fashion" portraits of Chinese women. The inspiration for this print, and full oil paintings on the same theme, came from a series of photographs of Chinese prostitutes from the early 1900s that Hung Liu discovered on a recent return trip to China. When the Communist revolution took hold and all able-bodied individuals were forced into labor, these women were forced into prostitution because the tradition of oppression that led to the practice of binding their feet made them unfit for physical toil. They could barely walk.

Hung Liu feels the need to make known the pain, suffering, and degradation of generations of women before her:

> Although I do not have bound feet, the invisible spiritual burdens fall heavy on me. . . . I communicate with the characters in my paintings, prostitutes—these completely subjugated people—with reverence, sympathy, and awe. They had no real names. Probably no children. I want to make up stories for them. Who were they? Did they leave any trace in history?

In Hung Liu's work, we come to understand a piece of history. We are challenged to reflect, as she does, upon human rights and freedoms, spiritual and physical oppression, political expression, and silenced voices. ●

7-11 HUNG LIU. *Untitled* (1992). Photo-etching, mixed media. 33" × 22½".

1 ft.

Mezzotint and Aquatint

Engraving, drypoint, and etching are essentially linear mediums. With these techniques, designs or images are created by cutting lines into a plate. The illusion of tonal gradations is achieved by altering the number and concentration of lines. Sometime in the midseventeenth century, the Dutchman Ludwig von Siegen developed a technique whereby broad tonal areas could be achieved by nonlinear engraving, that is, engraving that does *not* depend on line. The medium was called **mezzotint**, from the Italian word meaning "half tint."

With mezzotint engraving, the entire metal plate is worked over with a curved, multitoothed implement called a **hatcher**. The hatcher is "rocked" back and forth over the surface, producing thousands of tiny pits that will hold ink. If printed at this point, the plate would yield an allover consistent, velvety black print. But the mezzotint engraver uses this evenly pitted surface as a point of departure. The artist creates an image by gradually scraping and burnishing the areas of the plate that are meant to be lighter. These areas will hold less ink and therefore will produce lighter tones. The more persistent the scraping, the shallower the pits and the lighter the tone. A broad range of tones is achieved as the artist works from the rich black of the rocked surface to the highly polished pitless areas that will yield bright whites. Mezzotint is a rarely used, painstaking, and time-consuming procedure.

The subtle tonal gradations achieved by the mezzotint process can be duplicated with a much easier and quicker etching technique called **aquatint**. In aquatint, a metal plate is evenly covered with a fine powder of acid-resistant resin. The plate is then heated, causing the resin to melt and adhere to the surface. As in line etching, the matrix is placed in an acid bath, where its uncovered surfaces are eaten away by the solution. The depth of tone is controlled by removing the plate from the acid and covering the pits that have been sufficiently etched.

Aquatint is often used in conjunction with line etching and is frequently manipulated to resemble tones produced by wash drawings. In *The Painter and His Model* (Fig. **7-12**), Pablo Picasso brought the forms out of void space by defining their limits with dynamic patches of aquatint. These tonal areas resemble swaths of ink typical of wash drawings. Descriptive details of the figures are rendered in fine or ragged lines, etched to varying depths.

7-12 PABLO PICASSO. *The Painter and His Model* (1964). Etching and aquatint. 12⅝" × 18½". Museum of Fine Arts, Boston, MA. © 2011 Estate of Pablo Picasso/Artists Rights Society (ARS), NY.

1 in.

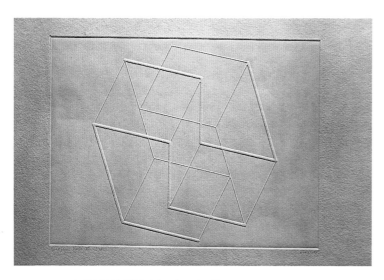

7-13 JOSEF ALBERS. *Solo V* (1958). Inkless intaglio. 6 ⅝" × 8 ⅝". Brooklyn Museum, Brooklyn, NY.

Solo V, the geometric image shown in Figure **7-13**, by etching the lines of his design to two different depths. Furrows in the plate appear as raised surfaces when printed. We seem to feel the image with our eyes, as light plays across the surface of the paper to enhance its legibility. Perceptual shifts occur as the viewer focuses now on the thick, now on the thin lines. In trying to puzzle out the logic of the form, the viewer soon discovers that Albers has offered a frustrating illustration of "impossible perspective."

LITHOGRAPHY

Lithography was invented at the dawn of the nineteenth century by the German playwright Aloys Senefelder. Unlike relief and intaglio printing, which rely on cuts in a matrix surface to produce an image, the lithography matrix is flat.

Other Etching Techniques

Different effects may also be achieved in etching by using grounds of different substances. **Soft-ground etching**, for example, employs a ground of softened wax and can be used to render the effects of crayon or pencil drawings. In a technique called **lift-ground**, the artist creates the illusion of a brush-and-ink drawing by actually brushing a solution of sugar and water onto a resin-coated plate. When the plate is slipped into the acid bath, the sugar dissolves, lifting the brushed image off the plate to expose the metal beneath. As in all etching mediums, these exposed areas accept the ink.

Given that the printing process implies the use of ink to produce an image, can we have prints without ink? The answer is yes—with the medium called **gauffrage**, or inkless intaglio. Josef Albers, a twentieth-century American abstract artist, created

7-14 WANG GUANGYI. *Great Criticism: Coca-Cola* (1990–1992). Lithograph. 28¾" × 27⅛".

1 in.

Lithography is a surface or **planographic printing** process (Fig. 7-1C).

In lithography, the artist draws an image with a greasy crayon directly on a flat stone slab. Bavarian limestone is considered the best material for the slab. Sometimes a specially sensitized metal plate is used, but a metal surface will not produce the often-desired grainy appearance in the print. Small particles of crayon adhere to the granular texture of the stone matrix. After the design is complete, a solution of nitric acid is applied as a fixative. The entire surface of the matrix is then dampened with water. The untouched areas of the surface accept the water, but the waxy crayon marks repel it.

A roller is then used to cover the stone with an oily ink. This ink adheres to the crayon drawing but repels the water. When paper is pressed to the stone surface, the ink on the crayon is transferred to the paper, revealing the image. Different lithographic methods yield different results. Black crayon on grainy stone can look quite like the crayon drawing it is. On the other hand, lithographs with large blocks of colored ink can emphasize the commercial quality of the printmaking process.

Wang Guangyi's *Great Criticism: Coca-Cola* (Fig. **7-14**) reads like an anti-American propaganda poster, the kind that you could imagine seeing glued in multiples to plywood in an urban landscape. It features bold lines and a sharp definition of color and shape. The power of the image and its message are enhanced by the work's simplicity and directness, as well as our visual recognition of stereotypes—in this case the faces of Asian men, their standard laborer's overalls, and the Coca-Cola logo.

The impact of Käthe Kollwitz's lithograph *The Mothers* (Fig. **7-15**), which highlights the plight of lower-class German mothers left alone to fend for their children after World War I, could not be further removed from that of *Great Criticism: Coca-Cola*. The high contrast of the black and white and the coarse quality of the wax crayon yield a sense of desperation suggestive of a newspaper documentary photograph. All the imagery is thrust toward the picture plane, as in high relief. The harsh contours of protective shoulders, arms, and hands contrast with the more delicately rendered faces and heads of the children—all contributing to the poignancy of the work.

7-15 KÄTHE KOLLWITZ. *The Mothers* (1919). Lithograph. 17¾" × 23". The Philadelphia Museum of Art, Philadelphia, PA. © 2011 Artists Rights Society (ARS), NY/VG Bild-Kunst, Bonn.

1 in.

7-16 ALEX KATZ. *Red Coat* (1983). Silkscreen, printed in color. 58" × 29". The Museum of Modern Art, NY. John B. Turner Fund. Art © Alex Katz/ Licensed by VAGA, NY.

1 ft.

SERIGRAPHY

In **serigraphy**—also known as **silkscreen printing**—stencils are used to create the design or image. Unlike the case with other graphic processes, these images can be rendered in paint as well as ink.

One serigraphic process begins with a screen constructed of a piece of silk, nylon, or fine metal mesh stretched on a frame. A stencil with a cutout design is then affixed to the screen, and paper or canvas is placed beneath (Fig. 7-1D). The artist forces paint or ink through the open areas of the stencil with a flat, rubber-bladed implement called a **squeegee**, similar to those used in washing windows. The image on the support corresponds to the shape cut out of the stencil. Several stencils may be used to apply different colors to the same print.

Images can also be "painted" on a screen with use of a varnishlike substance that prevents paint or ink from passing through the mesh. This technique allows for more gestural images than cutout stencils would provide. Recently, a serigraphic process called **photo silkscreen** has been developed; it allows the artist to create photographic images on a screen covered with a light-sensitive gel.

Serigraphy was first developed as a commercial medium and is still used as such to create such things as posters and labels on cans of food. The American Pop artist Andy Warhol raised the commercial aspects of serigraphy to the level of fine art in many of his silkscreen prints of the 1960s, such as *Four Marilyns* (see Fig. 1-9). These faithful renditions of celebrities and everyday items satirize the mass media's bombardment of the consumer with advertising. They also have their amusing side.

Alex Katz defines his forms with razor-sharp edges, fixing his subjects in an exact time and place by the details of their clothing and hairstyles. At the same time, he transcends their temporal and spatial limits by simplifying and transforming their figures into something akin to icons. For example, the subject's intense red lips in his silkscreen *Red Coat* (Fig. **7-16**) serve as a symbol of contemporary glamour. *Red Coat* looks something like a photograph transported into another medium. The individual shapes seem carved into a single plane like sawed jigsaw puzzle pieces. As in a photo, the edges of the silkscreen crop off parts of the image. The woman looks like a supermodel, with her features exaggerated as they might be in a cover girl image.

1 in.

7-17 EDGAR DEGAS. *The Ballet Master* (c. 1874). Monotype in black ink. 22" × 27½". National Gallery of Art, Washington, D.C.

MONOTYPE

Monotype is a printmaking process, but it overlaps the other two-dimensional mediums of drawing and painting. Like drawing and printmaking, monotype yields but a single image, and like them, therefore, it is a unique work of art.

In monotype, drawing or painting is created with oil paint or watercolor on a nonabsorbent surface of any material. Brushes are used, but sometimes fine detail is rendered by scratching paint off the plate with sharp implements. A piece of paper is then laid on the surface, and the image is transferred by hand rubbing the back of the paper or passing the matrix and paper through a press. The result, as can be seen in a monotype by Edgar Degas (Fig. **7-17**), has all the spontaneity of a drawing and the lushness of a painting.

Look at the things around you, the immediate world around you. If you are alive, it will mean something to you, and if you care enough about photography, and if you know how to use it, you will want to photograph that meaning.

—Edward Weston

IMAGING: PHOTOGRAPHY, FILM, VIDEO, AND DIGITAL ARTS

8

Technology has revolutionized the visual arts. For thousands of years, one of the central goals of art was to imitate nature as exactly as possible. Today, any one of us can point a camera at a person or an object and capture a realistic image. Point-and-shoot cameras no longer even require that we place the subject in proper focus or that we regulate the amount of light so as not to overexpose or underexpose the subject. Technology can do all of these things for us.

Similarly, the art of the stage was once available only to those who lived in the great urban centers. Now and then a traveling troupe of actors might come by, or local groups might put on a show of sorts, but most people had little or no idea of the ways in which drama, opera, dance, and other performing arts could affect their lives. The advent of motion pictures, or cinematography, suddenly brought a flood of new imagery into new local theaters, and a new form of communal activity was born. People from every station of life could flock to the movie theater on the weekend. Over time, cinematography evolved into an art form independent of its beginnings as a mirror of the stage.

More recently, television has brought this imagery into the home, where people can watch everything from the performing arts to sporting events in privacy and from the multiple vantage points that several cameras, rather than a single set of eyes, can provide. Fine artists have also appropriated television—or, more precisely, the technology that makes television possible—to produce **video art**. Technology has also given rise to the computer as a creative video-mediated tool. With the aid of artificial intelligence, we can instantly view models of objects from all sides. We can be led to feel as though we are sweeping in on our solar system from the black reaches of space, then flying down to the surface of our planet and landing where the programmer would set us down.

Millions of children spend hours playing video games, such as Tetris, which challenges them to rotate plummeting polygons to construct a solid wall, or Mario Brothers and Tomb Raider, which require them to evade or blast a host of enemies before their computer-drawn heroes and heroines plunge into an abyss. Computer technology and computer-generated images have likewise been appropriated by fine artists in the creation of **digital art**. In illustrations of blue jeans that rocket through space, snappy graphics that headline sporting events, and the web design that greets us every time we go online, computer-generated images punctuate our daily lives. DVDs, multimedia computers, and software that can blend or distort one shape or face into another are bringing a "virtual reality" into our lives that is in some ways more alluring than, well, "real reality."

In this chapter, we discuss photography, film (cinematography), video, and digital arts. These mediums have given rise to unique possibilities for artistic expression.

PHOTOGRAPHY

Photography is a science and an art. The word *photography* is derived from Greek roots meaning "to write with light." The scientific aspects of photography concern the ways in which images of objects are made on a **photosensitive** surface, such as film, by light that passes through a **lens**. Chemical changes occur in the film so that the images are recorded. This much of the process—the creation of an objective image of the light that has passed through the lens—is mechanical.

It would be grossly inaccurate, however, to think of the *art* of photography as mechanical. Photographers make artistic choices, from the most mundane to the most sophisticated. They decide which films and lenses to use, and which photographs they will retain or discard. They manipulate lighting conditions or printing processes to achieve dazzling or dreamy

effects. Always, they are in search of subjects—ordinary, extraordinary, universal, personal.

Photography is truly an art of the hand, head, and heart. Before the advent of digital photography, the photographer had to understand films and grasp skills related to developing **prints**. The photographer must also have the intellect and the passion to search for and to see what is important in things—what is beautiful, harmonious, universal, and worth recording.

Photography is a matter of selection and interpretation. Similar subjects seen through the eyes of different photographers will yield wildly different results. In Ansel Adams's *Moon and Half Dome, Yosemite National Park, California* (Fig. **8-1**), majestic cliffs leap into a deep, cold sky. From our earthbound vantage point, the perfect order of the desolate, spherical moon contrasts with the coarseness of the living rock. Yet we know that its geometric polish is an illusion wrought by distance—the moon's surface is just as rough and chaotic. Adams's composition is as much about design elements (shape, texture, value) as it is a visual document of the California landscape. Distance and scale come sharply into focus: This is a story of humans dwarfed by nature and nature dwarfed by the stars.

8-1 ANSEL ADAMS. *Moon and Half Dome, Yosemite National Park, California* (1960).

Photography records the gamut of feelings written on the human face, the beauty of the earth and skies that man has inherited and the wealth and confusion man has created.
—Edward Steichen

8-2 Crescent Earth, seen by Apollo 17.

In the early nineteenth century, when photography was invented, the technology that made Figure 8-2 possible would have been only fantasy. In this NASA photograph, taken during the first manned mission to the moon in July 1969, the crescent shape of sunlight blanketing a distant Earth is silhouetted against a velvet black sky. Its perfect geometry is a dramatic counterpoint to the irregular textured surface of the moon. Although only a sliver of Earth's blue color is evident at the point where light turns abruptly to shadow, it is enough to suggest a sense of life in contrast to the barren, unforgiving lunar landscape.

Both the Adams photograph and the one taken from space have artful compositions, even though the NASA photograph was not taken by an artist. Adams chose a specific moment, when shadows were deep, the sky was clear, and the position of the sun exaggerated the textures of the rock. The black shadows and the uniform steel gray sky have such precise contours that they read as flat puzzle pieces. The NASA photograph is striking for two reasons. First, the "composition" is dramatically simple: a field bisected into two zones by the sharp diagonal created by the contour of the moon. Second, the perspective is intriguing: we sense the fluid glide of the ship through the stillness of space.

The aesthetic aspect of both photographs is not all they have in common. The history of photography is full of evidence of the artist-photographer boldly going where no man (or woman) has gone before or challenging the viewer to see anew the familiar and ubiquitous. The mood, stylistic inclinations, cultural biases, and technical preferences influence the nature of the creative product. As observers, we are as enriched by the diversity of this medium as much as any other in the visual arts.

Cameras

Cameras may look very different from one another and boast a variety of equipment, but they all possess certain basic features. As you can see in Figure **8-3**, the camera is similar to the human eye. In both cases, light enters a narrow opening and is projected onto a photosensitive surface.

The amount of light that enters the eye is determined by the size of the *pupil*, which is an opening in the muscle called the *iris*; the size of the pupil responds automatically to the amount of light that strikes the eye. The amount of light that enters a camera is determined by the size of the opening, or **aperture**, in the **shutter**. The aperture opening can be adjusted manually or, in advanced cameras, automatically. The size of the aperture, or opening, is the so-called **F-stop**. The smaller the F-stop, the larger the opening. The shutter can also be made to remain open to light for various amounts of time, ranging from a few thousandths of a second—in which case **candid** shots of fast action may be taken—to a second or more.

When the light enters the eye, the *lens* keeps it in focus by responding automatically to its distance from the object. The light is then projected onto the retina, which consists of cells that are sensitive to light and dark and to color. Nerves transmit visual sensations of objects from the retina to the brain.

In the same way, the camera lens focuses light onto a photosensitive surface such as **film**. A camera lens can be focused manually or automatically. Many photographers purposely take pictures that are out of focus, for their soft, blurred effects. **Telephoto lenses** magnify faraway objects and tend to collapse the spaces between distant objects that recede from us. **Wide-angle lenses** allow a broad view of objects within a confined area.

In their early days, cameras tended to be large and were placed on mounts. Today's cameras are usually small and held by hand. *The Steerage* (see Fig. 1-27) was shot with an early handheld camera. Many contemporary cameras contain angled mirrors that allow the photographer to see directly through the lens and thereby to be precisely aware of the image that is being projected onto the film.

Film

When an image is "shot," it is recorded on a device such as film or an electronic memory device such as a disk or memory stick. Contemporary black-and-white films are very thin, yet they contain several layers, most of which form a protective coating and backing for the photosensitive layer. The active layer contains an **emulsion** of small particles of a photosensitive silver salt (usually silver halide) suspended in gelatin.

After the film is exposed to light and treated chemically, it becomes a **negative**, in which metallic silver is formed from the crystals of silver halide. In this negative, areas of dark and light are reversed. Because the negatives are transparent, light passes through them to a print surface, which becomes the final photograph, or print. Here the areas of light and dark are reversed again, now matching the shading of the original subject. Prints are also usually made significantly larger than the negative.

Black-and-white films differ in color sensitivity (the ability to show colors such as red and green as different shades), in contrast (the tendency to show gradations of gray as well as black and white), in graininess (the textural quality, as reflective of the size of the silver halide crystals), and in speed (the amount of exposure time necessary to record an image). Photographers select films that will heighten the effects they seek to portray.

Color film is more complex than black-and-white film, but similar in principle. Color film also contains several layers, some of which are protective and provide backing. There are two basic kinds of color film: **color reversal film** and **color negative film**. Both types of color film contain three light-sensitive layers.

Prints are made directly from *color reversal film*. Therefore, each of the photosensitive layers corresponds to one of the primary colors in additive color mixtures: blue, green, or red. When color reversal film is exposed to light and treated

retina (photosensitive surface)

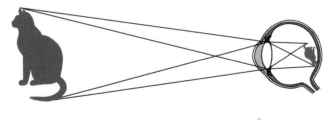

film (photosensitive surface)

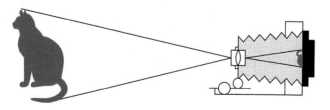

8-3 The camera and the human eye compared.

Imaging: Photography, Film, Video, and Digital Arts

chemically, mixtures of the primary colors emerge, yielding a full-color image of the photographic subject.

Negatives are made from *color negative film.* Therefore, each photosensitive layer corresponds to the complement of the primary color it represents. (Additive color mixtures and primary and complementary colors are explained in Chapter 2.)

Color films, like black-and-white films, differ in color sensitivity, contrast, graininess, and speed. But color films also differ in their appropriateness for natural (daylight) or artificial (indoor) lighting conditions.

Digital Photography

Today, **digital photography** abounds. Digital cameras translate the visual images that pass through the lens into bits of digital information, which are recorded onto an electronic storage device such as a disk, not on film. High-quality (translation: extremely expensive) digital cameras take photos whose **resolution**—that is, sharpness—rivals that of images recorded on film. The stored information can then be displayed on a computer monitor. Rather than have several prints made, the photographer can "back up" the information repeatedly. It can also be sent over the Internet in digital form. Printed images can also be scanned, which converts them into digital formats, and then stored on computer hard drives or sent over the Internet.

Digital photography has some advantages. One is that the photographer need not deal with film—loading and unloading it and having it developed. The images can be displayed immediately on a display built into the camera or on a computer monitor. Software then permits you to manipulate the images as desired. You can also print them out as you would print out any other image or text.

The disadvantages are that (most) digital images do not have the sharpness of film images. Images take up a tremendous amount of storage space (several megabytes each!) on your hard drive. Also, your printer may not print images that approach the quality of film images, even if you have stored enough information to do so. To get professional-quality prints, you may have to invest in professional equipment or take your disk elsewhere, just as you have to take film to a lab or processor to be developed. But the price of this equipment is falling steadily, and we seem to be arriving at a point at which nearly anyone will be able to afford digital equipment that rivals the resolution of more traditional photography.

History of Photography

The cameras and films described previously are rather recent inventions. Photography has a long and fascinating history. Although true photography does not appear much before the mid-nineteenth century, some of its principles can be traced back another 300 years, to the camera obscura.

THE CAMERA OBSCURA The **camera obscura**—literally, the covered-over or darkened room—was used by Renaissance artists to help them accurately portray depth, or perspective, on two-dimensional surfaces. The camera obscura could be a box, as shown in Figure **8-4**, or an actual room with a small hole that admits light through one wall. The beam of light projects the outside scene upside down on a surface within the box. The artist then simply traces the scene, as shown, to achieve a proper perspective—to truly imitate nature.

DEVELOPMENT OF PHOTOSENSITIVE SURFACES The camera obscura could only temporarily focus an image on a surface while a person labored to copy it by tracing. The next developments in photography concerned the search for photosensitive surfaces that could permanently affix images. These developments came by bits and pieces.

In 1727, the German physicist Heinrich Schulze discovered that silver salts had light-sensitive qualities, but he never tried to record natural images. In 1802, Thomas Wedgwood, son of the well-known English potter, reported his discovery that paper soaked in silver nitrate did take on projected images as a chemical reaction to light. However, the images were not permanent.

HELIOGRAPHY In 1826, the Frenchman Joseph-Nicéphore Niepce invented **heliography**. **Bitumen**, or asphalt residue, was placed on a pewter plate to create a photosensitive surface. The bitumen was soluble in **lavender oil** if kept in the dark, but insoluble if struck by light. Niepce used a kind

8-4 The camera obscura.

8-5 LOUIS-JACQUES-MANDÉ DAGUERRE. *The Artist's Studio* (1837).

of camera obscura to expose the plate for several hours, and then he washed the plate in lavender oil. The pewter showed through where there had been little or no light, creating the image of the darker areas of the scene. The bitumen remained where the light had struck, however, leaving lighter values.

THE DAGUERREOTYPE The **daguerreotype** resulted from a partnership formed in 1829 between Niepce and another Frenchman, Louis-Jacques-Mandé Daguerre. The daguerreotype used a thin sheet of silver-plated copper. The plate was chemically treated, placed in a camera obscura, and exposed to a narrow beam of light. After exposure, the plate was treated chemically once more.

Figure 8-5 shows the first successful daguerreotype, taken in 1837. Remarkably clear images could be recorded by this process. In this work, called *The Artist's Studio*, Daguerre, a landscape painter, sensitively assembled deeply textured objects and sculptures. The contrasting light and dark values help create an illusion of depth.

There were drawbacks to the daguerreotype. It had to be exposed from 5 to 40 minutes, requiring long sittings. The recorded image was reversed, left to right, and was so delicate that it had to be sealed behind glass to remain fixed. Also, the plate that was exposed to light became the actual daguerreotype. There was no negative, and consequently, copies could not be made. However, some refinements of the process did come rapidly. Within 10 years, the exposure time had been reduced to about 30 to 60 seconds, and the process had become so inexpensive that families could purchase two portraits for a quarter. Daguerreotype studios opened

all across Europe and the United States, and families began to collect the rigid, stylized pictures that now seem to reflect days gone by.

THE NEGATIVE The negative was invented in 1839 by British scientist William Henry Fox Talbot. Talbot found that sensitized paper, coated with emulsions, could be substituted for the copper plate of the daguerreotype. He would place an object, such as a sprig of a plant, on the paper and expose the arrangement to light. The paper was darkened by the exposure in all areas except those covered by the object. Translucent areas, allowing some passage of light, resulted in a range of grays. Talbot's first so-called photogenic drawings (Fig. 8-6), created by this process, seem eerie, though lyrically beautiful. The delicacy of the image underscores the impracticality of the process: How on earth would you "photograph" an elephant?

As with the daguerreotype, this process produced completed photographs in which the left and right of the image were reversed. In Talbot's photogenic drawings, the light and dark values of the image were also inverted. Talbot improved

8-6 WILLIAM HENRY FOX TALBOT. *Botanical Specimen* (1839). Photogenic drawing.

8-7 UNKNOWN (ATTR. LOUIS LUMIÈRE). *Young Lady with an Umbrella* (1906-1910). Autochrome. Institut Lumière, Lyon, France.

a burgeoning business in portrait photography. Having a likeness of oneself was formerly reserved for the wealthy, who could afford to commission painters. Photography became the democratic equalizer. The rich, the famous, and average bourgeois citizens could now become memorable, could now make their presence known long after their flesh had rejoined the elements from which it was composed.

Photographic studios spread like wildfire, and many photographers, such as Julia Margaret Cameron and Gaspard Felix Tournachon—called "Nadar"—vied for famous clientele. Cameron's impressive portfolio included portraits of Charles Dickens; Alfred, Lord Tennyson; and Henry Wadsworth Longfellow. Nadar's 1859 portrait of the actress Sarah Bernhardt (Fig. 8-8) was printed from a glass plate, which could be used several times to create sharp copies. Early portrait photographers such as Nadar imitated both nature and the arts, using costumes and props that recalled Romantic paintings or sculpted busts caressed by flowing drapery. The photograph is soft and smoothly textured, with middle-range values predominating; Bernhardt is sensitively portrayed as pensive, intelligent, and delicate.

on his early experiments with his development of the **contact print**. He placed the negative in contact with a second sheet of sensitized paper and exposed them both to light. The resultant print was a "positive," with left and right, and light and dark, again as in the original subject. Many prints could be made from the negative. Unfortunately, the prints were not as sharp as daguerreotypes, because they incorporated the texture of the paper on which they were captured. Subsequent advances led to methods in which pictures with the clarity of daguerreotypes could be printed from black-and-white as well as color negatives.

Photography improved rapidly for the next 50 or 60 years—faster emulsions, glass-plate negatives, better camera lenses—and photographs became increasingly more available to the general public. The next major step in the history of photography came with the introduction by Louis Lumière of the autochrome color process in 1907. Autochromes were glass plates coated with a layer of tiny potato starch grains dyed in three different colors. A layer of silver bromide emulsion covered the starch. When the autochrome was developed, it yielded a positive color transparency. Due to the technical limitations of the process Autochrome Lumière photographs, such as *Young Lady with an Umbrella* (Fig. 8-7), evoke late nineteenth-century French paintings in subject, palette, and texture. Autochrome technology was not replaced until 1932, when Kodak began to produce color film that applied the same principles to more advanced materials.

PORTRAITS By the 1850s, photographic technology and the demands of a growing middle class in the wake of the American and French revolutions came together to create

8-8 NADAR. *Sarah Bernhardt* (1859). Bibliothèque Nationale, Paris, France.

The American photographer Alfred Stieglitz (Fig. 1-27) expressed the view that portraits ought to be taken over the course of the subject's lifetime because that was only way to reveal the personality. Over a period of two decades, he photographed Georgia O'Keeffe (see Fig. 20-14) extensively; this body of work contains some 500 negatives. Contemporary photographer Nicholas Nixon began his documentary-portrait series *The Brown Sisters* (Fig. 8-9) in 1975 and has taken one black and white photograph of the group each year since. The format never changes—the sisters are always in the same position from left to right—but the locations do. More than family snapshots, although not unlike them, the series reads like a private diary of sibling relationships and the subtlety of the aging process.

PHOTOJOURNALISM Prior to the nineteenth century, there were few illustrations in newspapers and magazines. Those that did appear were usually in the form of engravings or drawings. Photography revolutionized the capacity of the news media to bring realistic representations of important events before the eyes of the public. Pioneers such as Mathew Brady and Alexander Gardner first used the camera to record major historical events such as the U.S. Civil War. The photographers and their crews trudged down the roads alongside the soldiers, horses drawing their equipment behind them in wagons referred to by the soldiers as "Whatsits."

Equipment available to Brady and Gardner did not allow them to capture candid scenes, so there is no direct record of the bloody to-and-fro of the battle lines, no photographic

8-9 NICHOLAS NIXON. *The Brown Sisters* (2010). Gelatin silver print. 7 11/16" × 9½". The Museum of Modern Art, NY. The Family of Man Fund.

Documentary photography records the social scene of our time. It mirrors the present and documents [it] for the future. Its focus is man in his relation to mankind. It records his customs at work, at war, at play. . . . It portrays his institutions. . . . It shows not merely their facades, but seeks to reveal the manner in which they function, absorb the life, hold the loyalty, and influence the behavior of human beings.

—Dorothea Lange

record of each lunge and parry. Instead, they brought home photographs of officers and of life in the camps along the lines. Although battle scenes would not hold still for Gardner's cameras, the litter of death and devastation caused by the war and pictured in Gardner's *Home of a Rebel Sharpshooter, Gettysburg* (Fig. **8-10**) most certainly did. Despite their novelty and their accuracy, not many works of such graphic nature were sold. There are at least three reasons for this tempered success. First, the state of the art of photography made the photographs high priced. Second, methods for reproducing photographs on newsprint were not invented until about 1900; therefore, the works of the photojournalists were usually rendered as drawings, and the drawings translated into woodcuts before they appeared in the papers. Third, the American public might not have been ready to face the brutal realities they portrayed. In a similar vein, social commentators have suggested that the will of many Americans to persist in the Vietnam War was sapped by the incessant barrage of televised war imagery.

During the Great Depression of the 1930s, the conscience of the nation was stirred by the work of many photographers hired by the Farm Security Administration. Dorothea Lange

1 in.

8-11 DOROTHEA LANGE. *Migrant Mother, Nipomo, California* (1936). Gelatin silver print. 12½" × 9⅞". The Oakland Museum of Art, Oakland, CA.

8-10 ALEXANDER GARDNER. *Home of a Rebel Sharpshooter, Gettysburg* (July 1863). Wet-plate photograph. Chicago History Museum, Chicago, IL.

and Walker Evans, among others, portrayed the lifestyles of migrant farmworkers and sharecroppers. Lange's *Migrant Mother* (Fig. **8-11**) is a heartrending record of a 32-year-old woman who is out of work but cannot move on because the tires have been sold from the family car to purchase food for her seven children. The etching in her forehead is an eloquent expression of a mother's thoughts; the lines at the outer edges of her eyes tell the story of a woman who has aged beyond her years. Lange crops her photograph close to her subjects; they fill the print from edge to edge, forcing us to confront them rather than allowing us to seek comfort in a corner of the print not consigned to such an overt display of human misery. The migrant mother and her children, who turn away from the camera and heighten the futility of their plight, are as much constrained by the camera's viewfinder as they are by their circumstances.

In the very year that Lange photographed the migrant mother, Robert Capa's fearless coverage of the Spanish Civil War resulted in such incredible photographs as *Death of a Loyalist Soldier* (see Fig. 3-17). During the early 1940s, photographers such as Margaret Bourke-White carried their hand-held cameras into combat and captured tragic images of the butchery in Europe and in the Pacific. In 1929, Bourke-White became a staff photographer for *Fortune*, a new magazine published by Henry Luce. When Luce founded *Life* in 1936, Bourke-White became one of its original staff photographers. Like Dorothea Lange, she recorded the poverty of the Great Depression, but in the 1940s, she traveled abroad to become

one of the first female war photojournalists. As World War II was drawing to an end in Europe, Bourke-White arrived at the Nazi concentration camp of Buchenwald in time for its liberation by Gen. George S. Patton. Her photograph *The Living Dead of Buchenwald* (Fig. 8-12), published in *Life* in 1945, has become a classic image of the Holocaust, the Nazi effort to annihilate the Jewish people. The indifferent countenance of each survivor expresses, paradoxically, all that he has witnessed and endured. In her book *Dear Fatherland, Rest Quietly*, Bourke-White put into words her own reactions to Buchenwald. In doing so, she showed how artistic creation, an intensely emotional experience, can also have the effect of objectifying the subject of creation:

> I kept telling myself that I would believe the indescribably horrible sight in the courtyard before me only when I had a chance to look at my own photographs. Using the camera

8-12 MARGARET BOURKE-WHITE. *The Living Dead of Buchenwald, April 1945* (1945).

was almost a relief; it interposed a slight barrier between myself and the white horror in front of me . . . it made me ashamed to be a member of the human race.[1]

Dorothea Lange traveled rural America to photograph the effects of the Depression, and Margaret Bourke-White followed the U.S. troops abroad during World War II. As Bourke-White discovered, one of the keys to photojournalism is being in the presence of history in the making. On September 11, 2001, when terrorists hijacked commercial aircraft and flew them into the World Trade Center towers, Ron Berard was living on an upper floor of an apartment directly across from the devastation. His photograph (Fig. **8-13**) captures the hellish and almost surreal nature of the event in which almost 3,000 people lost their lives—the shard of the curtain wall that remained, the pile of rubble, the charred facade of a still-standing neighbor. The eerie smoke that rose from the pit would continue to rise for two months.

Another of Berard's photographs—an American flag flying, flapping, snapping against the grim background of the devastation of the World Trade Center site—was published by *Time* magazine. Yet perhaps the best-known photo from the tragedy of September 11 is the one taken a day later by Thomas E. Franklin, a staff photographer for *The Record*, a local New Jersey newspaper. That image of firefighters raising the flag amidst the rubble—a symbol of survival, heroism, and pride—was commemorated in a U.S. postage stamp. Its content, design, and emotional impact have been compared with the equally famous photograph of U.S. Marines raising the flag on the Pacific island of Iwo Jima during World War II.

PHOTOGRAPHY AS AN ART FORM Photographers became aware of the potential of their medium as an art form more than 100 years ago. Edward Weston (see Fig. 2-3), Paul Strand, Edward Steichen, and others argued that photographers must not attempt to imitate painting (as Lumière had) but must find modes of expression that are truer to

8-13 RON BERARD. *Untitled* (2001).

their medium. Synergistically, painters moved toward abstraction because the obligation to faithfully record nature was now assumed by the photographer. Why, after all, do what a camera can do better? In 1902, Alfred Stieglitz founded the Photo-Secession, a group dedicated to

---

[1] Margaret Bourke-White, *Dear Fatherland, Rest Quietly* (New York: Simon and Schuster, 1946), 73.

8-14 EDWARD STEICHEN. *The Flatiron Building—Evening* (1906).

cannot readily see, there is nothing gloomy or frightening about the scene. Rather, it seems pregnant with wonderful things that will happen as the rain stops and the twentieth century progresses.

It was not long before artists began to manipulate their medium so that they, too, could venture beyond imitation. The first steps were tentative, building on the familiar and the readily acceptable. Some portrait photographers, for example, experimented with double-exposed images and tableaus— elaborate painted backdrops against which people and objects were thoughtfully and deliberately arranged. The tableau form is also seen in the works of contemporary artists.

Sandy Skoglund's *Radioactive Cats* (Fig. 8-15) portrays a phlegmatic elderly couple live out their colorless lives amidst an invasion of neon green cats. Skoglund sculpted the plaster cats herself and painted the room gray, controlling every aspect of the set before she photographed the scene.

Artist-photographer William Wegman happened upon his most famous subject when his Weimaraner puppy virtually insisted on performing before his lights. Man Ray, named by Wegman after the Surrealist photographer, posed willingly in hundreds of staged sets that range from the credible to the farcical. *Blue Period* (Fig. 8-16) is a riff on Pablo Picasso's painting *The Old Guitarist* (see Fig. 20-5), enframed in a souvenir-sized reproduction in the left lower foreground. In both works, a guitar cuts diagonally across the composition, adding the only contrasting color to the otherwise mono-

advancing photography as a separate art form. Stieglitz enjoyed taking pictures under adverse weather conditions and at odd times of day to show the versatility of his medium and the potential for expressiveness.

Edward Steichen's *The Flatiron Building— Evening* (Fig. 8-14), photographed a century ago, is among the foremost early examples of the photograph as a work of art. It is an exquisitely sensitive nocturne of haunting shapes looming in a rain-soaked atmosphere. The branch in the foreground provides the viewer with a psychological vantage point as it cuts across the composition like a bolt of lightning or an artery pulsing with life. The values are predominantly middle grays, although here and there, beacon-like, streetlamps sparkle in the distance. The infinite gradations of gray in the cast-iron sky-scraper after which the picture is named, and in the surrounding structures, yield an immeasurable softness. Although much is present that we

8-15 SANDY SKOGLUND. *Radioactive Cats* (1980). Cibachrome. 30" × 40".

1 ft.

8-16 WILLIAM WEGMAN. *Blue Period* (1981). Color Polaroid photograph. 24" × 22".

view of the fashion industry. Sherman appears as a disheveled model with a troubling expression. Something here is very wrong. Regimented stripes go awry as the fabric of her dress is stretched taut across her thighs and knees. Her hands rest oddly in her lap, fingertips red with what seems to be blood. And then there is the smile—an unsettling leer implying madness.

Iranian American photographer and video artist Shirin Neshat came to the United States as a teenager, before the shah, or monarch, was removed from power in 1979, and returned in 1990 to witness a nation transformed by the rule of Islamic clergy. She was particularly concerned about how life had changed for Iranian women, who now had limited opportunities outside the home and were veiled behind black

chromatic blue background. The heads of the old man and of Man Ray hang, melancholy, over the soulful instrument. As Picasso gave the old man's flesh a bluish cast, so did Wegman tint the Weimaraner's muzzle. In Wegman's photograph, however, we find the pièce de résistance—an object laden with profound meaning for the guitarist's stand-in: a blue rubber bone.

Cindy Sherman is her own exclusive subject, adopting diverse personae for her photographs. Sherman recalls a mundane, early inspiration for her approach: "I had all this makeup. I just wanted to see how transformed I could look. It was like painting in a way."[2] Soon she set herself before elaborate backdrops, costumed in a limitless wardrobe. Dress designers began to ask her to use their haute couture in her photographs, and works such as *Untitled* (Fig. **8-17**) were actually shot as part of an advertising assignment for French *Vogue*. The result is less a sales device than a harsh

1 ft.

8-17 CINDY SHERMAN. *Untitled* (1984). Color photograph. 71" × 48½".

[2] Cindy Sherman, in Gerald Marzorati, "Imitation of Life," *Artnews* 82 (September 1983): 84–85.

1 in.

8-18 SHIRIN NESHAT. *Untitled (Women of Allah)* (1994).
Gelatin silver print, ink. 14⅛" × 11".

chadors. Figure **8-18** is one of a series called *Women of Allah*, in which guns or flowers are frequently juxtaposed with vulnerable though rebellious faces and hands that emerge from beneath the veil. The exposed flesh is overwritten with sensual or political texts by Iranian women in the native tongue of Farsi. To a non-Arabic-speaking Westerner, the calligraphic writing may first appear to be little more than a mélange of elegant and mysterious patterns and designs. Yet there is no mistaking its purpose as one of resistance. The photos are unlikely to be seen and "decoded" by the eyes of Iranians living in Iran, but the message of the artist to the world outside is clear.

In contrast to Skoglund, Wegman, and Neshat, who stage their artistic photographs, Andreas Gursky infers the artistic from existing circumstances, often relying on the absence of context to focus the viewer's attention on lines, patterns, or textures rather than on subject. *Bahrain I* (Fig. **8-19**) is titled after the Middle Eastern island country in which Gursky cap-

tured an aerial view of a racetrack in the sprawling desert. Thick lines and shapes of black asphalt crisscross the sand, resembling the broad strokes of an abstract painting. The allusion to works on canvas is underscored by sheer size of his prints: *Bahrain I* is almost 10 feet high.

Evolving technology has made it possible for photographers to achieve dazzling images such as the one in Harold Edgerton's *Milk Drop Coronet* (Fig. **8-20**), featured in the Museum of Modern Art's first exhibition of photography in 1937. Edgerton, called the father of high-speed and stop-action photography, was an electrical engineer at MIT who pioneered the use of the stroboscope—a device that emits brief and brilliant flashes of light that seem to slow or stop the

1 ft.

8-19 ANDREAS GURSKY. *Bahrain I* (2005). Chromogenic color print. 9' 10⅞" × 7' 2½". © 2011 Andreas Gursky/Artists Rights Society (ARS), NY/VG Bild-Kunst, Bonn.

action of people or objects in motion—for photography. He would synchronize the flashes with the movements of objects and capture them with an open shutter at many flashes per second. Edgerton applied the technology to capture ordinary and extraordinary events—water coming out of a faucet, a simple drop of milk splashing into a pool of the liquid, bullets penetrating helium balloons, and athletes in motion.

Edgerton's process was the opposite of what photographer Eadweard Muybridge aimed to do in his early experiments in filmmaking. Edgerton froze each and every fraction of actual motion in a single image. Muybridge combined numerous individual photographs of a moving object into a sequence that, if viewed in rapid succession, gave the illusion of actual motion. The door to cinema was open.

8-20 HAROLD EDGERTON. *Milk Drop Coronet* (1957, printed later). Silver gelatin print. 16" × 20".

FILM

Eadweard Muybridge's *Galloping Horse* (Fig. **8-21**) sequence was shot in 1878 by 24 cameras placed alongside a racetrack and was made possible by new fast-acting photosensitive plates. (If these plates had been developed 15 years earlier, Brady could have bequeathed us a photographic record of Civil War battle scenes.) Muybridge had been commissioned to settle a bet as to whether racehorses ever had all four hooves off the ground at once. He found that they did, but also that they never assumed the rocking-horse position in which the front and back legs are simultaneously extended.

Muybridge is generally credited with performing the first successful experiments in making motion pictures. He fashioned a device that could photograph a rapid sequence of images, and he invented the **Zoopraxiscope**, which projected these images onto a screen.

The birth of cinema was the result, then, of specific inventions. In 1889, Henry Reichenbach, working as an inventor for George Eastman's Kodak company, created film: images printed on celluloid and cut into strips. Two years later,

8-21 EADWEARD MUYBRIDGE. *Galloping Horse* (1878). George Eastman House, International Museum of Photography, Rochester, NY.

Thomas Alva Edison (who had met Muybridge in 1888) patented the **Kineto-scope**, a motion-picture viewing device. A sequence of images on film (something like Muybridge's galloping horse) was passed over a lamp, the light from which was broken into quick flashes by a revolving shutter placed between the film and the lamp. The light flashes illuminated each frame, and the rapidity of the progression of the frames, along with the phenomenon of persistence of vision, created the illusion of motion.

Edison's Kinetoscope was a box into which a viewer would peer to see a moving picture. The next step in the evolution of cinema was projection of the moving picture; this happened with the Cinematographe, a camera and projector in one piece of equipment, patented by the brothers August and Louis Lumière in France in 1895. Their first public motion-picture projection took place the same year, a 20-minute program of 10 short films. Among them was *The Demolition of a Wall*, a film that is known as the first to feature special effects: Lumière reversed the film to suggest that the wall was going up rather than going down. Soon after, the appearance of trick photography became the staple of Georges Melies, who used stop-motion and superimposed images to create true special effects in films that included adaptations of two novels by Jules Verne—*A Trip to the Moon* and *Twenty Thousand Leagues under the Sea*.

Within a few short years of these inventions, commercial movie houses sprang up in France and in the United States and motion pictures were distributed for public viewing. These were silent films accompanied by live orchestral music and stage shows. The next big step in movie making occurred with the first feature film incorporating sound—*The Jazz Singer* (1927). From then on, sound on film recording shaped the future of cinema.

CINEMATOGRAPHY

Cinematography is the art of making motion pictures by manipulating the technology and processes to achieve desired effects. As in any other medium, cinematography involves artistic choices. The specific cameras and lenses, lighting, "in camera" (multiple exposures, time lapse, or a dissolve or fade-to-black, for example) and postproduction effects, and the film stock that directors and cinematographers use will determine the character of a film. In *Under the Table* (Fig. **8-22**),

8-22 JORDAN RATHUS. Film still from *Under the Table* (2005). 16mm film. 11 min, 10 sec.

which posits the lives and intimate interactions of a family of four holed up in a post-apocalyptic shelter, filmmaker Jordan Rathus used Kodak Vision2 500T stock to obtain a grainy feel that would match the family's environment—what she describes as "a claustrophobic and long-forgotten bunker filled with retro objects and stale relationships." This film stock also enabled the use of fewer and smaller lights to fill in shadows. Additional methods were employed to "pump up the saturation" of color and achieve a warm look.

Varieties of Cinematographic Techniques

Motion pictures, then, begin with the creation of the illusion of movement; this is accomplished via stroboscopic motion or the presentation of a rapid progression of images of stationary objects. An audience is shown 16 to 24 pictures or frames per second, and each picture or frame differs slightly from the one preceding it. At a rate of 22 or 24 frames per second, the motion in a film seems smooth and natural. But what if a cinematographer wants to tweak that aspect and create the illusion of **slow motion**? It is not a matter of slowing down the rate of frames per second because at fewer than 16 or so the movement will seem choppy. Rather, slow motion is achieved by shooting 100 or more frames per second. When the films are played back at 22 or 24 frames per second, movement appears to be very slow yet smooth and natural. This is one example of the ways in which directors and cinematographers manipulate the materials and processes of the film medium for artistic purposes.

FIXED CAMERAS AND STAGED PRODUCTIONS With a stage play, the audience is fixed and observes the action from a single vantage point. Similarly, many early motion

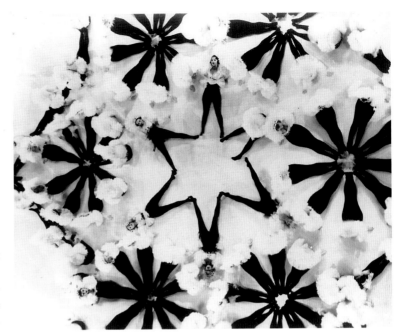

8-23 BUSBY BERKELEY. Tutti Frutti number from *Dames* (1934).

pictures used a single camera that was more or less fixed in place. The first film that the Lumière brothers shot used a fixed camera to record workers, animals, and a man on a bicycle leaving the Lumière Factory (1895). In other early films, actors entered and exited a stage before a fixed camera, much as they do in plays.

For the most part, the Busby Berkeley musicals of the 1930s (Fig. **8-23**) were shot on indoor stages that pretended to be nothing but stages. The motion picture had not yet broken free from the stage that had preceded it. Many directors used cinematography to bring the stages of the great urban centers to small cities and rural towns. We can note that the musicals of the 1930s were everything that the photographs of Dorothea Lange and the other Depression photographers were not: they were bubbly, frivolous, light, even saucy. Perhaps they helped Americans make it through these difficult times. Some musicals of the 1930s showed apple-cheeked kids getting their break on the Great White Way. Others portrayed the imaginary shenanigans of the wealthy few in an innocent era when Hollywood believed that they would offer amusement and inspiration to destitute audiences rather than stir feelings of social conflict through depiction of conspicuous consumption and frivolity.

THE MOBILE CAMERA Film critics usually argue that motion pictures should tell their stories in ways that are inimitable through any other medium. One way is through the mobile camera. Film pioneer D. W. Griffith is credited with making the camera mobile. He attached motion-picture cameras to rapidly moving vehicles and used them to **pan** across expanses of scenery and action, as in the battle scenes in his *Birth of a Nation* (Fig. **8-24**). Today it is not unusual for cameras to be placed aboard rapidly moving vehicles and also to **zoom** in on and away from their targets.

EDITING Griffith is also credited with making many advances in film editing. **Editing** is the separating and assembling, sometimes called "patching

8-24 D. W. GRIFFITH. Scene from *Birth of a Nation* (1915).

8-26 ORSON WELLES. Film still from *Citizen Kane* (1941).

and pasting," of sequences of film. Editing helps make stories coherent and heightens dramatic impact.

In **narrative editing**, multiple cameras are used during the progress of the same scene or story location. Then shots are selected from various vantage points and projected in sequence. Close-ups may be interspersed with **longshots**, providing the audience with abundant perspectives on the action while advancing the story. Close-ups usually better communicate the emotional responses of the actors, whereas longshots describe the setting, as in Alfred Hitchcock's thriller *North by Northwest* (Fig. **8-25**).

In **parallel editing**, the story shifts back and forth from one event or scene to another. Scenes of one segment of a battlefield may be interspersed with events taking place at another location or back home, collapsing space. Time may also be collapsed through parallel editing, with the cinematographer shifting back and forth between past, present, and future.

In the **flashback**, one form of parallel editing, the story line is interrupted by the portrayal or narration of an earlier episode, often through the implied fantasies of a principal character. Orson Welles's *Citizen Kane* (Fig. **8-26**) innovated the use of the flashback, which usually gives current action more meaning. In the **flash-forward**, editing permits the audience to see glimpses of the future. The flash-forward is frequently used at the beginning of dramatic television shows to capture the interest of the viewer who may be switching channels.

Motion pictures may proceed from one scene to another by means of **fading**. The current scene becomes gradually dimmer, or *fades out*. The subsequent scene then grows progressively brighter, or *fades in*. In the more rapid, current technique of the **dissolve**, the subsequent scene becomes brighter and the current scene fades out so that the first scene seems to dissolve into the second.

In **montage**, a sequence of abruptly alternating images or scenes conveys associated ideas or the passage of time. Images can suddenly flash into focus or whirl about for impact, as in a series of newspaper headlines meant to show the progress of the actors over time.

8-28 Film still from *Toy Story 3* (2010).

COLOR Color came into use in the 1930s. One early color film, *The Wizard of Oz*, depicted the farm world of Kansas in black and white and the imaginary Oz in glorious, often expressionistic color. Madonna sort of reverses the pattern in *Truth or Dare*, where her stage performances (fantasy?) are in color and her (real?) backstage life is in black and white. Yet interestingly, this pattern is now frequently reversed in music videos, where fantasy is often portrayed in black and white and reality in (everyday, natural?) color.

The screen version of Margaret Mitchell's *Gone with the Wind* (Fig. **8-27**) was one of the first color epics, or "spectaculars." It remains one of the highest-grossing works of all film eras. In addition to the sweeping **panoramas** of the Civil War battlefield wounded and the burning of Atlanta, *Gone with the Wind* included close-ups of the passion and fire communicated by Clark Gable as Rhett Butler and Vivien Leigh as Scarlett O'Hara.

ANIMATION Animation is the creation of a motion picture by photographing a series of drawings, each of which shows a stage of movement that differs slightly from the one preceding it. As a result, projecting the frames in rapid sequence creates the illusion of movement. The first cartoons were in black and white and employed a great deal of repetition.

During the 1930s, Walt Disney's studios began to produce full-color stories and images that have become part of our collective unconscious mind. Disney characters such as Mickey Mouse, Donald Duck, Bambi, Snow White, and Pinocchio are national treasures. In recent years, Disney has collaborated with Pixar Animation Studios to create a new generation of computer-animated films, including *Toy Story*; *Finding Nemo*; *Monsters, Inc.*; *The Incredibles*; *Up* (winner of two Academy Awards in 2010); and *Toy Story 3* (also winner of two Academy Awards, in 2011) (Fig. **8-28**). These films represent a dramatic technological departure from earlier animated features: they are created using computer graphics, more specifically three-dimensional computer-generated imagery (CGI). *Toy Story 3* was also the first animated film to be released in theatres with 7.1 surround sound, a system of eight speakers placed throughout the theater carrying eight channels of sound.

8-27 VICTOR FLEMING. "The Burning of Atlanta," film still from *Gone with the Wind* (1939).

8-29 CHRISTOPHER NOLAN. Film still from *Inception* (2010).

SPECIAL EFFECTS In a turn-of-the-century example of special effects, George Melies made a film in which a music master removes his own head, soon to be replaced by a succession of heads that he persistently takes off one after the other. He tosses the heads onto a telegraph wire, each of which forms a musical note. Over the years, filmmakers have raised the technical bar for special effects in their action movies. The industry has come a long way, from Melies's trick photography and tiny exploding capsules planted in the ground to simulate gunfire to the extravaganzas of effects in films such as *Avatar* (2009) and *Inception* (2010; winner of 2011 Academy Award for special effects) (Fig. **8-29**). Complex motorized sets and remote-controlled models as well as extensive computer graphics combine to create an extreme illusion of the director's reality. Notable scenes in *Inception* (the hotel corridor and the outdoor Paris café) feature complex movable sets, location explosions, sophisticated camera work, and postproduction enhancements using digital technology.

Varieties of Cinematographic Experience

No discussion of cinematography can hope to recount adequately the richness of the motion-picture experience. Broadly speaking, motion pictures are visual experiences that entertain or move us. For example, as in novels, we identify with characters and become wrapped up in plots. Like other artists, cinematographers make us laugh (consider the great films of the Marx brothers and Laurel and Hardy); create propaganda, satire, social commentary, fantasy, and symbolism; express artistic theories; and reflect artistic styles. Let us consider some of these more closely.

PROPAGANDA Although there are some early (and choppy) film records of World War I, cinematography was ready for World War II. In fact, while many American actors were embattled in Europe and the Pacific, former president Ronald Reagan was making films for the United States that depicted the valor of the Allied soldiers and the malevolence of the enemy.

8-30 LENI RIEFENSTAHL. Film still from *Triumph of the Will* (1936).

Our adversaries were active as well. Before the war, in fact, German director Leni Riefenstahl made what is considered one of the greatest (though also most pernicious) propaganda films of all time, *Triumph of the Will* (Fig. **8-30**). Riefenstahl transformed the people and events of an historic event, the 1935 Nuremberg Congress, into abstract, symbolic patterns through the juxtaposition of longshots and close-ups, and aerial and ground-level views. Her montage of people, monuments, and flag-bedecked buildings unified flesh and stone into a hymn to Nazism. The United States, England, Canada, and some other nations paid a backhanded compliment to the power of *Triumph of the Will* by banning it.

SATIRE Satire is the flip side of propaganda. Although Riefenstahl glorified national socialism in Germany, American filmmakers derided it. In one cartoon, for example, Daffy Duck clubs a realistic-looking, speechifying Adolf Hitler over the head with a mallet. Hitler dissolves into tears and calls for his mommy. British American filmmaker Charlie Chaplin added to the derision of the Führer in *The Great Dictator* (Fig. **8-31**). The film and television series *M*A*S*H* was set during the Korean War, but it satirized authoritarianism through the ages.

SOCIAL COMMENTARY Filmmakers, like documentary photographers, have made their social comments. *The Grapes of Wrath* (Fig. **8-32**), based on the John Steinbeck novel, depicts one family's struggle for survival during the Great Depression, when the banks failed and the Midwest farm basket of the United States turned into the Dust Bowl. Like a Dorothea Lange photograph, the camera comes in to record hopelessness and despair. Cinematographers have commented on subjects as varied as *Divorce, American Style*; *The Killing Fields* of Southeast Asia; and the excesses of *Wall Street*.

8-31 CHARLES CHAPLIN. Film still from *The Great Dictator* (1940).

8-32 JOHN FORD. Film still from *The Grapes of Wrath* (1940).

FANTASY Fantasy and flights of fancy are not limited to paintings, drawings, and the written word. In the experimental films of Robert Wiene and Salvador Dalí and Luis Buñuel, events are not confined to the material world as it is; they occupy and express the innermost images of the cinematographer. The sets for Wiene's *The Cabinet of Dr. Caligari* (Fig. **8-33**) were created by three painters who employed Expressionist devices such as angular, distorted planes and sheer perspectives. The hallucinatory backdrop removes the protagonist, a carnival hypnotist who causes a sleepwalker to murder people who displease him, from the realm of reality. The muddy line between the authentic and the fantastic is further obscured by the film's ending, in which the hypnotist becomes a mental patient telling an imaginary tale. (It is akin to the ravings of the mad Salieri, who, through flashbacks, recounts his actual and fantasized interactions with Mozart in the film *Amadeus*.)

Caligari has a story, albeit an unusual one, but Dalí and Buñuel's surrealistic *Un Chien Andalou* (Fig. **8-34**) has a script (if you can call it a script) without order or meaning in the traditional sense. In the shocking opening scene, normal vision is annulled by the slicing of an eyeball. The audience is then propelled through a series of disconnected, dreamlike scenes.

8-34 SALVADOR DALÍ AND LUIS BUÑUEL. Film still from *Un Chien Andalou* (1928). © Salvador Dalí, Fundació Gala-Salvador Dalí/Artists Rights Society (ARS), NY, 2011.

SYMBOLISM In writing about *Un Chien Andalou*, Buñuel claimed that his aims were to evoke instinctive reactions of attraction and repulsion in the audience, but that nothing in the film *symbolized* anything.[3] Fantastic cinematographers often portray their depths of mind literally. They create on the screen the images that dwell deep within their minds. Other cinematographers, such as Ingmar Bergman, frequently express aspects of their inner world through symbols.

Since the 1950s, filmgoers have been struck by Bergman's mostly black-and-white films (Fig. **8-35**). As in so much other art, nature serves as counterpoint to the vicissitudes of the human spirit in Bergman's films. The Swedish summers are short and precious. The bleak winters seem, to Bergman, to be the enduring fact of life. Against their backdrop, he portrays modern alienation from comforting religion and tradition. Bergman's films have ranged from jocular comedies to unrelieved dark dramas, and his bewitching screen images have brought together Nordic mythology and themes of love, death, and ultimate aloneness.

8-33 ROBERT WIENE. Film still from *The Cabinet of Dr. Caligari* (1919).

[3] Luis Buñuel, "Notes on the Making of *Un Chien Andalou*," in Art in Cinema, a symposium held at the San Francisco Museum of Art (repr., New York: Arno Press, 1968).

8-35 INGMAR BERGMAN. Film still from *The Seventh Seal* (1956).

VIDEO

Video technology was invented for television, which debuted to the masses in 1939 at the New York World's Fair in Flushing Meadows, Queens. As with film, video cameras capture and record a series of still images that are then reconstructed into a moving picture. With video, sights and sounds are transformed into electronic messages in the form of lengthy codes (a pattern of ones and zeros). Video also differs from film in the format of its storage systems. Today, analog video formats (VHS and Betamax, for example) have been largely replaced by digital formats (including DVD, Blu-Ray, QuickTime, and MPEG-4). Digital information can also be transmitted wirelessly or by cable; the television set then reconstructs the digital information into visual images and sounds.

Over about 60 years, television has radically altered American life and placed the American lifestyle before the world. Commercial television broadcasts many of the images that reflect and create our common contemporary culture—from reality programming like MTV's *Jersey Shore*, Bravo's *Real Housewives of* (fill in your favorite location), and Fox Network's *So You Think You Can Dance* to original program-

ming like HBO's *Sopranos*, *The Wire*, and *True Blood*; AMC's *Mad Men*, or ABC's cult classic *Lost*. Children spend as many hours in front of a TV set as they do in school, as congressional committees debate potential effects such as childhood obesity and the impact of televised violence.

"Live" TV coverage enabled hundreds of millions of viewers to witness Neil Armstrong's first steps on the moon in 1969. Millions watched in horror the live assassination of John F. Kennedy in 1963 and the explosion of the space shuttle *Challenger* in 1986. Viewers who came to be called "gulf potatoes" seemed to be addicted to the televising of the Gulf War, the nation's first real video war—which began with CNN's live description of fighter-bombers over Baghdad in 1991. In 2001, viewers watched the destruction of the World Trade Center live—whether from the suburbs of New York or from Chicago or Los Angeles—and in January 2011, the world witnessed the peaceful protests leading to revolution in the country of Egypt. Viewers become, so to speak, a single community connected by wireless broadcasting and by cable.

Commercial television programming, broadcast in the United States by privately owned media corporations, offers a wide variety of options to viewers, including news and

8-36 DARA BIRNBAUM. *Rio Videowall* (1989). Installation view of videowall in the public plaza of the Rio Shopping/Entertainment Complex, Atlanta, GA.

8-37 BILL VIOLA. *The Crossing* (1996). Two-channel color video and stereo-sound installation, continuous loop. 192" × 330" × 684". Solomon R. Guggenheim Museum, NY.

commentary, sporting events, situation comedies, reality programming, and films.

Video as a medium, distinguished from the commercial efforts of the television establishment, was introduced in the 1960s. Almost 30 years later, Dara Birnbaum addressed the relationship between television and video art, between the media and its mass-culture consumerism on the one hand and the discourse of contemporary art on the other. *Rio Videowall* (Fig. **8-36**), an interactive public work of art commissioned by the developers of the Rio Shopping/Entertainment Complex in Atlanta, Georgia, consists of 25 monitors arranged in a five-by-five grid, in which individual moving images are unified into a single, although shifting composition. Movement of the shoppers triggers a change of imagery on the screens that includes snippets of live news feeds juxtaposed with an almost nostalgic reflection on nature at its most pristine—the land before the onslaught of the shopping mall.

Just as the Lumière brothers used film primarily as a documentary medium, artists first used video to record and document performances that were site specific and of limited duration. And just as Melies favored fantasy over reality in his early artistic films, generations of contemporary artists have appropriated video as their medium in the creation of works of art—video art.

Fantasy and documentary continue to be approaches to video art. Consider the works of Bill Viola and Gillian Wearing. Bill Viola's *The Crossing* (Fig. **8-37**) is a video/sound installation that engulfs the senses and aims to transport the viewer into a spiritual realm. In this piece, the artist simultaneously projects two video channels onto separate 16-foot-high screens or on the back and front of the same screen. In each video, a man enveloped in darkness appears and approaches until he fills the screen. On one channel, a fire breaks out at his feet and grows until the man is apparently consumed in flames (the content is not what we would call graphic or disturbing, however). On the other channel, the one shown here, drops of water fall onto the man's head, develop into rivulets, and then inundate him. The sound tracks accompany the screenings with audio of torrential rain and of a raging inferno. The dual videos wash over the viewer with their contrasts of cool and hot colors and their encompassing sound. Critics speak about the spiritual nature

of Viola's work, but it is also about the here-and-now reality of the viewer's sensory experience elicited by the encounter with the work.

By contrast, Gillian Wearing often incorporates a documentary style in her video art. In the multiscreen *Family History* (Fig. **8-38**), she juxtaposes footage from a 1974 BBC documentary series called *The Family* with a present-day interview with one of the original cast/family members, and a staged narrative in which someone posing as a young Gillian Wearing is watching the old TV show. The work invites reflection on the definition of reality and the limitations of the documentary genre. It also penetrates the relationship between the private and public realms, of intimate family dynamics with spectatorship.

8-38 GILLIAN WEARING. *Family History* (2006). Shown at Brindley House, Newhall Street, Birmingham, England.

8-40 YAEL KANAREK. *Copy: Potentially Endless A* (2007). Lambda print. 44½" × 70". Edition of 3.

8-39 RUANE MILLER. *Blue Door* (2008). Archival limited edition digital print. 38" × 22¾".

DIGITAL ART

Most readers undoubtedly have toyed with computer programs such as Microsoft's Paint or Paintbrush or Apple's iPhoto or iMovie. Software such as this, typically part of the computer manufacturer's standard package, enables the user—artistic or otherwise—to create illustrations by manipulating stock shapes, drawing "freehand," "spray painting" color fields, or enhancing the images with a variety of textural patterns—all of which are selected by directing the mouse to a menu of techniques and design elements. The resultant shapes or drawings can be flipped and rotated or stretched in any direction. Even word-processing programs can be used to distort and otherwise play with images. Other

programs enable one to manipulate digital photographs and edit videos. In today's computer-tech-savvy environment, it is no longer unusual for the average teenager to be familiar with Adobe Photoshop software. Artistic results are only a point-and-click away.

Today computer graphics software programs offer palettes of tens of millions of colors, which can be selected and produced on the monitor almost instantaneously. Compositions can be recolored in seconds. Effects of light and shade and simulated textured surfaces can be produced with the point and click of a mouse. Software programs enable artists to create three-dimensional representations with such astounding realism that they cannot be distinguished from photos or films of real objects in space. They can be viewed from any vantage point and in any perspective. Images can be saved or stored in any stage of their development, be brought back into the computer's memory at will, and modified as desired, without touching the original image. It is difficult to believe that these images are stored in computers as series of zeroes and ones, and not as pictures, but they are.

Broadly speaking, digital art is the production of images by artists with the assistance of the computer. Ruane Miller's *Blue Door* (Fig. 8-39) begins with a photograph taken by the artist that is then altered using Photoshop painterly manipulations and compositing techniques. She is "interested in creating a coherent image with a convincing reality, though, after all . . . a virtual reality." Describing her work, Miller notes "Harmony, tension, complexity and counterbalance in the use of color, detail, and form are basic to the structure of [her] images."

Yael Kanarek's digital landscape in *Copy: Potentially Endless A* (Fig. 8-40) is a screenshot of an interactive digital journal containing entries by a virtual character whose gender and ethnicity remain hidden to us. The viewer finds love letters and travel logs that have been written by the character in the course of an expedition to find treasure in a fantastic desert landscape. The work is constructed of networked interfaces featuring text, photography, sculpture, and performance.

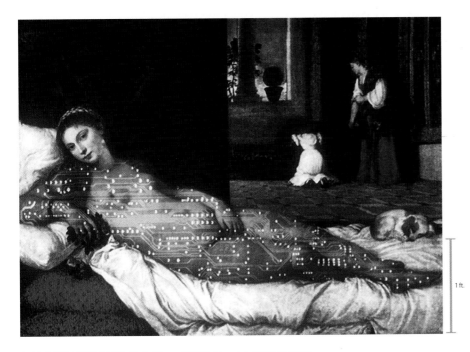

8-41 LYNN HERSHMAN. *Digital Venus* (1996). Iris print. 40⅛" × 59¾".

ums that narrow the gap, as it were, between them and the rest of us who are just seeking to express ourselves in some way. Portuguese-born artist, Jorge Colombo, creates his so-called "finger paintings" (Fig. 8-42) on an Apple iPad using an "app" called Brushes. Because of the responsiveness of the app to quick, loose drawing, Colombo has used his device, on location, as an electronic sketchbook and diary of his impressions of New York City. Some of these drawings, which have garnered much attention and recognition as covers for *The New Yorker* magazine, are printed with special programs that allow for high-resolution large-format images.

Artists not only appropriate the technology of the day, but they also appropriate images that have special meaning within a culture. Lynn Hershman's *Digital Venus* (Fig. 8-41) starts with Titian's well-known Renaissance painting *Venus of Urbino* (see Fig. 16-27) and substitutes digital imagery for the sumptuous glazes that defined the body. Many of Hershman's works comment on the voyeurism we find in the video medium, and *Digital Venus* is a way of showing how frequently the images that affect us are composed of pixels—microscopically small bits of digital information that fool our senses into believing we are somehow connecting with a corporeal reality. And like the work of Dara Birnbaum, *Digital Venus* addresses feminist issues pertaining to the male gaze and the exploitation of women.

Artists are now only scratching the surface of digital art as a medium. Art courses in digital arts and interactive multimedia have never been more in demand. Just as photography was once termed a "democratizer" in the visual arts—enabling anyone with a camera to capture anything— so has the ubiquitousness of the digital camera and computer opened the door to limitless experimentation among artists and outsiders alike.

The relative accessibility to non-artists of technology and software that will yield "artistic results" has spawned any number of manipulated digital photographs and videos appearing on social media sites. Apple's iPhoto, for example, allows you to take a picture of yourself and then transform it with options such as "Color Pencil," "Comic Book," or even "Pop Art"—which renders a single image into multiples in a grid that is a throwback to Andy Warhol. It is no surprise, then, that contemporary artists are creating works in medi-

8-42 JORGE COLOMBO. *42nd Street* (2009). Finger painting (using Brushes on Apple iPad). Pixel dimensions: 1024 × 768 (7.75 × 5.82 inches). Originally published as the June 2009 cover image in *The New Yorker*.

A sculptor is a person obsessed with the form and shape of things, and it's not just the shape of one thing, but the shape of anything and everything: the hard, tense strength, although delicate form of a bone; the strong, solid fleshiness of a beech tree trunk.

—Henry Moore

SCULPTURE

9

In *Metamorphosis*, Ovid's poetic narrative of the creation of the world, we meet a young Cypriot sculptor named Pygmalion. Now Pygmalion is pretty cynical about love. He vows never to marry, instead devoting his life to the perfection of his craft. Never say never. Pygmalion outdoes himself in carving a sculpture of a beautiful woman in ivory—so stunning, so lifelike, that he falls in love with his statue (Fig. 9-1). He makes a wish that his idol be brought to life and Venus hears his plea—the sculpture becomes flesh and Pygmalion finds his bride.

The myth of Pygmalion has been depicted in many versions and mediums, a subject that has suggested both the technical prowess of sculptors and the power to create the illusion of reality in spite of the harsh, seemingly unforgiving materials with which they work: marble, stone, bronze. Seeing Bernini's *Apollo and Daphne* (Fig. 2-72) in the flesh dispels any doubt that his skill was nothing short of transformative. The brain can hardly register as marble that which the eye sees.

Realism is, of course, only one stylistic dimension of sculpture, and marble, bronze, and wood are only a few examples of the wealth of materials that sculptors use. This chapter considers the definitions, materials, and techniques of sculpture—the carving, modeling, casting, constructing, and assembling of materials and objects into (primarily) three-dimensional works of art.

MICHELANGELO. The Cross-Legged Captive (c. 1530–1534). Marble. H: 7'6½". Galleria dell'Accademia, Florence, Italy.

1 ft.

9-1 JEAN-LÉON GÉRÔME. *Pygmalion and Galatea* (c. 1890). Oil on canvas. 35" × 27". The Metropolitan Museum of Art, NY.

SCULPTURE

A viewer's relationship to a sculpture is often much more complex than it is to a drawing or painting. Two-dimensional works generally are viewed from a single, optimal perspective—head-on. Sculpture, on the other hand, exhibited—as it often is—in the open space of a gallery, museum, or the great outdoors, beckons the viewer to participate in the revelation of its form by walking around the work and observing it from multiple viewpoints.

Not all sculpture is three-dimensional, nor is all of it intended to be viewed from more than one vantage point. Sculpture is broadly categorized into two types: **relief sculpture** and **free-standing sculpture**, or **sculpture-in-the-round**. In a relief, figures or images project to varying degrees from a two-dimensional plane (a plank of wood or a slab of marble, for example). If the imagery does not project significantly from the surface, we refer to the technique as **low or bas-relief**. In **high relief**, by contrast, figures project dramatically from the plane of the relief, so much so that they barely seem attached to the background. It is not uncommon to see a combination of high, middle, and bas-relief in a single sculpture (see Fig. 16-9) and reliefs can be created in any material, including

bronze. As with two-dimensional works of art, though, reliefs are intended to be viewed primarily from one perspective. It is true that some freestanding sculpture or sculpture-in-the-round is meant to be seen head-on, from an optimal vantage point, or is installed in such a way that a viewer cannot walk completely around it (Fig. 17-7). But sculpture-in-the-round is not connected to a two-dimensional surface and, importantly, it is carved or cast or assembled in three dimensions.

Sculpture is also described, in the broadest of terms, by the basic process used to create it: subtractive or additive. With a **subtractive process**, such as carving, material is removed from the original, raw mass in order to define a figure or an image. With an **additive process**, such as modeling, material is added or built up to reach a desired form. These processes are linked to a wide variety of sculptural techniques.

Carving

In **carving**, a subtractive process, the sculptor begins with a block of material and chips or cuts portions of it away until the desired result takes shape. Carving is a demanding technique that requires intense physical labor. The idiosyncrasies of materials—stone, wood, ivory—influence the mechanics of the carving process, the sculptor's choice of tools, and the overall effect of the final product.

Michelangelo carved all of his sculptures from single blocks of marble, leading a fellow artist to say that "You could roll them down a mountain and no piece would come off." Sure and confident in his skill, Michelangelo said that he was simply "liberating the figure from the marble that imprisons it." This description of his technique is clearly illustrated in *The Cross-Legged Captive* (Fig. **9-2**), one of a series of unfinished sculptures intended for the tomb of his patron Pope Julius II. Because so much of the marble block remains around the partially embedded figure, we can see that Michelangelo worked from front-to-back; it is as if the figure is materializing from the stone before our eyes or wrestling to break free of it. The contrast between the gouged surfaces of the marble block and the supple flesh and smooth planes of muscle reveals a clash of raw energy and meticulous attention to realistic detail. There is a tension in *The Cross-Legged Captive*—movement balanced by restraint—that creates a sense of anticipation in the work. We seem to await the liberation of a slave from bondage, the emergence of perfection from the imperfect.

Carving, by its very nature, is subtractive. But this does not mean that all carved works of sculpture that you will view have necessarily been hewn from a single block of material. Although Michelangelo is renowned for having worked exclusively (and almost flawlessly) with single blocks of marble, other sculptors were known to cover up mistakes in carving by adding pieces of marble to their compositions. Too much subtraction sometimes resulted in addition.

> *No painter ought to think less of sculpture than of painting*
> *and no sculptor less of painting than of sculpture.*
> —Michelangelo

9-2 MICHELANGELO. *The Cross-Legged Captive* (c. 1530–1534). Marble. H: 7′6½″. Galleria dell'Accademia, Florence, Italy.

error or redirection, modeling enables the artist to work and rework the material until desired forms begin to emerge. The tactile nature of modeling leaves evidence of the artist's fingerprints as the soft material is pushed and gouged. Materials used in modeling are soft and, in the case of wax or unbaked clay, impermanent. Modeling is often the first step in the concept or creation of a sculpture in a more permanent medium such as bronze. Small **maquettes** are sometimes fashioned in clay by sculptors as a "first draft" of their final project.

Casting

The relationship between modeling and **casting** can be seen in Louise Bourgeois's *Portrait of Robert* (Fig. **9-3**). The artist began by modeling a pliable material and then converted the work to bronze through a casting process. The white patina Bourgeois applied to the surface curiously subverts

9-3 LOUISE BOURGEOIS. *Portrait of Robert* (1969). Bronze, painted white. 13″ × 12½″ × 10″. Art © Louise Bourgeois Trust/Licensed by VAGA, NY.

Modeling

In **modeling**, a pliable material such as clay or wax is built up, added, and shaped into a three-dimensional form. The artist may manipulate the material by hand and use a variety of tools. Unlike carving, which offers less of a margin for

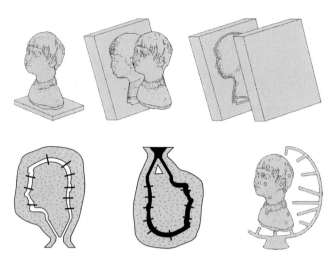

9-4 The lost-wax technique.

the shape of the mold. Once it cools, the mold is removed, leaving the cast piece, a more permanent version of the original object used to make the mold. Any liquid material that hardens can be used to in casting—molten metal, plaster, liquid plastics, paper pulp, clay diluted with water, and more. Once a mold has been made, the casting process may be duplicated, resulting in multiple casts of a single work.

THE LOST-WAX TECHNIQUE Pouring molten bronze into a mold results in a solid bronze cast. This is fine for small objects, like *Robert*, but what if the artist is creating a larger-than-life-size piece? The weight and expense, even the availability of bronze for a large sculpture, makes simple casting as previously described untenable. A hollow-casting technique was developed to create large-scale works in bronze and smaller works of precious metals like gold. It is seen in sculpture from ancient Greece and Rome and in Asian and Southeast Asian art, as well as in pre-Columbian and African art. In hollow casting, works of sculpture consist of thin shells of metal.

The process used for hollow casting, **lost-wax** or ***cire perdu*** ("lost wax" in French; Fig. **9-4**), has changed little over the centuries. This method, like casting, begins with a full-sized model, in this case usually sculpted in clay. A mold, also of clay, is made around the model. The mold is removed, in pieces, from the model, and molten wax is applied to the inside, negative surfaces of the mold. These individual pieces will eventually be reassembled to form the entire, completed work. When the molten wax is hard, the mold is removed and what remains

the typical look of bronze and imparts, instead, a claylike appearance, referencing the very material with which she began the piece.

In casting, a **mold** is first made by pressing a softish material around the wax or clay object that will record the impressions—in a kind of negative—of the surface of the object. This soft material becomes an inner mold, which is then surrounded by a more rigid material like plaster. The object is removed and liquid material is then poured into the hollow form of the mold. The liquid hardens into

1 ft.

9-5 GEORGE CONDO. *The Butcher and His Wife* (2008–2009). Bronze. 43" × 48" × 85". Collection of the Artist. Shown at Whitney Biennial (2010).

9-6 SHERRIE LEVINE. *Fountains after Duchamp* (1991). Bronze. Installation view at Sherrie Levine Exhibition in the Zürich Kunsthalle (February 11, 1991—March 1, 1992). Zürich, Switzerland.

is a hollow wax model that reflects the shape of the original clay model. The wax model will bear the marks and textures of the original clay sculpture, but the surface is malleable enough to be reworked with finer detail. The metal shell of the final product, let us note and keep in mind, will be equivalent in thickness to that of the hollow, molten wax model.

There are two next steps. One is to turn the hollow wax model upside down and fill it with liquid clay, allowing it to harden. The other is to create a clay mold, called an **investment**, around the hollow wax model. The investment and the clay core are separated, then, by the thin layer of the wax model and connected to each other with metal pins. The whole thing is heated so that the wax melts out (or is lost), leaving a space between the clay core and the investment—a space into which a molten metal such as bronze or gold can be poured. The metal hardens, the investment (mold) is removed, and the clay core is broken up and mostly extracted. The individual parts of the sculpture, now replicated in bronze, are rejoined with molten metal used to fill the gaps. The surface is then smoothed, polished, or treated with chemicals that yield a particular finish.

The appearance of cast bronze sculpture, reflecting the nature of the processes used to create it, is anything but consistent or predictable. Consider the visual contrast of works by contemporary artists George Condo and Sherrie Levine. *The Butcher and His Wife* (Fig. **9-5**) preserves the aggressively worked surface of the clay from which the work was cast, so much so that the technique dominates the overall appearance of the sculpture and obscures the legibility of the figures. Levine's *Fountains after Duchamp* (Fig. **9-6**) creates a completely different impression. The gleaming, flawless surfaces of her row of bronze urinals have the look of

factory-tooled, mass-produced utilitarian objects. Whereas the tactile quality of Condo's work conveys the immediacy of the artist's expressive gestures and close contact with his material—his signature, so to speak—Levine's work seems almost absent an author. She takes advantage of that quality to great effect. The urinals pay homage to Marcel Duchamp's infamous Dada work, a found object that he titled *Fountain* (see Fig. 1-36). Levine's "fountains" represent what lies at the heart of her artistic concept and strategy: the critical appropriation of objects and images that already exist in the visual lexicon of high art and mass culture. If Duchamp invested his readymades with a new *idea*—the reconsideration of ordinary objects in the artist's self-defined and self-imposed context of fine art—Levine's objects and reproductions are invested with a reconsideration of issues such as authorship and originality in relation to art making.

CASTING OF HUMAN MODELS *Three Figures and Four Benches* (Fig. **9-7**) by George Segal features an intriguing variation on the casting process. Segal produced ghostlike replicas of human beings by means of plaster casts. Live models were covered in plaster-soaked cloth, which was molded and kneaded by the artist's hands. When the plaster was dry, the cast was removed in sections and then reassembled into whole figures that consist of a hollow plaster shells. The plaster sculptures, with their rough surface textures of strips of gauze bandaging, were hauntingly juxtaposed with found objects—buses, gas stations, diners, and other settings, creating a kind of limbo of contemporary urban life. His work suggests an unimaginable aloneness. His figures do not seem to speak to one another or interact in any way. They are at once connected and disconnected, sharing a place and time and yet lost in their inner worlds.

9-7 GEORGE SEGAL. *Three Figures and Four Benches* (1979). Painted bronze. 52" × 144" × 58". Theo Anderson, Allentown, PA. Art © The George and Helen Segal Foundation/Licensed by VAGA, NY.

TYPES OF MATERIALS

Sculpture as a medium is approached through any number of materials. Historically, wood, clay, stone, and metal are most typical. But the list of materials sculptors can employ and have employed is limitless and anything but typical—fiberglass, fluorescent tubes, high-heeled shoes, even human blood in the form of ice sculpture. The raw materials, possibilities, and products are endless in variety, appearance, and effect.

Stone

Stone is an extremely hard, earthen material that can be carved, scraped, drilled, and polished. The durability that makes stone, or rock—in all of its myriad aggregates including granite, marble, limestone, jade, and basalt—so appropriate for monuments and statues meant to outlive generations is also what makes working with it a tedious process. The harshness of the granite used by ancient Egyptians—mostly quarried near Aswan—made it almost impossible to render fine detail, one reason that their figures were simplified and stay close to the shape of quarried blocks. Marble, by contrast, is a relatively soft stone and more conducive to carving and delicate detail. The Greeks, who manipulated marble with great facility, acquired most of their material from islands in the Aegean.

The hand tools used to carve stone—such as the chisel, mallet, and **rasp**—have not changed much over the centuries. Contemporary sculptors have the advantage of specialized power tools that enable them to remove large areas of unwanted material with relative ease and to polish a finished piece to a high gloss.

Carving in stone goes back to the Stone Age and small limestone figurines such as the *Venus of Willendorf* (see Fig. 13-2). In spite of the primitive nature of the sculptor's flint tools, an impressive amount of detail delineates arms, a torso, and a rounded head covered with either curly hair or a woven cap. The roundness of the sculpture suggests that its overall shape was determined by—and stays close to—the shape of the stone from which it was carved. *Venus* is just a bit over four inches high.

It is a dramatic leap from the *Venus of Willendorf* to, say, Bernini's *Apollo and Daphne* (see Fig. 2-72), a work that illustrates the potential of marble as a sculptural material. In the hands of an artist with breathtaking skill, marble can suggest a gamut of textures—the softness and sensuousness of flesh, the silky textures of hair, smooth-skinned leaves, and rugged, splintered bark. Imagine the intricacy of cutting away the obstinate stone to reveal the delicate leaves sprouting from Daphne's fingertips and locks of hair. Bernini portrays the exact moment from classical mythology when the nymph, Daphne, pursued by an adoring Apollo, beseeches her father, a river god, to change her form so that Apollo will not capture her. Just as Apollo reaches Daphne and puts his arm around her waist, she is transformed into a laurel tree. The fright and disbelief on the faces of the characters pushes the illusion of realism to its absolute limit.

Marble continues to be a favored material for contemporary sculptors. *Eyes* (Fig. **9-8**), by Louise Bourgeois, features two precisely tooled spheres perched atop a marble cube, some of which has been chiseled to create hollows and irregularities. Two deeply carved circular openings in the spheres suggest the penetrating pupils of eyes, a commonly used symbol among Surrealist artists

1 ft.

9-8 LOUISE BOURGEOIS. *Eyes* (1982). Marble. 74¾" × 54" × 45¾". The Metropolitan Museum of Art, NY. Art © Louise Bourgeois Trust/Licensed by VAGA, NY.

9-9 URSULA VON RYDINGSVARD. *Droga* (2009).

(see Chapter 20). Although Bourgeois's technique results in a finished work that remains close to the quarried marble block, the perfectly round eyes, the polish of the surfaces, and the carved interruptions create a striking contrast between a deliberate absence and an assertive presence of the artist's hand.

Wood

Wood, like stone, may be carved using a variety of tools and, like stone, possesses different degrees of hardness that affect its workability and durability. Sculptors carve works from solid blocks of wood or, in the case of very large works, laminate pieces of wood together using adhesive, heat, and pressure. Wood's **tensile strength** exceeds that of stone, so parts of a wood sculpture that protrude are less likely than their stone counterparts to break off. On the other hand, stone is less impervious to disintegration over time.

Sculptors working in wood take into consideration types of wood (hard or soft), their grain patterns (straight or wavy), and their color. Tools for carving and finishing wood blocks include gouges, saws, knives, chisels, planes, mallets, sanders, and polishers. In carving wood, artists particularly study the direction of the grain, as the strength of the wood is connected to its grain.

Plywood, a familiar building material, is also used for sculpture. Sheets of plywood are made by stacking and glu-ing thin strips of wood (veneers), laid in such a way that the grain of each individual sheet is at a right angle to the ones below and above it. The process yields a strong product that is resistant to warping, twisting, shrinking, or cracking. Under heat, plywood can be bent into any shape, making it a very flexible material.

Wood is a versatile material that yields dramatically different results depending on its type and the tools used to manipulate it. Barbara Hepworth's *Two Figures* (see Fig. 4-8), carved from elm wood, are highly polished and smooth to the touch. The natural wood grain of the outer "shells" imparts warmth to the surface that contrasts with the pure white, marblelike finish of the concavities. The shapes possess an organic roundness and sense of lightness that are enhanced by this color contrast. The hollowed-out, void spaces complete a composition that is has pleasing balance of positive and negative shapes.

The smoothness, sensuousness, and apparent suppleness of *Two Figures* could not be more sharply different from the aggressively worked surface of Ursula von Rydingsvard's *Droga* (Fig. **9-9**). Beginning by taking a chainsaw to commercially milled cedar beams, the artist then cut, gouged, glued, and assembled pieces into a sprawling, faceted, monumental whole (it is 10 feet high and 18 feet long). *Droga* may resemble strata of the earth's crust or a sci-fi monster taking shape from the mud and rock of a creepy underworld, but, more simply, in *Droga*, the audience never loses sight of the tactile aspects of wood as a raw material.

the medium, such as fingerprints and handprints, as we saw in works by Bourgeois and Condo in the section on casting earlier in this chapter. Compared to stone or wood, clay has little strength, and it is not typically considered a permanent material—unless it is exposed to heat, as in ceramics. Sculptors have always used clay to make three-dimensional sketches, or models, for works that are then cast in more durable materials such as bronze.

Clay can be fired in a kiln at high temperatures so that it becomes hard and nonporous, making the material more suitable to sculpture and ceramics. Before firing, clay can be coated with glazes that can be manipulated to create different designs and surface textures. Michael Doolan's *A Cautionary Tale Continuum* (*Yellow*) (Fig. **9-11**) is created through a process that begins with hand-modeling and hand-building techniques to create a hollow stoneware figure. The figures are then often completed out of the studio by factory professionals with expertise in surface finishes such as automotive

9-10 PO SHUN LEONG. *Figure* (1993). Mahogany with hidden drawers. H: 50".

Carving, gouging, cutting, assembling, and polishing are used to a very different effect by Po Shun Leong in his *Figure* (Fig. **9-10**). The rich mahogany surfaces have a complexity, delicacy, and intricacy. There is a restlessness to the patterns and the myriad angles at which the pieces are set in relation one another. Coupled with the punctuation of hidden drawers that can be opened or closed, the handling of the surfaces creates a feeling of constant motion.

Clay

Clay is a naturally occurring material that is more pliable than stone or wood. Works in clay often preserve the evidence of the artist's direct handling of

9-11 MICHAEL DOOLAN. *A Cautionary Tale Continuum* (*Yellow*) (2010). Hand-modeled earthenware, adhered automotive nylon.

nylon and metallic lusters. Doolan's earthenware sculptures have a *Toy Story* quality to them—familiar images of children's play objects caught in circumstances in which things seem to have gone terribly wrong. We shall consider ceramics further in our discussion in Chapter 12, Craft and Design.

Metal

The process of casting metals such as bronze, gold, silver, or iron has changed little over the centuries. Sculptors use any number of techniques including **extruding**, **forging**, **stamping**, **drilling**, **filing**, and **burnishing** to manipulate the material, mark it, and polish it. Contemporary artists have also assembled **direct-metal sculptures**, often of steel, by welding, riveting, and soldering. Modern adhesives have also made it possible to glue sections of metal together into three-dimensional constructions.

Different metals have different properties. Bronze, an alloy of copper, has been the most popular casting material because of its surface and color characteristics. A bronze finish can be dull or glossy, and chemical treatments can pro-

duce colors ranging from greenish blacks to golden or deep browns. Because of oxidation, bronze and copper surfaces age to a rich green or greenish blue **patinas**.

For decades, Richard Serra has worked with steel, an alloy of iron, to create minimalist sculpture that expresses the physical properties and capabilities of his material. Like the installation at the Guggenheim Museum in Bilbao, Spain (Fig. **9-12**), many of his works have been monumental in scale and site-specific. Serra's steel surfaces grow more richly textured over time and with oxidation so that subsequent encounters with the same work reveals new visual dimensions. Serra's sculpture is intended to be experienced and not simply viewed, to be walked into, around, and through. Serra has said that one of his goals as an artist is the "opening up of the continuum of space." In some works, sheets of steel alternately enclose the visitor in a protected, almost private space and lead that same visitor, by way of an undulating path, to a more public, socially interactive space. The mass is solid and the texture is palpable, but the concept seems to reflect a nonmaterial realm—a gateway to something other within the real worlds we traverse every day.

9-12 RICHARD SERRA. Installation view, Guggenheim Museum, Bilbao, Spain. © 2011 Richard Serra/Artists Rights Society (ARS), NY.

Types of Materials   **185**

MODERN AND CONTEMPORARY MATERIALS AND METHODS

During the past century, technological changes have over-leaped themselves, giving rise to new materials, such as plastics and fluorescent lights, and to new ways of working with traditional materials. Experimentation has led to new approaches to sculpture and to redefinitions.

Until the early years of the twentieth century, sculpture was defined by a handful of techniques and processes—all of which we have encountered in this chapter: carving, modeling, and casting. Pablo Picasso expanded that technical vocabulary when he introduced constructed sculpture, built up of scraps of wood and found objects, in his Cubist works. Sculpture would never be the same. Assemblage,

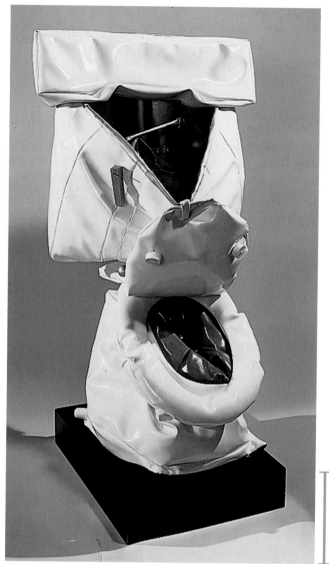

9-14 CLAES OLDENBURG. *Soft Toilet* (1966). Vinyl filled with kapok painted with Liquitex, and wood. 57 1/16" × 27 5/8" × 28 1/16". Whitney Museum of American Art, NY.

1 ft.

readymades, mixed-media installations, light sculpture, and kinetic sculpture are a sampling of contemporary approaches that followed. The list is by no means exhaustive.

Constructed Sculpture

Constructed sculpture is built or constructed from an assortment of materials—pieces of wood, sheet metal, wire, plastic, cardboard, found objects, just about anything. Picasso inspired experimentation with relief sculptures such as his 1913 *Mandolin and Clarinet* (Fig. **9-13**). As critic Robert Hughes remarked, such works were "everything that statues

9-13 PABLO PICASSO. *Mandolin and Clarinet* (1913). Wood construction and paint. Musée Picasso, Paris, France. © 2011 Estate of Pablo Picasso/Artists Rights Society (ARS), NY.

had not been: not monolithic, but open, not cast or carved, but assembled from flat planes."[1] In spirit and style, reliefs from this era were very close to Picasso's paintings. But the unorthodox materials challenged all traditions in art making.

A Russian visitor to Picasso's Paris studio, Vladimir Tatlin, is credited with having realized the three-dimensional potential of constructed sculpture, which was then further developed in Russia by the brothers Antoine Pevsner and Naum Gabo. Naum Gabo's *Column* (see Fig. 20-16) epitomizes a characteristic of many constructed works: the ascendance of shape and volume over sculptural mass. Gabo's translucent planes of plastic and glass encircle, frame, and slice into the surrounding space.

The precision of Gabo's *Column*, its simultaneously architectural and ethereal qualities—its overall look of perfection—

could not be more unlike the technique and sensibility that drove Pop artist Claes Oldenburg's construction *Soft Toilet* (Fig. 9-14). Stitched of vinyl and stuffed with kapok, a silky natural fiber, a familiar object that we know to be hard, cold, and unmovable is rendered soft, supple, and pliable. Our senses are utterly subverted.

Assemblage

Assemblage is a form of constructed sculpture in which pre-existing, or found objects, recognizable in shape, are integrated and combined in novel combinations that take on meaning of their own—meaning separate from their constituent parts. Louise Nevelson's *Royal Tide IV* (Fig. 9-15) is a compartmentalized assemblage of rough-cut geometric shapes and lathed wooden pieces including posts and finials, barrel staves, and chair slats—the pieces of a personal or collective

[1] Robert Hughes, "The Liberty of Thought Itself," *Time*, September 1, 1986, 87.

1 ft.

9-15 LOUISE NEVELSON. *Royal Tide IV* (1960). Wood, with gold-spray technique. 127" × 175½" × 21½".

past, of lonely introspective journeys amid the cobwebs of Victorian attics. Even though some of the objects are familiar and recognizable, Nevelson's unifying coat of paint deemphasizes their distinct identities. The whole—an exercise in variety within unity—is greater than the sum of the parts.

Willie Cole's assemblages show us the degree to which discreet, familiar, found objects can lose themselves utterly in their second lives as works of fine art. In *House Pet* (Fig. **9-16**), brightly colored and wildly patterned women's high-heeled shoes are stacked, squashed, and nestled into an overall shape that resembles an adorable—if completely weird—crouching animal. Cole's early assemblages were built of vintage and modern clothes irons, and he has used shoes and multiple versions of other objects in his works as well. He challenges himself to find new resolutions by identifying and adhering to a constant—a particular object—and producing visually complex variations on it.

Found objects are at the root of these assemblages by Nevelson and Cole, but they are built on the concept of the **readymade** as art introduced by Marcel Duchamp during the **Dada** movement—"an ordinary object elevated to the dignity of a work of art by the mere choice of an artist." Duchamp created

an uproar in 1917 when he submitted *Fountain* (Fig. 1-36), a porcelain urinal turned on its side and signed "R. Mutt," to an exhibition of the Society of Independent Artists. After a debate on the justification of the readymade as a valid work of art, the board decided not to show it. For Duchamp, the dimension of taste, good or bad, was irrelevant. Art could be defined by an idea, and the very action of choosing an object and creating a new context for it invested it with new meaning.

Mixed Media

Mixed media is a catchall category that describes constructions and assemblages in which artists use a combination of **mediums** and materials, sometimes in combination with found objects. Picasso's *Mandolin and Clarinet*, Miriam Schapiro's *Wonderland* (Fig. 1-35), Robert Rauschenberg's *Bed* (Fig. 21-11), Judy Pfaff's *Dragon* (Fig. 21-30), and Hew Locke's *El Dorado* (Fig. 22-5) are only a few examples of mixed-media works that you will find in your textbook. Note that not all mixed-media works are classified as sculpture; they can be two or three dimensional, reliefs, freestanding works, or installations. Ann Sperry's series *My Piano: The Fragmen-*

9-16 WILLIE COLE. *House Pet* (2010). Canvas, high-heeled shoes, resin.

9-17 ANN SPERRY. *My Piano: The Fragmentation of Memory* (2002). Galvanized metal, piano parts. 7½" × 21" × 15½".

Light Sculpture

Sculptors, regardless of their techniques, are aware of the ways in which light influences the nature and perception of their work. Alternating between deep and shallow carving will yield gradations of tone from dark to light, as in Michelangelo's *Cross-Legged Captive*. Light plays an integral part in the perception of Helene Brandt's *Mondrian Variations* (Fig. 2-13). Lines of steel project from the surface of the wall, intersecting to form a three-dimensional grid. Under a spotlight, the grid creates a shadow that reads as the ghostly presence of the Dutch painter Piet Mondrian—the muse, as it were, who inspired Brandt's series of works based on his renowned grid paintings.

It is only in the past century that sculptors began to experiment with the use of artificial light as a material, taking advantage of its physical properties, psychological effects, and potential to create visual illusions. Dan Flavin worked principally with fluorescent tubes, exploring the

tation of Memory (Fig. 9-17), features sculptures assembled from piano parts, sheets of galvanized metal, steel, and brass. One work in the series even incorporates **monoprints** (see Chapter 7, Printmaking, Fig. 7-17). Critic Rebecca Fenton said of the series that "Ann Sperry seeks to manipulate her materials away from their previous uses and, therefore, our preconceived expectations. Still, she relates new artwork to 'past life,' the associations and memories of her materials."

Kinetic Sculpture

Sculptors have always been concerned with the portrayal of movement, but **kinetic sculptures** incorporate actual movement caused by the wind, magnetic fields, jets of water, electric motors, variations in the intensity of light, or the active manipulation of the audience. During the 1930s, the American sculptor Alexander Calder introduced motion as a basic element—like line, shape, or color—into the compositions he called **mobiles** (see Fig. 2-71). Carefully balanced weights are suspended on wires such that the gentlest current of air sets them moving in prescribed orbits.

George Rickey's name has become synonymous with contemporary kinetic sculpture. The stainless steel shapes of his *Five Open Squares Gyratory* (Fig. 9-18) are weighed and balanced to move silently and effortlessly with the slightest bit of breeze. As they rise, fall, and twirl, the squares frame shifting bits of the surrounding landscape, evoking the feeling of snapshots that capture the fleeting aspects of nature.

9-18 GEORGE RICKEY. *Five Open Squares Gyratory* (1981). Stainless steel. 9'4" × 6' × 42". Art © Estate of George Rickey/Licensed by VAGA, NY.

The body is our common denominator for our pleasures and our sorrows.
I want to express through it who we are, how we live and die.
—Kiki Smith

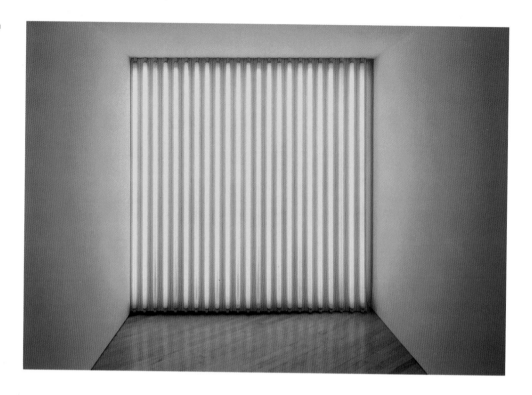

9-19 DAN FLAVIN. *Untitled* (to Jan and Ron Greenberg) (1972–1973). Fluorescent light. 96" × 96". Installation view at the Dan Flavin Art Institute, Bridgehampton, NY. © 2011 Stephen Flavin/Artists Rights Society (ARS), NY.

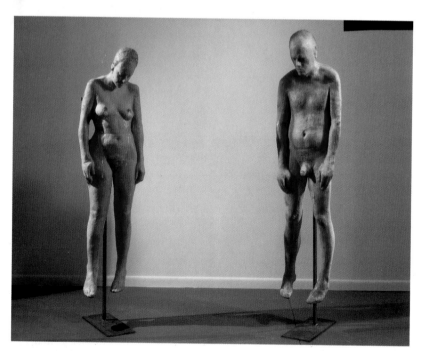

9-20 KIKI SMITH. *Untitled* (1990). Beeswax and microcrystalline wax figures on metal stands; female figure installed height 6'1½"; male figure installed height 6'4 15/16". Whitney Museum of American Art, NY.

resonance of color and its ability to define space. In his untitled piece seen in Figure **9-19**, the installation room seems to dead-end with a screen of yellow light tubes placed back-to-back with a matching screen of green tubes (which you cannot see from this side). Because the sculpture blocked passage from one part of the room to another, only a glimpse of the light filling the space on the other side of the screen could be seen through the narrow spaces on either side of the piece. The result was an intriguing juxtaposition of regimented tubes of yellow and the unfettered glow of green light. The opposite effect was observed in viewing the work from the other side.

Other Materials

The trajectory of sculpture as a medium in the twentieth and twenty-first centuries has been dramatic and dynamic with new definitions of art and the artist's use of unconventional materials. This section considers a scant few examples of unexpected materials and techniques.

The figures in Kiki Smith's *Untitled* (Fig. **9-20**) were constructed of beeswax and microcrystalline wax. The artist's realism is, in a sense, more realistic than realism has ever been—even when compared to the technical skills of a Bernini or the illusionism of a sculptor like Duane Hanson (see Fig. 21-26). The realism in Kiki Smith's couple is almost too painful to observe, too close to the realities of our own physical selves. Smith has written that as "Most of the functions of the body are hidden . . . from society," she aims to bring them out into the open, focusing on body parts and body by-products. In their state of deterioration, the effigies in Smith's untitled work have lost control over their bodily functions. The woman's figure is stained with, or drained of, milk that drips from her nipples. Semen drips down the man's leg. They are suspended in space, isolated in their loss of control, sharing the frailties of the human condition.

Sylvie Fleury constructed her *Dog Toy 4 (Gnome)* (Fig. **9-21**) from Styropor, little balls of polystyrene that expand and stick together when heated. Styropor is commonly used for packaging and insulation because it can be shaped and molded and is almost weightless. Chances are, the last time you purchased

9-22 JANINE ANTONI. *Gnaw* (1992). Detail: (installation) 600 lb. lard, gnawed by the artist; 600 lb. collapsed lard, gnawed by the artist; 45 heart-shaped packages for chocolate made from chewed chocolate removed from the chocolate cube and 400 lipsticks made with pigment, beeswax, and chewed lard removed from the lard cube. The Museum of Modern Art, NY.

9-21 SYLVIE FLEURY. *Dog Toy 4 (Gnome)* (2000). Styropor. 78¾" × 74⅞" × 59 1/16".

a flat-screen TV or other electronics, they were surrounded by protective panels of the same material. Fleury's point of departure was a familiar, nonthreatening, squeaky animal toy, blown up to the same nightmarish proportions that turned the smiling marshmallow man in the film *Ghostbusters* into a menacing monster crushing everything in its wake. In the tradition of Andy Warhol and the Pop artists, who had in turn been influenced by the found objects of the Dada artists before them, Fleury elevates consumer products of a "disposable society" to the level of fine art.

Janine Antoni's *Gnaw* (Fig. **9-22**) may pay tongue-in-cheek homage to a **minimalist** geometric sculpture, but it holds some sensory surprises: Antoni's material is chocolate and her "carving" tools consist of what nature has endowed her with—a strong set of teeth. The surface texture of the piece records the process, what Antoni has characterized as the most important element of her art. *Gnaw* was one of two companion pieces—the other was a cube of lard—which she bit and chewed, refashioning gnawed chunks into small objects such as lipstick tubes and chocolate boxes.

Perhaps because we are surrounded in our daily lives by monuments, we are accustomed to thinking of sculpture as a permanent and enduring. *Gnaw* is a work in which the notion of permanence is insignificant. Chocolate will melt in your mouth or, with a bit of heat, into a nondescript and gooey pool. Permanence is not necessarily a concern of some artists in particular works. In the next chapter, we will consider site-specific art, much of which exists in the moment.

THE STORM KING ART CENTER in Mountainville, New York, is a sculpture garden located about one hour north of Manhattan. But this sculpture garden consists of 500 acres of landscaped lawns and fields, hills, and woodlands, including views of the mountains of the lower Hudson Valley. There are permanent installations of works by sculptors including Isamu Noguchi, Alexander Calder, Henry Moore, Magdalena Abakanowicz, Mark di Suvero, Roy Lichtenstein, and Louise Nevelson. Works by Andy Goldsworthy and Richard Serra were commissioned for their sites. The Goldsworthy wall winds its way across more than 2,200 feet, dipping into ponds and climbing out. The four partially buried Serra shards of steel, *Schunnemunk Fork*, named after nearby Schunnemunk Mountain, occupy 10 acres. Whereas the Goldsworthy and Serra sculptures seem to have the permanence of the ages, the huge di Suvero sculptures, of steel but also airy, look as though they might without notice decide to pick themselves up and search out different prospects in the fields.

All this was founded by Ralph E. Ogden in 1960 as a museum for Hudson Valley painters. The landscape was wrecked from careless farming, and hundreds of truckloads of soil were brought in; grasses were planted. Fortunately, some woodlands with hills and boulders were in place. Ponds were dug and filled

9-23 MENASHE KADISHMAN. *Suspended* (1977). Weathering steel. 276" × 396" × 48".

with water. A 1935 Normandy-style house was renovated, and it houses offices, temporary exhibitions, and a museum store. Early on, works were acquired

9-24 RICHARD SERRA. *Schunnemunk Fork* (1990–1991). Weathering steel. © 2011 Richard Serra/Artists Rights Society (ARS), NY.

A 96" × 589" × 2½".

B 96" × 421" × 2½".

C 96" × 460" × 2½".

D 96" × 652" × 2½".

Among sculpture parks of the world, Storm King is King.
—J. Carter Brown

9-25 Mark di Suvero sculptures at Storm King Art Center.

from the estate of the sculptor David Smith, and these alone became a magnet for visitors.

The place is like no other: Visit once and you are ensnared. Visit twice and you are mesmerized, because no two visits are alike. The times of the day cast their own shadows, changing patterns of cloud cover dim or brighten sunlight, and the changing seasons bring a distinctive palette to grasses and leaves. What lay in shade may suddenly gush into radiance with a burst of sunlight. There is no good weather or bad weather for this art—only different weather with variable, sometimes capricious, degrees of illumination. Come and observe the play of the sky across the fields, as did the artists of the Hudson River School two centuries ago .◉

9-26 ALEXANDER CALDER. *Five Swords* (1976). Sheet metal, bolts, and paint. 213" × 264" × 348". © 2011 Calder Foundation, NY/Artists Rights Society (ARS), NY.

9-27 MAYA LIN. *Storm King Wavefield* (2007–2008).

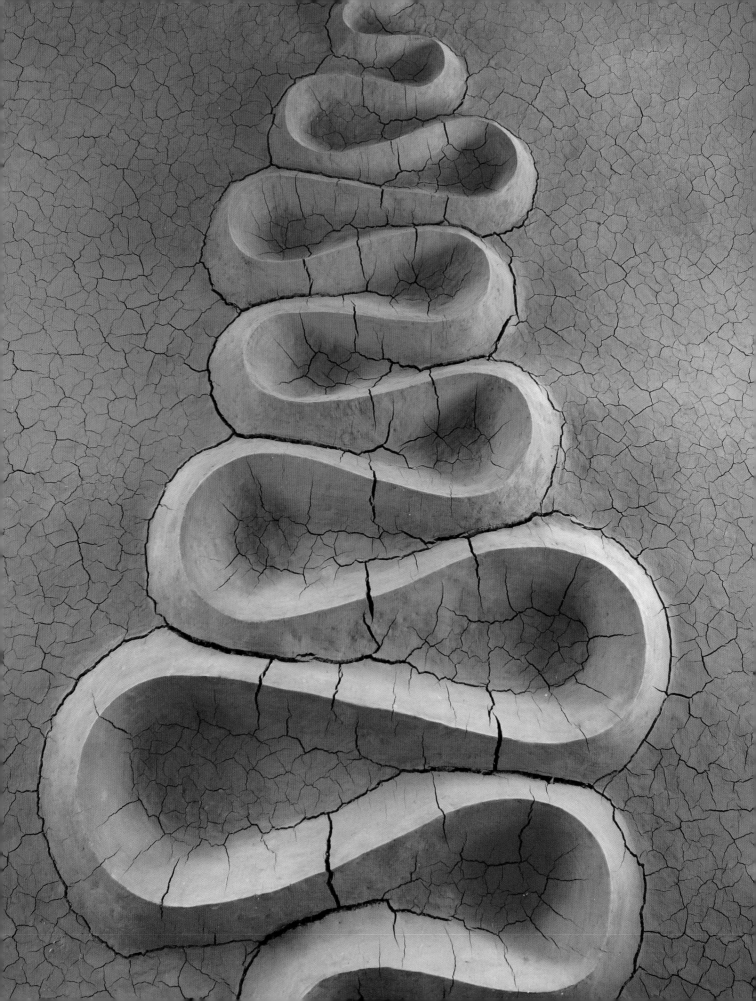

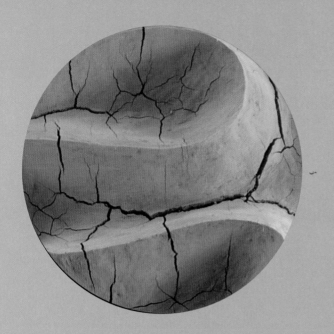

Give me a place to light and I will invent an installation that will bring it out.

—Dan Flavin

SITE-SPECIFIC ART

10

Site-specific works are distinguished from other artworks that are typically created in a studio with no particular spatial context in mind. Site-specific art is produced in or for one location and—in theory, at least—is not to be relocated. The work is in and of its site, and often the content and meaning of the work is inextricably bound to it. By this description, the history of art is full of examples of site-specific art, ranging from the sculptural decoration on the Parthenon (Fig. 14-10) and Michelangelo's Sistine Chapel ceiling (Figs. 16-21 to 16-22) to a mural by Orozco commissioned for Dartmouth College (Fig 1-39), or Kozloff's mosaic for a Philadelphia train station (Fig. 1-37). But the term *site-specific* came into use in the 1960s and 1970s as a blanket category for art that was created for or in a specific location. That location might be a museum or gallery, a public space, or a site in the natural landscape.

ANDY GOLDSWORTHY. Detail of a 2005 installation. One of a series of "refuges d'art" accessible by hiking trails in Provence, France.

As coincidence would have it, nearly all of these possibilities were met in *Big Bambú: You Can't, You Don't, and You Won't Stop* (Fig. **10-1**), a temporary, site-specific work for the B. Gerald Cantor Roof Garden at the Metropolitan Museum of Art by twin-brother artists Mike and Doug Starn. Seasonal installations on the Met's rooftop have become a warm-weather must-see for New Yorkers for years. But repeated visits over the six months in 2010 when *Big Bambú* was in town offered unique rewards. It would never look the same twice. The installation, which ultimately rose 50 feet off the terrace floor and sprawled more than 100 feet, was a work in progress from start to finish. The artists and their team of collaborators—rock climbers—continually constructed the piece from bamboo poles and stalks that were meticulously knotted together with brightly colored lengths of nylon rope. The effect, according to the artists, was one of "chaos" and "interdependence," an "ever-changing living organism" that morphed and grew on its perch above Central Park—a dramatic counterpoint to the stone facades of the Met and the New York City skyline.

The junglelike environment offered another irresistible element: visitors were allowed to climb up into the work. A central concept of *Big Bambú* was audience participation. Guided tours brought the intrepid up bamboo ramps to lookout platforms and across a bridge that spanned a 25-foot gap in the network of poles. Viewing the work and understanding it was to experience it, to be a physical part of it. Six months after construction began, *Big Bambú* was gone, recorded in documentary photographs and films and imprinted on the minds of those who were there.

Site-specific art consists of many types, goals, and styles, including land and environmental art, ephemeral art, public art, and monuments.

LAND ART

Land art is site-specific work that is created or marked by an artist within natural surroundings. Sometimes large amounts of earth or land are shaped into sculptural forms, as in the earthworks of the 1960s and 1970s. These works could be temporary or permanent and included great trenches and drawings in the desert, bulldozed configurations of earth and rock, and delicately constructed compositions of ice, twigs, and leaves. What such works have in common is the artist's use of local materials to create pieces that are unified with or contrapuntal to the landscape.

Robert Smithson's *Spiral Jetty* (Fig. **10-2**) is composed of basalt and earth bulldozed into a spiral formation in Utah's Great Salt Lake. The spiral shape of the jetty was inspired by a whirlpool, as well as the configuration of salt deposits that

10-1 MIKE AND DOUG STARN. *Big Bambú: You Can't, You Don't, and You Won't Stop* (2010). Approx. 5,000 interlocking 30- and 40-foot-long fresh-cut bamboo poles, lashed together with 50 miles of nylon rope. Approx. 100' long, 50' wide, and 40' high. The Iris and B. Gerald Cantor Roof Garden, The Metropolitan Museum of Art, NY

10-2 ROBERT SMITHSON. *Spiral Jetty* (1970). Black rocks, salt, earth, water, and algae. L: 1,500'; W: 15'. Great Salt Lake, UT. Art © Estate of Robert Smithson/Licensed by VAGA, NY.

10-3 ANDY GOLDSWORTHY. *Ice Star* (12 January 1987). Cibachrome photograph. 30" × 30". Scaur water, Penpoint, Dumfriesshire, Scotland.

accumulate on rocks bordering the lake. After its creation, the jetty lay submerged underwater for many years. With a prolonged drought, the spiral began to reemerge in 1999 and, depending on the water levels of the lake, now "comes and goes."

The delicacy of many of Andy Goldsworthy's constructions stands in marked contrast with Smithson's bulldozed mounds of earth. They communicate, from another perspective, the fragility and changeability of nature. Goldsworthy works with materials he finds on site—leaves, sticks, stones, ice fragments—manipulating them with a soft, controlled touch or even, as with *Ice Star*, his breath (Fig. **10-3**). The following documentary narrative accompanied the piece:

thick ends dipped in snow then water
held until frozen together
occasionally using forked sticks as
support until stuck
a tense moment when taking them
away
breathing on the stick first to release it

Goldsworthy explores both the transitory and the timeless in his varied works. *Storm King*

Wall (Fig. **10-4**) incorporates the remains of a dilapidated farm fence found on the site of the Storm King Art Center into a 2,278-foot-long fieldstone wall. The work snakes through fields and around trees, at one point dipping into a pond and reappearing at the other side to continue its march along the landscape. As with many of Goldsworthy's pieces, the viewer experiences a quiet human presence—sometimes fleeting, sometimes enduring—in the midst of the natural world.

Art that "makes marks" in nature is often temporary. In March 2004, Danish artist Marco Evaristti set sail in two icebreakers to find the perfect "frozen canvas" among the icebergs off the coast of Greenland. For two hours, a crew of 20 sprayed 780 gallons of red dye onto an almost 10,000-square-foot iceberg (Fig. **10-5**). The dye, diluted with seawater, was the same that is used for tinting meat. Evaristti's work can be found—for the time being, at least—near Ilullissat (which means "icebergs" in the Greenlandic language), a town of 4,000 that is popular among tourists for its spectacular and *artistic* scenery.

Another approach to land art can be seen in the works of Robert Smithson and Nancy Holt (see Fig. 2-24). Rather than creating works from natural materials present on the site, these artists interrupt the landscape with objects consisting of man-made materials. In so doing, the viewer is encouraged to consider the relationship between the environment and human activity. Holt's placement of gargantuan concrete cylinders on a desert floor is designed to enframe and focus the sun's light. In Smithson's *Yucatan Mirror Displacements* (Fig. **10-6**), topographic shifts, like vignettes, became the context for the placement of clusters of mirrors as the artist traveled through the landscape. The interactivity between nature and technology is clear. The mirrors transform the environment by interrupting the natural setting, and the environment in turn transforms them. The anonymity of the mirror surfaces is lost as they reflect the shapes, colors, and textures of their host environment.

One of the most spectacular examples of land art that combines nature and man-made materials is Walter de Maria's *The Lightning Field* (Fig. **10-7**). The field is constructed of 400 stainless steel poles (lightning rods) anchored in a 1-by-0.62-mile plot of earth. As with Holt's *Sun Tunnels*, nature's

10-6 ROBERT SMITHSON. *Yucatan Mirror Displacements* (April 1969). Color photographs. Nine parts, 10½" × 10½" each. Solomon R. Guggenheim Museum, NY. Art © Estate of Robert Smithson/Licensed by VAGA, NY.

10-7 WALTER DE MARIA. *The Lightning Field* (1977). 400 polished stainless steel poles installed in a grid array measuring 1 mile × 1 km. The poles—2" in diameter and averaging 20'7½" in height—are spaced 220' apart and have solid pointed tips that define a horizontal plane. Quemado, NM.

A CLOSER LOOK CHRISTO AND JEANNE-CLAUDE:
THE GATES, CENTRAL PARK, NEW YORK CITY, 1979–2005

AS IF INTENTIONALLY TIMED TO SHAKE New York City out of its winter doldrums, 7,503 sensuous saffron panels were gradually released from the tops of 16-foot-tall gates along 23 miles of footpaths throughout Central Park. It was the morning of February 12, 2005—a date that marked the end of artists Christo and Jeanne-Claude's 26-year odyssey to bring a major project to their adopted city. For a brief 16 days, the billowy nylon fabric fluttered and snapped and obscured and enframed our favorite park perspectives (Fig. 10-8). The park's majestic plan of ups and downs, of lazy loops and serpentine curves (as originally designed by Frederick Law Olmsted and Calvert Vaux), was being seen or reseen for the first time as we—the participants—wove our walks according to the patterns of the gates. The artists have said that "the temporary quality of their projects is an aesthetic decision," that it "endows the works of art with a feeling of urgency to be seen." For a brief 16 days, it was clear from the crowds in a winter park, from the constant cluster of buses at the 72nd Street entrance, and from the rubbernecking traffic on the streets and avenues bordering the park that the urgency of which Christo and Jeanne-Claude speak was very real.

As with all of Christo and Jeanne-Claude's works of environmental art, every aspect of the *Gates* project was financed and fought for by the artists. They developed the concept for *The Gates* in 1979, but their first proposal to the city in 1981 was rejected. Mayor Michael R. Bloomberg granted permission for the 2005 version of the project on January 22, 2003. The vital statistics of *The Gates, Central Park, New York City, 1979–2005* are staggering. Placed at 12- to 15-foot intervals, 7,503 vinyl gates, 16 feet high, varying in width from 5 feet 6 inches to 18 feet, covered 23 miles of footpaths (Fig. 10-9). The free-hanging, saffron-colored fabric panels dropped from the top of each rectangular vinyl gate to 7 feet above the ground—just low enough for small children on their father's

shoulders to sneak a touch. The project required more than 1 million square feet of vinyl and 5,300 tons of steel. Hundreds of paid volunteers assembled, installed, maintained, and removed the work, and most of the materials were to be recycled. The estimated cost of the project—borne by the artists alone—was $20 million.

The artists finance their environmental sculptures, which have included Wrapped Reichstag, Berlin, 1971–1995; Surrounded Islands, Biscayne Bay, Greater Miami, Florida, 1980–1983; Running Fence, Sonoma and Marin Counties, California, 1972–1976; and others, by selling preparatory drawings and early works by Christo. Much of the funds thus accumulated have been used to cover the cost of the materials used in the project, to pay workers, and, when necessary, for legal fees to combat suits brought by concerned environmentalists (as was the case with the *Running Fence* project).

The environmental art projects of artists Christo and Jeanne-Claude have been seen by

10-8 CHRISTO AND JEANNE CLAUDE. *The Gates, Central Park, New York City (1979–2005).*

millions, who have been enticed to experience their familiar surroundings with a heightened sensibility. Like the artists, I, too, live in New York City. I walked *The Gates* many times over 16 days, each time with a group of family members and friends who made the pilgrimage. When asked why it was so important to realize this work in Central Park, Christo responded, "When our son was a little boy, we used to take him to Central Park every day—he loved to climb the beautiful rocks. Central Park was a part of our life." I think of my own daughter, whose school held gym class on the park's Great Lawn. The Central Park that she will remember as a part of her life growing up in New York will forever include the 16 days when, in clear and in cold and a glorious snowfall, a "golden river" snaked through a barren winter scene, lighting the landscape with flashes of color. ●

10-10 Christo with your author in Central Park on the day after *The Gates* officially closed.

"behavior" in the grandest sense gives shape and meaning to the work. The enduring as well as transitory aspects of nature are woven into the varied experience of land art.

The intimate physical relationship between the individual artist and the environment forms the basis of the work of yet another group of land artists. Ana Mendieta's series of self-portraits (Fig. 10-11) consisted of marking the presence of her body in the landscape using materials and methods such as impressions in the snow and mud and hollowed-out, body-shaped depressions filled with gunpowder and lit afire.

In a work that evokes the literary character Gulliver and his encounter with the tiny Lilliputians, Charles Simonds used his body as a building site for the miniature dwellings of an imagined civilization of little people (Fig. 10-12). The artist lay

10-12 CHARLES SIMONDS. *Landscape–Body–Dwelling* (1971). Artist's body, clay. Life size.

down on the earth and covered himself with clay, providing a convoluted landscape setting for the diminutive structures. Simonds's work can also be seen in an inconspicuous corner of a ledge in the stairwell of New York's Whitney Museum of American Art.

EPHEMERAL ART

Hippocrates' oft-quoted words were intended to laud the significance of art, attributable in part to its longevity and survival across generations. Is its sentiment outdated? Consider much of the work we have discussed so far in this chapter, which did not last long beyond its creation. Goldsworthy's *Ice Piece* remained frozen just long enough for him to document it with his camera. Many artists work with ephemeral materials—in other words, materials that do not endure.

The term **ephemeral art** is used specifically to describe works that have a temporal immediacy or are built with the recognition that they will disintegrate. You see them one minute and the next they're gone. Most of this work is viewed only in photographs after the fact, unless one happens to be lucky enough to be present when the piece is crafted or performed. How does such work differ from land art? Sometimes it doesn't. Goldsworthy's *Ice Piece* comes under the cat-

egory of land art that is ephemeral, but his *Storm King Wall*, made of stone, is intended to endure.

Cai Guo Qiang's fireworks pieces (Fig. **10-13**) are classic examples of ephemeral art. *Transient Rainbow*, commissioned by the Museum of Modern Art (undergoing renovation at the time) was planned to coincide with the opening of its temporary space in Queens—across the East River from Manhattan. As Cai wrote:

> In my hometown every significant social occasion of any kind, good or bad—weddings, funerals, the birth of a baby, a new home—is marked by the explosion of fireworks. They even use fireworks when they elect Communist party officials, or after someone delivers a speech. Fireworks are like the town crier, announcing whatever's going on in town.

The project was a masterpiece of coordination in conception, creation, and documentation. After several iterations, shaped by the concerns of the New York City Fire Department, Transit Authority, Coast Guard, and Federal Aviation Administration, Qiang's piece came and went, in some 15 seconds, on June 29, 2002. The fireworks display consisted of 1,000 shells that were launched in sequence from the Manhattan side of the river, ascending and descending in an arc toward Queens, on the opposite side. The brilliant color palette unfolded so that, for a moment, a transient moment, the fireworks rainbow spanned the river.

Anyone who has tried to capture a fireworks display with a camera knows that it's a tough thing to do. The vibrancy and shimmer that send "ooooos" through the crowd never seem to measure up in our photographic record. With a work that is literally there one minute and gone the next, its documentation becomes extremely important. Qiang hired 20 photographers in all—three of whom were specialized fireworks photographers from Japan—to capture *Transient Rainbow*. The video document and still photographs have become an essential part of the work: tangible records of an ephemeral art performance.

10-13 CAI GUO QIANG. *Transient Rainbow* over East River, New York City (2002).

HEIZER'S *RIFT* WITH LIBESKIND'S JEWISH MUSEUM

IN 1967, MICHAEL HEIZER took to the bottom of a dry lakebed for *Rift* (Fig. 10-14), one piece in his land art series called *Nine Nevada Depressions*. Almost three decades later, Daniel Libeskind used a startlingly similar shape for his extension of the Berlin Museum dedicated to the Holocaust and Jewish art and life (Fig. 10-15). Libeskind's zigzag design was derived mathematically by plotting the Berlin addresses of Jewish writers, artists, and composers who were killed during the Holocaust. The building's jagged shape reads as a painful rift in the continuity of the neighborhood in which it stands; it is punctuated by voids that symbolize the absence of Jewish people and culture in Berlin.

Heizer's *Rift* consists of a displacement of local materials such that the normalcy of the landscape is interrupted. For Heizer, the process is perhaps less about symbolism than it is about artistic elements. His depressions play with the relative scale of humans and nature; he is as much interested in the disintegration of his piece by natural processes over time as he is with the initial creative act. Heizer's jagged "scar" on the earth faded over time and then disappeared. How did Libeskind use this shape to try to ensure that the story of the Jews of Berlin would not fade or disappear? Is there something inherent in these shapes in contrast to their surroundings that suggests a certain symbolism or elicits a certain emotional response? How much do content and context influence our analysis of works with such visual congruities? ●

10-14 MICHAEL HEIZER. *Rift* (deteriorated). First of *Nine Nevada Depressions* (1968). 1.5-ton displacement on the bottom of a dry lake bed. 6220½" × 177³⁄₁₆" × 118⅛". Massacre Dry Lake, NV.

10-15 DANIEL LIBESKIND. Extension of the Berlin Museum (1989–1996). Berlin, Germany.

PUBLIC ART

The history of art is also full of works created for public spaces. Michelangelo's *David* (Fig. 16-25), even though it now has sanctuary in the Galleria dell'Accademia in Florence, was installed as a public work of art for the Piazza della Signoria, just outside the building that served as the political center of the city. A bit farther south, in Rome, one can see some of the most famous, most elaborate fountains in the world. They were created for the pleasure of the public (though often too for the glory of a pope). It is common also today for institutions (including the U.S. federal government) to allot a percentage of the overall cost of their building programs for works of art destined for the public spaces in and around buildings. You are probably familiar with works of public art in your own cities and towns, some dating back decades and some installed for a particular occasion or just for the season, as was Olafur Eliasson's *New York City Waterfalls* (Fig. **10-16**). Constructed under the Brooklyn Bridge in the summer of 2008, it was one of four sites featuring freestanding waterfalls funded by New York's Public Art Fund.

New York's Central Park forms the geographic and spiritual heart of that city and serves as the backdrop for one of its most beloved public sculptures. *Angel of the Waters* (Fig. **10-17**) (also known as Bethesda Fountain), by Emma Stebbins, towers above a circular brick plaza bordering a large lake. Warm weather brings sunbathers, break-dancers, newlyweds, and

10-16 OLAFUR ELIASSON. *The New York City Waterfalls*, Brooklyn Bridge, NY (2008).

10-17 EMMA STEBBINS. *Angel of the Waters* (Bethesda Fountain) (1873). Central Park, NY.

10-18 ANTONI GAUDÍ. *Serpent/Salamander* (1900–1914). *Parc Güell*, Barcelona, Spain.

10-19 ANTONI GAUDÍ. Detail of mosaic sunburst in ceiling of hypostyle hall (1900–1914). *Parc Güell*, Barcelona, Spain.

10-20 ANTONI GAUDÍ. Detail of mosaic serpentine bench, which sits in plaza above hypostyle hall (1900–1914). *Parc Güell*, Barcelona, Spain.

10-21 ANISH KAPOOR. *Cloud Gate* (2004–2006). *Cloud Gate*'s exterior consists of 168 highly polished stainless steel plates. It is 33' × 66' × 42' tall. Millennium Park, Chicago, IL.

splashing dogs to this public gathering space that seems to sit protectively beneath the outspread wings of an angel.

At the beginning of the twentieth century in Barcelona, one of its most famous native sons—Antoni Gaudí—was asked by his patron, Eusebi Güell, to create a gardenlike suburb for the very rich overlooking the city. The project was abandoned, but not before completion of what is now one of Barcelona's most treasured public sites, *Parc Güell*. A lively mosaic serpent (Fig. **10-18**) stands at the entrance of the park and has become one of the recognizable symbols of the city. Flights of steps lead to a variation on a hypostyle hall, with a forest of columns ornamented with lavish mosaic bases. The undulating ceiling is punctuated with mosaic discs called sunbursts (Fig. **10-19**). This space was originally intended to serve as a public market. Resting on top of the columned hall is an esplanade, the perimeter of which is lined with its serpentine, mosaic-clad stone bench (Fig. **10-20**). Gaudí was known for his playful, organic forms (see also his *Casa Mila*, Fig. 19-39) that helped define the Modernista style in Catalunya (or Catalonia), Spain.

Chicago's Millennium Park has its own very popular and very new gathering space, the focal point of which is Anish Kapoor's *Cloud Gate* (Fig. **10-21**). Nicknamed "the bean"

because of its elliptical, beanlike shape, the work consists of highly polished, mirrorlike stainless steel plates that reflect the people, places, and things surrounding it, both permanent and transient. Kapoor has called his piece "a gate to Chicago, a poetic idea about the city it reflects." The work inspired a new jazz composition (*Fanfare for Cloud Gate*) by Orbert Davis, performed in Millennium Park on the occasion of the dedication of Kapoor's sculpture.

A bit of controversy surrounding *Cloud Gate* proves interesting with regard to the nature of land and environmental art, including commissioned public works of art. Kapoor owns the rights to the piece, and therefore photographs of it cannot be reproduced commercially (as in this book) without his permission. One particular photographer learned this the hard way, when he was not permitted to photograph "the bean" without a prepaid permit. The public response to limits on publishing personal photographs of this public work of art was strong; photographs began to appear all over the Internet (you can find them on Google Images or Flickr, a photo-sharing website). If public art is public (and sometimes supported in real dollars by the public), where, in your opinion, should the artist's rights end and the public's begin?

10-22 A woman in Copley Square passes one of about 100 painted cows that were to be found around Boston as part of CowParade Boston '06, Saturday, June 10, 2006. Each cow is painted in its own unique design. Many of them are creations of local artists. The cows were on display throughout the summer. In September the cows were rounded up and auctioned off to raise money for charity.

The Bethesda Fountain and *Cloud Gate* have become icons of their respective cities; there are permanent installations of comparable works of art in public spaces all over the globe. Public art can also be temporary, like the pandemic *Cow Parades*—installations of fiberglass cows painted in every conceivable style, on every imaginable theme, turning up in almost too many cities to mention: New York, Chicago, London, Brussels, Sydney, Stockholm, Athens, Sao Paolo, and Moscow, to name some on the list (Fig. **10-22**). In all, it is estimated that Cow Parade has been seen by more than 100 million people worldwide. Some of the cows have been purchased after exhibition, raising money for charities. *Waga-Moo-Moo*, one of the Dublin *Cow Parade*, fetched $148,000 for a good cause. The cow craze has spawned many imitators, with different creatures popping up in cities everywhere.

MONUMENTS

The few examples of site-specific public art that we have looked at were designed or installed to enhance a particular open, public space. Their main purpose is or was aesthetic—to create beauty or to enhance the environment. Monuments comprise another category of site-specific public art. Their purpose is to preserve the memory of a person or an event.

The category of monuments is so broad that the few works we are able to concentrate on here represent an absurdly small percentage of what we live with in our communities. Equestrian monuments—men on horseback—seem almost ubiquitous in cities and towns, even though the identities of those memorialized are often forgotten. One of the purposes of monuments is to institutionalize memory. Monuments serve as expressions of the need or desire of a city, a country, or perhaps of a generation to "never forget."

The Oklahoma City National Memorial and Museum was created to remember the victims, survivors, and rescuers of the 1995 bombing of the Alfred P. Murrah Federal Building in that city. It is a multipart memorial site that incorporates various symbolic elements, the most arresting of which is the *Field of Empty Chairs* (Fig. **10-23**). One hundred sixty-eight chairs representing the individual victims were placed in nine rows corresponding to the floors they inhabited. The chairs are crafted of stone and bronze on a glass base, each etched with a victim's name. The field of chairs overlooks a reflecting pool that is adjacent to a Rescuer's Orchard honoring those who risked their lives and rushed to the scene to help. The focal point of the orchard is the Survivor Tree, an elm that withstood the blast of the explosion and now honors the survivors of the attack. The memorial site, which occupies the footprint of the Murrah building, also includes a museum. The memorial was designed to touch everyone who experienced the event, reflecting the impact of the violence on the community. It is an interactive type of monument, a place where one comes to witness history and to remember the dead and the living. The grief and the mourning are col-

10-23 The Field of Empty Chairs (2000). Oklahoma City National Memorial and Museum, Oklahoma City, OK.

lective, but the relationship to the victims—through the symbol of the chair—is personal. The empty chair represents loss and literal absence—a father or mother or friend who is no longer at the table, no longer sharing in life's moments.

This sense of loss and absence is central to Peter Eisenman's Holocaust Memorial in Berlin (Fig. 10-24), erected in memory of the European Jews murdered by the Nazis. Within view of the Brandenburg Gate and the Reichstag—

two architectural monuments associated with Adolf Hitler and Nazism—Eisenman placed 2,711 gray, concrete **stelae** side by side in claustrophobic rows. The stelae are the same length and width but vary in height and are placed on slabs that are tilted in different directions. The paths between the slabs slope up and then down so that the journey among these stones shifts and changes. The concentration of stelae is greatest at the center of the monument, creating a

10-24 PETER EISENMAN. Holocaust Memorial (2004). Berlin, Germany.

disturbing sense of confinement. In sunlight, the shadows are sharp and harsh; shady areas that ought to provide welcome respite from the sun are, instead, menacing. On an overcast day, the relentless grayness of the stones and the sky is somber, ashen, and funereal. The site is also home to an exhibition space, underground beneath the stelae, that is dedicated to the historical background of the Holocaust. The feeling is cryptlike, but there are no bodies, no objects that belonged to the deceased, and therein lies a point of the memorial. The Nazis planned to annihilate the Jews of Europe and any memory of them.

As the competitions ensued for the commission of Berlin's Holocaust Memorial, questions were raised about the relevance of a modern, abstract design. Would it be understood? Would it have meaning? The same questions haunted Maya Lin's proposal for the Vietnam Veterans Memorial in Washington, D.C., decades earlier (see A Closer Look: The Vietnam Veterans Memorial—A Woman's Perspective).

The Oklahoma City Memorial, the Berlin Holocaust Memorial, and the Vietnam Veterans Memorial all have a very different feeling from traditional triumphal monuments. Rather than looking at stylized images of heroic figures, we are called upon to reflect quietly and intimately on acts of human courage in the face of death. Although an antitriumphal approach represents a significant trend in contemporary monument design, it is not by any means universal. The National World War II Memorial (Fig. **10-25**) in Washington, D.C., was dedicated in 2004, more than 50 years after the Allied victories in Europe and Japan. The design for the memorial, with its pavilions and pillars, stirred a different kind of controversy in that its traditional, classical forms were reminiscent, to one journalist, of the pompous style embraced by the Fascist regimes of the 1930s, the very regimes that the Allies fought to defeat. One critic went so far as to refer to the memorial as a "monument on steroids—vainglorious, demanding of attention and full of trite imagery."[1]

The reception of the National World War II Memorial was not all negative, although the controversy raises an interesting question about the ways in which people relate to memorials and critics evaluate them. Many contemporary artists have gravitated toward designs that are interactive, educational, and reflective. Artists working in a more traditional mode emphasize the larger-than-human, the heroic. Reactions to memorials are highly personal, and the way memory is institutionalized is a very sensitive topic. Critics can find themselves in a situation in which their criticism is viewed, at best, as politically incorrect or, at worst, as unpatriotic.

---

[1] Thomas M. Keane Jr., *Boston Herald*, 2004.

10-25 FRIEDRICH ST. FLORIAN. National World War II Memorial (2004). Washington, D.C.

WHEN WE VIEW THE EXPANSES of the Washington Mall, we are awed by the grand obelisk that is the Washington Monument. We are comforted by the stately columns and familiar shapes of the Lincoln and Jefferson memorials. But many of us do not know how to respond to the two 200-foot-long black granite walls that form a V as they recede into the ground. There is no label—only the names of 58,000 victims chiseled into the silent walls:

> As we descend along the path that hugs the harsh black granite, we enter the very earth that, in another place, has accepted the bodies of our sons and daughters. Each name is carved not only in the stone, but by virtue of its highly polished surface, in our own reflection, in our physical substance. We are not observers, we are participants. We touch, we write [letters to our loved ones], we leave parts of ourselves behind. This is a woman's vision—to commune, to interact, to collaborate with the piece to fulfill its expressive potential. . . .

> Maya Ying Lin has foregone the [format of the triumphal monument]. She has given us [the earth mother] Gaea, who, pierced by the ebony scar of suffering death, takes back her children, as she has done since the dawn of humanity.*

This is Maya Ying Lin's Vietnam Veterans Memorial (Fig. 10-26), completed in 1982 on a two-acre site on the Mall. In order to read the names, we must descend gradually into the earth, and then just as gradually work our way back up. This progress is perhaps symbolic of the nation's involvement in Vietnam. The eloquently simple design of the memorial also stirs controversy, as did the war it commemorates.

This dignified understatement in stone has offended many who would have preferred a more traditional memorial. One conservative magazine branded the design a conspiracy to dishonor the dead. Architecture critic Paul Gapp of the *Chicago Tribune* argued, "The so-called memorial is bizarre . . . neither a building nor sculpture." One Vietnam veteran had called for a statue of an officer offering a fallen soldier to heaven. The public expects a certain heroic quality in its monuments to commemorate those fallen in battle. Lin's work is anti-heroic and antitriumphal. Whereas most war monuments speak of giving up our loved ones to a cause, her monument speaks only of giving up our loved ones.

How did the Vietnam Memorial come to be so uniquely designed? It was chosen from 1,421 entries in a national competition. The designer, Maya Ying Lin, is a Chinese American woman who was all of 22 years old at the time she submitted her entry. A native of Ohio, Lin had just graduated from Yale University, where she majored in architecture. Lin recognized that a monumental sculpture or another grand building would have been intrusive in the heart of Washington. Her design meets the competition criteria of being "neither too commanding nor too deferential" and is yet another expression of the versatility of stone. ●

It terrified me to have an idea that was solely mine to be no longer a part of my mind, but totally public.

—Maya Ying Lin, on her design for the Vietnam Veterans Memorial in Washington, D.C.

10-26 MAYA YING LIN. Vietnam Veterans Memorial (1982). Polished black granite. L: 492'. Washington, D.C.

---

* Lois Fichner-Rathus, "A Woman's Vision of the War," *New York Times*, August 18, 1991, H6.

The mother art is architecture. Without an architecture of our own we have no soul of our own civilization.

—Frank Lloyd Wright

ARCHITECTURE

11

The earliest humans found shelter in nature's protective cocoons—the mouth of a yawning cave, the underside of a rocky ledge, the dense canopy of an overspreading tree. But the construction of dwellings goes back to the Stone Age. In the words of author Howard Bloom, "first came the mammoth, then came architecture." Before we became capable of transporting bulky materials over vast distances, we had to rely on local possibilities. Ice Age humans dragged the skeletal pieces of woolly mammoths to a protective spot and piled them into domelike structures (Fig. 11-1). Native Americans carved complex communities into the sides of mesa cliffs (Fig. 11-2). Later, they built huts from sticks and bark and conical teepees from wood poles sheathed in animal skins. African villagers wove sticks and grass into cylindrical walls, plastered them with mud, and capped them with geometrically pure cone roofs. Desert inhabitants fashioned sun-baked clay into bricks, and the Inuit stacked blocks of ice with precision to create igloos.

Architecture is the art and science of designing buildings, bridges, and other structures. Of all the arts, architecture probably has the greatest impact on our daily lives. It shapes the immediate environments in which we live, work, or entertain ourselves. And, as the history of architecture reveals, it reflects and symbolizes our concept of self and the societies in which we live, past and present.

FRANK GEHRY. Ray and Maria Stata Center for Computer, Information, and Intelligence Sciences at MIT (2005). Cambridge, MA.

Architects work within the limits of their materials and the technology of the day. Although architects are visionaries and designers with artistic skills, they also possess technical knowledge necessary to determine how materials may be used to span and enclose vast spaces efficiently and safely. Architects are collaborators. They work with other professionals—engineers, contractors and builders, tradespeople, and interior designers.

Architects are also compromisers. The architect mediates between a client and civic planning boards and build-

11-1 This house was built of hundreds of mammoth bones by hunters on windswept, treeless plains in Ukraine, about 15,000 years ago. Working as a team, hut builders needed only a few days to haul together hundreds of massive mammoth bones, then stack them into a snug home.

ing departments, historic preservation committees, and, of course, the properties and aesthetic possibilities of the site itself. Today's technology may make possible the erection of a 20-story-high, 20-foot-wide "sliver skyscraper" on an expensive, narrow urban site, but with what aesthetic impact on a neighborhood? Since the 1930s, architects in New York City have had to comply with the so-called setback law and step back or contour their high-rises from the street in order to let the sun shine in on an environment that seemed in danger of devolving into a maze of blackened canyons. For an architect, negotiation is part of the job description. Climate, site specifics, materials, building codes, **service systems**, funding, and human personalities are just some of the variables that the architect encounters in an attempt to create a functional and aesthetically interesting structure.

In this section, we will explore ways in which architects have come to terms with these variables. We will survey the use of building materials and methods including stone, wood, cast iron, steel, concrete, and new technologies.

STONE ARCHITECTURE

As a building material, stone is massive and virtually indestructible. Contemporary wood-frame homes frequently sport stone fireplaces, perhaps as a symbol of permanence and strength as well as of warmth. The Native American cliff dwellings at Mesa Verde, Colorado (Fig. **11-2**), could be considered something of an "earthwork high relief." The cliff itself becomes the back wall or "support" of more than 100 rect-

11-2 Cliff dwellings, Mesa Verde, CO.

angular apartments. Circular, underground **kivas** served as community centers. Construction with stone, **adobe**, and timber creates a mixed-media functional fantasy. Early humans also assembled stone temples and memorials.

Post-and-Lintel Construction

The prehistoric Stonehenge (see Fig. 13-3) probably served religious or astronomical purposes. Its orientation toward the sun and its layout in concentric circles are suggestive of the amphitheaters and temples to follow. Stonehenge is an early example of **post-and-lintel construction** (Fig. **11-3A**). Two stones were set upright as supports, and a third was placed across them, creating an opening beneath. How the massive blocks of Stonehenge were transported and erected remains a mystery.

Early stone structures were erected without benefit of mortar. Their dry **masonry** relied on masterly carving of blocks, strategic placement, and sheer weight for durability. Consider the imposing ruin of the fortress of Machu Picchu, perched high above the Urubamba River in the Peruvian Andes. Its beautiful granite walls (Fig. **11-4**), constructed by the Incas, are pieced together so perfectly that not even a knife blade can pass between the blocks. The faces of the Great Pyramids of Egypt (see Fig. 13-12) are assembled as miraculously, perhaps even more so considering the greater mass of the blocks.

Stone became the favored material for the public buildings of the Egyptians and the Greeks. The Egyptian Temple of

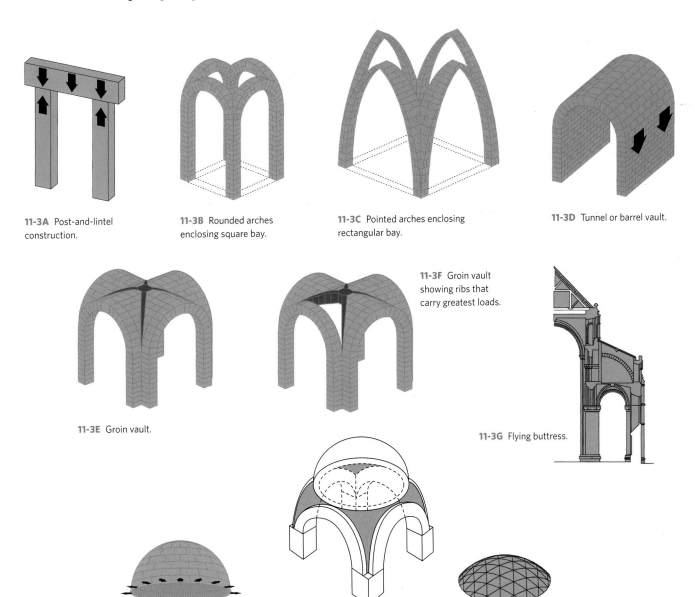

11-3A Post-and-lintel construction.

11-3B Rounded arches enclosing square bay.

11-3C Pointed arches enclosing rectangular bay.

11-3D Tunnel or barrel vault.

11-3E Groin vault.

11-3F Groin vault showing ribs that carry greatest loads.

11-3G Flying buttress.

11-3H Dome.

11-3I Pendentives.

11-3J Geodesic dome.

11-4 Walls of Fortress of Machu Picchu, Urubamba Valley, Peru. (1490–1530).

11-5 Hypostyle Hall, Temple of Amen-Re (1570-1342 BCE). Karnak, Egypt.

Amen-Re at Karnak (Figs. **11-5** and **11-6**) and the Parthenon (see Fig. 14-10) of the Classical period of Greece begin to speak of the elegance as well as the massiveness that can be fashioned from stone. The Temple of Amen-Re is of post-and-lintel construction, but the paintings, relief sculptures, and overall smoothness of the columns belie their function as bearers of stress. The virtual forest of columns was a structural necessity because of the weight of the massive stone lintels. The Parthenon is also of post-and-lintel construction. Consistent with the Greeks' emphasis on the functional purpose of columns, the surfaces of the marble shafts are free from ornamentation. The Parthenon, which may be the most studied and surveyed building in the world, is discussed at length in Chapter 14.

Arches

Architects of stone also use **arches** to span distances (Figs. **11-3B** and **11-3C**). Arches have many functions, including supporting other structures, such as roofs, and serving as actual and symbolic gateways. An Arch of Triumph, as in the city of Paris, provides a visual focus for the return of the conquering hero. Eero Saarinen's Gateway Arch (Fig. **11-7**), completed in St. Louis in 1966, stands 630 feet tall at the center and commemorates the westward push of the United States after the Louisiana Purchase of 1803. The Pont du Gard (see Fig. 14-22) near Nîmes, France, employs the arch in a bridge that is part of an aqueduct system. It is a marvel of Roman engineering. Early masonry arches were fashioned from **bricks**; each limestone block of the Pont du Gard weighs up to two tons, and they were assembled without benefit of mortar. The bridge stands and functions today, two millennia after its creation.

An arch is two curves trying to fall.

—Andy Rooney

11-6 Hypostyle Hall, Temple of Amen-Re (1570-1342 BCE). Karnak, Egypt.

11-7 EERO SAARINEN. Jefferson National Expansion Memorial, Gateway Arch (1966). St. Louis, MO.

In most arches, wedge-shaped blocks of stone, called **voussoirs**, are gradually placed in position ascending a wooden scaffold called a **centering**. When the center, or **keystone**, is set in place, the weight of the blocks is all at once transmitted in an arc laterally and downward, and the centering can be removed. The pull of gravity on each block serves as "cement"; that is, the blocks fall into one another so that the very weight that had made their erection a marvel now prevents them from budging. The **compressive strength** of stone allows the builder to place additional weight above the arch. The Pont du Gard consists of three **tiers** of arches, 161 feet high.

Vaults

An extended arch is called a **vault**. A tunnel or **barrel vault** (Fig. **11-3D**) simply places arches behind one another until a desired depth is reached. In this way, impressive spaces may be roofed, and tunnels may be constructed. Unfortunately, the spaces enclosed by barrel vaults are dark, because piercing them to let in natural light would compromise their strength. The communication of stresses from one arch to another also requires that the centering for each arch be kept in place until the entire vault is completed.

Roman engineers are credited with the creation of the **groin vault**, which overcame limitations of the barrel vault, as early as the third century CE. Groin vaults are constructed by placing barrel vaults at right angles to cover a square space (Fig. **11-3E**). In this way the load of the intersecting vaults is transmitted to the corners, necessitating **buttressing** at these points but allowing the sides of the square to be open. The square space enclosed by the groin vault is called a **bay**. Architects could now construct huge buildings by assembling any number of bays. Because the stresses from one groin vault are not transmitted to a large degree to its neighbors, the centering used for one vault can be removed and reused while the building is under construction.

The greatest loads in the groin vault are thrust onto the four arches that compose the sides and the two arches that run diagonally across them. If the capacity of these diagonals is increased to carry a load, by means of **ribs** added to the vault (Fig. **11-3F**), then the remainder of the roof can be fashioned from stone **webbing** or other materials much lighter in weight. A true stone skeleton is created.

Note in Figure 11-3B that rounded arches can enclose only square bays. One could not use rounded arches in rectangular bays because the longer walls would have higher arches. Architects over the centuries solved the rectangular bay problem in several ingenious ways. The most important of these is found in **Gothic** architecture, discussed in Chapter 15, which

uses ribbed vaults and **pointed arches**. Pointed arches can be constructed to uniform heights even when the sides of the enclosed space are unequal (Fig. 11-3C). Gothic architecture also employed the so-called flying buttress (Fig. **11-3G**), a masonry strut that transmits part of the load of a vault to a buttress positioned outside a building.

Most of the great cathedrals of Europe achieve their vast, open interiors through the use of vaults. Massive stone rests benignly above the heads of worshippers and tourists alike, transmitting its brute load laterally and downward. The **Ottonian** St. Michael's (see Fig. 15-19), built in Germany between 1001 and 1031 CE, uses barrel vaulting. Its bays are square, and its walls are blank and massive. The **Romanesque** St. Sernin (see Fig. 15-21), built in France between about 1080 and 1120, uses round arches and square bays. The walls are heavy and blunt, with the main masses subdivided by buttresses. St. Étienne (see Fig. 15-23), completed between 1115 and 1120, has high, rising vaults—some of the earliest to show true ribs— that permit light to enter through a **clerestory**. Stone became a fully elegant structural skeleton in the great Gothic cathedrals, such as those at Laon (see Figs. 15-28 and 15-29) and Chartres (see Fig. 15-31) and in the Notre-Dame of Paris (see Fig. 15-30). Lacy buttressing and ample **fenestration** lend these massive buildings an airy lightness that seems consonant with their mission of directing upward the focus of human awareness.

Domes

Domes are hemispherical forms that are rounded when viewed from beneath (see Figs. **11-3H** and **11-3J**). Like vaults, domes are extensions of the principle of the arch and are capable of enclosing vast reaches of space. (Buckminster Fuller, who designed the United States Pavilion [Fig. 11-25] for the 1967 World's Fair in Montreal, proposed that the center of Manhattan should be enclosed in a weather-controlled transparent dome two miles in diameter.) Stresses from the top of the dome are transmitted in all directions to the points at which the circular base meets the foundation, walls, or other structures beneath.

The dome of the Buddhist temple or Stupa of Sanchi, India, completed in the first century CE, rises 50 feet above the ground and causes the worshipper to contemplate the dwelling place of the gods (see Fig. 18-26). It was constructed from stones placed in gradually diminishing concentric circles. Visitors find the domed interior of the Pantheon of Rome (see Fig. 14-29), completed during the second century CE, breathtaking. Like the dome of the Stupa, the rounded inner surface of the Pantheon, 144 feet in diameter, symbolizes the heavens.

11-8 ANTHEMIUS OF TRALLES AND ISODORUS OF MILETUS. Interior of Hagia Sophia (532–537 CE). Istanbul, Turkey.

The dome of the vast Hagia Sophia (see Fig. **11-8**) in Constantinople is 108 feet in diameter. Its architects, building during the sixth century CE, used four triangular surfaces called **pendentives** (Fig. **11-31**) to support the dome on a square base. Pendentives transfer the load from the base of the dome to the **piers** at the corners of the square beneath.

Today, stone is rarely used as a structural material in developed nations. It is expensive to quarry and transport, and it is too massive to handle readily at the site. Metals are lighter and have greater tensile strength, so they are suitable as the skeletons or reinforcers for most of today's larger structures. Still, buildings with steel skeletons are frequently dressed with thin facades, or **veneers**, of costly marble, limestone, and other types of stone. Many tract homes are granted decorative patches of stone across the front facade, and slabs of slate are frequently used to provide minimum-care surfaces for entry halls or patios in private homes.

WOOD ARCHITECTURE

Wood is as beautiful and versatile a material for building as it is for sculpture. It is an abundant and, as many advertisements have proclaimed, renewable resource. It is relatively light in weight and is capable of being worked on at the site with readily portable hand tools. Its variety of colors and grains, as well as its capacity to accept paint or to weather charmingly when left in its natural state, make wood a ubiquitous material. Wood, like stone, can be used as a structural element or as a facade. In many structures, it is used as both.

Wood also has its drawbacks. It warps and cracks. It rots. It is also highly flammable and stirs the appetite of termites and other devouring insects. However, modern technology has enhanced the stability and strength of wood as a building material. Chemical treatments decrease wood's vulnerability to rotting from moisture. **Plywood**, which is built up from sheets of wood glued together, is unlikely to warp and is frequently used as an underlayer in the exterior walls of small buildings and homes. Laminated wood beams possess great strength and are also unlikely to become distorted in shape from exposure to changing temperatures and levels of humidity.

Architects, like artists and designers, use contrasting materials to create visual diversity and surface interest. They often reference textures found in nature in order to integrate a building with its site, or to create a dramatic counterpoint to it. The tree houses (Fig. **11-9**) designed by the German architect studio baumraum are extreme and playful examples of both. The designers refer to their endeavors as a blend of architecture, landscape design, and "arboriculture," aiming to integrate the structures into their forest surrounds and, at the same time, preserve the integrity of the host trees. In designing its lofty wood dwellings, baumraum—which literally means "tree space" in German—also takes into consideration

11-9 BAUMRAUM.

factors such as the species of a tree, its distance off the ground, and the amount of clear building space available in order to successfully suspend the structures. The result is a study in contrast and connection between humans and their natural surroundings.

Post-and-Beam Construction

Post-and-beam construction (Fig. **11-10A**) is similar to post-and-lintel construction. Vertical and horizontal timbers are cut and pieced together with wooden pegs. The beams span openings for windows, doors, and interior spaces, and they can also support posts for another story or roof trusses.

Trusses

Trusses are lengths of wood, iron, or steel pieced together in triangular shapes of the sort shown in Figure **11-10B** in order to expand the abilities of these materials to span distances. Trusses acquire their strength from the fact that the sides of a triangle, once joined, cannot be forced out of shape. In many buildings, roof trusses are exposed and become elements of the design.

Balloon Framing

Balloon framing (Fig. **11-10C**), a product of the industrial revolution, dates back to the beginning of the twentieth century. In balloon framing, factory-cut studs, including the familiar two-by-four, are mass-produced and assembled at the site using thousands of factory-produced metal nails. Several light, easily handled pieces of wood replace the heavy timber of post-and-beam construction. Entire walls are framed in place or on their sides and then raised into place by a crew of carpenters. The multiple pieces and geometric patterns of balloon framing give it a sturdiness that rivals that of the post and beam, permitting the support of slate or tile roofs. However, the term *balloon* was originally a derisive term: inveterate users of post and beam were skeptical that the frail-looking wooden pieces could provide a rugged building.

Balloon framing has now been used on millions of smaller buildings, not only homes. Sidings for balloon-framed homes include **clapboard**, asbestos shingle, brick and stone veneer, and aluminum. Roofs have included asphalt, cedar shingle, tile, and slate. These materials vary in cost, and each has certain aesthetic possibilities and practical advantages. Aluminum, for example, is lightweight, durable, and maintenance-free. However, when aluminum siding is shaped like clapboard and given a bogus grain, the intended trompe l'oeil effect usually fails and can create something of an aesthetic embarrassment.

Two other faces of wood are observable in American architect Richard Morris Hunt's J.N.A. Griswold House (Fig. **11-11**), built at Newport, Rhode Island, in 1862–1863 in the *Stick style*, and in the Cape Cod–style homes in Levittown, Long Island, a suburb of New York City (Fig. **11-12**). The Griswold House shows the fanciful possibilities in wood. The Stick style sports a skeletal treatment of exteriors that remind one of an assemblage of matchsticks, open interiors, and a curious interplay of voids and solids and horizontal and vertical lines. Shapes pro-

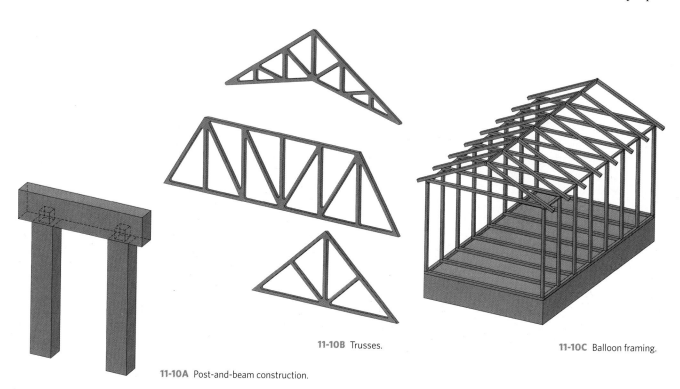

11-10B Trusses.

11-10C Balloon framing.

11-10A Post-and-beam construction.

liferate in this short-lived movement. Turrets and gables and dormers poke the roof in every direction. Trellised porches reinforce a certain wooden laciness. One cannot imagine the Griswold House constructed in any material but wood.

The house at Levittown (Fig. **11-13**) is more than a home; it is a socioaesthetic comment on the need for mass suburban housing that impacted so many metropolitan regions during the marriage and baby boom that followed World War II. This house and 17,000 others almost exactly like it were built, with few exceptions, on 60-foot by 100-foot lots that had been carved out from potato fields. In what was to become neighborhood after neighborhood, bulldozers smoothed already flat terrain and concrete slabs were poured. Balloon frames were erected, sided, and roofed. Trees were planted; grass was sown. The houses had an eat-in kitchen, living room, two tiny bedrooms, one bath on the first floor, and an expansion attic. Despite the tedium of the repetition, the original Levittown house achieved a sort of architectural integrity, providing living space, the pride of ownership, and an inoffensive facade for a modest price. Driving through Levittown today, it seems that every occupant thrust random additions in random directions as the family grew, despite the limitations of the lots. The trees only partly obscure the results.

11-12 Cape Cod–style houses built by Levitt & Sons (c. 1947–1951). Levittown, NY.

11-13 A family in front of their new Levitt home (1950).

11-14 Engraving of Sir Joseph Paxton's Crystal Palace (1851). London, England.

CAST-IRON ARCHITECTURE

Nineteenth-century industrialization also introduced **cast iron** as a building material. It was one of several structural materials that would change the face of architecture. Cast iron was a welcome alternative to stone and wood. Like stone, iron has great strength, is heavy, and has a certain brittleness, yet it was the first material to allow the erection of tall buildings with relatively slender walls. Slender iron beams and bolted trusses are also capable of spanning vast interior spaces, freeing them from the forests of columns that are required in stone.

At the mid-nineteenth-century Great Exhibition held in Hyde Park, London, Sir Joseph Paxton's Crystal Palace (Fig. **11-14**) covered 17 acres. Like subsequent iron buildings, the Crystal Palace was **prefabricated**. Iron parts were cast at the factory, not the site. The new railroads facilitated their transportation, and it was a simple matter to bolt them together at the exhibition. It was also a relatively simple matter to dismantle the structure and reconstruct it at another site. The iron skeleton, with its myriad arches and trusses, was an integral part of the design. The huge plate-glass paneled walls bore no weight. Paxton asserted that "nature" had been his "engineer," explaining that he merely copied the system of longitudinal and transverse supports that one finds in a leaf. Earlier architects were also familiar with the structure of the leaf, but they did not have the structural materials at hand that would permit them to build, much less conceptualize, such an expression of natural design.

The Crystal Palace was moved after the exhibition, and until heavily damaged by fire, it served as a museum and concert hall. It was demolished in 1941 during World War II, after officials discovered that it was being used as a landmark by German pilots on bombing runs.

11-15 GUSTAVE EIFFEL. Eiffel Tower (1889). Paris, France.

The Eiffel Tower (Fig. **11-15**) was built in Paris in 1889 for another industrial exhibition. At the time, Gustave Eiffel was castigated by critics for building an open structure lacking the standard masonry facade. Today the Parisian symbol is so familiar that one cannot visualize Paris without the tower's magnificent exposed iron trusses. The pieces of the 1,000-foot-tall tower were prefabricated, and the tower was assembled at the site in 17 months by only 150 workers.

Structures such as these encouraged **steel-cage construction** and the development of the skyscraper.

STEEL-CAGE ARCHITECTURE

Steel is a strong metal of iron alloyed with small amounts of carbon and a variety of other metals. Steel is harder than iron, and more rust and fire resistant. It is more expensive than other structural materials, but its great strength permits it to be used in relatively small quantities. Light, narrow, prefabricated I-beams have great tensile strength. They resist bending in any direction and are riveted or welded together into skeletal forms called **steel cages** at the site (Fig. **11-16**). Facades and inner walls are hung from the skeleton and frequently contribute more mass to the building than does the skeleton itself.

The Wainwright Building (Fig. **11-17**), erected in 1890, is an early example of steel-cage construction. Architect Louis Sullivan, one of the fathers of modern American architecture, emphasized the verticality of the structure by running **pilasters** between the windows through the upper stories. Many skyscrapers run pilasters up their entire facades. Sullivan also emphasized the horizontal features of the Wainwright Building. Ornamented horizontal bands separate most of the windows, and a severe decorated **cornice** crowns the structure. Sullivan's motto was "form follows function," and the rigid horizontal and vertical processions of the elements of the facade suggest the regularity of the rectangular spaces within. Sullivan's early "skyscraper"—in function, in structure, and in simplified form—was a precursor of the twentieth-century behemoths to follow.

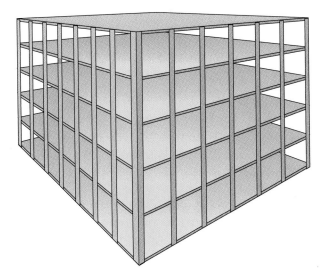

11-16 Steel-cage construction.

11-17 LOUIS SULLIVAN. Wainwright Building (1890-91). St. Louis, MO.

With steel-cage construction, the weight of the building is borne by its structural core and not its walls, allowing for an expansive use of glass—called a *curtain wall*—on a building's elevations (Figure **11-18**). New York City's Lever House (Fig. **11-19**), designed by Gordon Bunshaft of Skidmore, Owings, and Merrill, is a landmark example of steel-cage construction using a curtain wall. Although the skyscraper, by contemporary standards, barely "scrapes the sky"—it is only 24 stories high—the austere, minimalist, rectangular profile of Lever House, with its uninterrupted wrap of glass, became the model for hundreds of buildings by the 1960s. Lever House is also credited with an innovation in urban planning—the integration of the office building with a public, open plaza on the ground floor, complete with gardens and walkways that enable pedestrians to cut across part of the city block on

11-19 GORDON BUNSHAFT. Lever House (1951–1952). NY.

which the building sits. The plaza, covered by a flat roof only a couple of stories high, prevents the shaft of the office building from overwhelming its site. The evening light angles down across the plaza and illuminates the avenue beneath.

REINFORCED CONCRETE ARCHITECTURE

Although cement was first produced in the early 1800s, the use of **reinforced concrete** is said to have begun with a French gardener, Jacques Monier, who proposed strengthening concrete flower pots with a wire mesh in the 1860s. In reinforced concrete, or **ferroconcrete**, steel rods and/or steel mesh are inserted at the points of greatest stress into concrete

11-18 Building project in Wuhan, China, illustrating the relationship between the load bearing columns and the glass curtain exterior.

Architecture is the first manifestation of man creating his own universe.
—Le Corbusier

slabs before they harden. In the resultant slab, stresses are shared by the materials.

Ferroconcrete has many of the advantages of stone and steel, without some of the disadvantages. The steel rods increase the tensile strength of concrete, making it less susceptible to tearing or pulling apart at stress points. The concrete, in turn, prevents the steel from rusting. Reinforced concrete can span greater distances than stone, and it supports more weight than steel. Perhaps the most dramatic advantage of reinforced concrete is its capacity to take on natural curved shapes that would be unthinkable in steel or concrete alone. Curved slabs take on the forms of eggshells, bubbles, seashells, and other organic shapes that are naturally engineered for the even spreading of stress throughout their surfaces and are, hence, enduring.

Reinforced concrete, more than other materials, has allowed the architect to think freely and sculpturally. There are limits to what ferroconcrete can do, however; initial spatial concepts are frequently somewhat refined by computer-aided calculations of marginally more efficient shapes for distributing stress. Still, it would not be far from the mark to say that buildings of almost any shape and reasonable size are possible today, if one is willing to pay for them. The architects of ferroconcrete have achieved buildings that would have astounded the ancient stone builders—and perhaps Joseph Paxton as well.

Le Corbusier's chapel of Notre-Dame-du-Haut (Figs. **11-20** and **11-21**) is an example of what has been referred to as the

"new brutalism," deriving from the French *brut*, meaning "rough, uncut, or raw." The steel web is spun, and the concrete is cast in place, leaving the marks of the wooden forms on its surface. The white walls, dark roof, and white towers are decorated only by the texture of the curving reinforced concrete slabs. In places the walls are incredibly thick. Windows of various shapes and sizes expand from small slits and rectangles to form mysterious light tunnels; they draw the

11-22 FRANK LLOYD WRIGHT. Kaufmann House ("Fallingwater") (1936). Bear Run, PA. © 2011 Frank Lloyd Wright Foundation/Artists Rights Society (ARS), NY.

11-23 MOSHE SAFDIE. Habitat, Expo 67 (1967). Montreal, Québec, Canada.

observer outward more than they actually light the interior. The massive voids of the window apertures recall the huge stone blocks of prehistoric religious structures.

Frank Lloyd Wright's Kaufmann House (Fig. **11-22**), which has also become known as "Fallingwater," shows a very different application of reinforced concrete. Here cantilevered decks of reinforced concrete rush outward into the surrounding landscape from the building's central core, intersecting in strata that lie parallel to the natural rock formations. Wright's **naturalistic style** integrates his building with its site. In the Kaufmann House, reinforced concrete and stone walls complement the sturdy rock of the Pennsylvania countryside.

For Wright, modern materials did not warrant austerity; geometry did not preclude organic integration with the site. A small waterfall seems mysteriously to originate beneath the broad white planes of a deck. The irregularity of the structural components—concrete, cut stone, natural stone, and machine-planed surfaces—complements the irregularity of the wooded site.

Israeli architect Moshe Safdie's Habitat (Fig. **11-23**) is another expression of the versatility of concrete. Habitat was erected for Expo 67 in Montreal as one solution to the housing problems of the future. Rugged, prefabricated units were stacked like blocks about a common utility core at the site, so that the roof of one unit would provide a private deck for another. Only a couple of Safdie-style "apartment houses" have been erected since, one in Israel and one in Puerto Rico, so today Safdie's beautiful sculptural assemblage evokes more nostalgia than hope for the future. Its unique brand of rugged, blocky excitement is rarely found in mass housing, and this is our loss.

STEEL-CABLE ARCHITECTURE

The notion of suspending bridges from cables is not new. Wood-and-rope suspension bridges have been built in Asia for thousands of years. Iron suspension bridges, such as the Menai Strait Bridge in Wales and the Clifton Bridge near Bristol, England, were erected during the early part of the nineteenth century. But in the Brooklyn Bridge (Fig. **11-24**), completed in 1883, John Roebling exploited the great tensile strength of steel to span New York's East River with **steel cable**. In such a cable, many parallel wires share the stress. Steel cable is also flexible, allowing the roadway beneath to sway, within limits, in response to changing weather and traffic conditions.

Roebling used massive vaulted piers of stone masonry to support parabolic webs of steel, which are rendered lacy by

We may live without architecture, and worship without her, but we cannot remember without her.
—John Ruskin

11-24 JOHN A. ROEBLING. Brooklyn Bridge (1869–1883), NY. There is another stirring aspect to the photograph of the Brooklyn Bridge. In the background, you can see the twin towers of the World Trade Center, which collapsed in the terrorist attack of September 11, 2001.

the juxtaposition. In many more recent suspension bridges, steel cable spans more than a mile, and in bridges such as the Golden Gate, the George Washington, and the Verrazano Narrows, the effect is aesthetically stirring.

SHELL ARCHITECTURE

Modern materials and methods of engineering have made it possible to enclose spaces with relatively inexpensive shell structures. Masonry domes have been replaced by lightweight shells, which are frequently flatter and certainly capable of spanning greater spaces. Shells have been constructed from reinforced concrete, wood, steel, aluminum, and even plastics and paper. The concept of shell architecture is as old as the canvas tent and as new as the geodesic dome (Fig. **11-25**), designed by Buckminster Fuller for the United States Pavilion at Expo 67 in Montreal. In many sports arenas, fabric roofs are held up by keeping the air pressure inside the building slightly greater than that outside. Like balloons, these roof structures are literally inflated.

Fuller's shell is an assemblage of lightweight metal trusses into a three-quarter sphere that is 250 feet in diameter. Looking more closely, one sees that the trusses compose six-sided units that give the organic impression of a honeycomb. Light

floods the climate-controlled enclosure, creating an environment for any variety of human activity—and any form of additional construction—within. Such domes can be covered with many sorts of weatherproofing, including lightweight metals and fabric and translucent and transparent plastics and glass. Here the engineering requirements clearly create the architectural design.

11-25 BUCKMINSTER FULLER. United States Pavilion, Expo 67 (1967). Montreal, Québec, Canada.

EVERY EVENING, FOR A MONTH IN THE SPRING OF 2002, twin towers of light, composed of 88 searchlights, rose toward the blackened sky from Ground Zero. The installation was mounted in memory of the victims of the terrorist attack on the World Trade Center on September 11, 2001, and the twin towers of glass and steel themselves. *New York Times* critic Herbert Muschamp* described the *Tribute in Light* (Fig. 11-26) as "a moving piece of urban spectacle" whose "twin light towers . . . seemed to be looking for something." He praised the project for setting "a rhetorical tone worthy of emulation by those who [would] be shaping the future of Lower Manhattan" in the wake of the destruction. Intended to be a temporary installation, *Tribute in Light* shone yearly on September 11 until the tenth anniversary of the attacks in 2011.

---

*Herbert Muschamp, March 12, 2002. Copyright © 2002 by The New York Times Company.

In "My Lost City," the American novelist F. Scott Fitzgerald, writing in 1936 about the bygone New York he remembered as a younger man, lamented: ". . . I have lost my splendid mirage. Come back, come back, O glittering and white!" Construction is underway to do just that—to bring back the towers "glittering and white." Within months following September 11, dozens of architects and planners were submitting concepts to New York City for the rebuilding of the World Trade Center site, which included a memorial to those who had been killed in the attack and new buildings that might recapture the upward spirit of the city. Daniel Libeskind, for example, designed a light and airy steel and glass tower to replace the fallen ones. Even so, his design was to be significantly stronger than the original, taking into account the sobering realities of luring tenants into a super high-rise skyscraper in a post-9/11 world and the desire of most Americans to build high and build proud.

The final design of One World Trade Center (One WTC), however, is by the renowned architectural group

11-26 *Tribute in Light* (March–April 2002). NY.

11-27 Cross-section of One World Trade Center (projected completion year: 2013). Height: 1776'. NY. © Skidmore, Owings & Merrill LLP.

the office tower with what will surely become a bustling plaza designed of textured granite cobblestones. In addition to a restaurant, there are zones for relaxation and spaces for memory and reflection. The building meets or exceeds construction standards for safety and security, but the overall impression is one of openness and accessibility—a careful balance that will facilitate the revival of urban life in a location that has extraordinary meaning to New Yorkers and the country (Figs. 11-27 and 11-28).

11-28 Rendering of the completed One World Trade Center, with the National September 11 Memorial in the foreground, sited on the footprints of the towers that were destroyed. © Skidmore, Owings & Merrill LLP.

of Skidmore, Owings, and Merrill, which pioneered mid-twentieth century skyscraper architecture in buildings like Lever House (see Fig. 11-19). According to the firm, "the design solution is an innovative mix of architecture, structure, urban design, safety and sustainability." The tower, which is adjacent to the World Trade Center Memorial, rises a symbolic 1776 feet from a cubic base, supporting a structure with a prismatic glass curtain wall that captures refracted light in myriad ways, depending on the time of day and atmospheric conditions.

One WTC not only "recaptures" the lower Manhattan skyline, but also provides communal space that integrates

11-29 FRANK GEHRY. Ray and Maria Stata Center for Computer, Information, and Intelligence Sciences at MIT (2005). Cambridge, MA.

NEW MATERIALS, NEW VISIONS

In architecture studios and schools, the saying goes, "Convention gets built; innovation gets published." But this adage is systematically being proven wrong as scientists and engineers have combined forces to turn architects' dreams into reality: "If you can think it, we can build it."

In 1997, Frank Gehry transformed architectural design with the use of titanium in the same way that reinforced concrete altered the look of the exterior "skin" of buildings in the 1950s and 1960s. His Guggenheim Museum in Bilbao, Spain (see Fig. 2-18), set a new artistic course for Gehry in terms of his own style and nurtured the adaptation of high-tech metals by architects worldwide. Gehry's Ray and Maria Stata Center (Fig. **11-29**), which opened in 2005 on the Massachusetts Institute of Technology campus, stands as a visual summation of his most recent designs, materials, and theories of spatial relationships. The 730,000-square-foot complex will be a hub for research in the fields of computer science, linguistics, and philosophy. The assertive clashing of shapes signifies the disparate disciplines that will be housed in the structure, while communal lounges and shared interior spaces encourage interaction, collaboration, and the cross-fertilization of ideas. Gehry said of the Stata Center: "It reflects the different groups, the collision of ideas, the energy of people and ideas. . . . That's what will lead to the breakthroughs and the positive results."

Architect Peter Testa's view is that there is a "need to rethink how we assemble buildings" and that it is time to design in collaboration with materials manufacturers and to explore the potential of nascent technologies. Testa and his partner, Devyn Weiser, have designed a high-rise tower out of composite materials (Fig. **11-30**). Their skyscraper would be held erect by a cross-hatched lattice made of carbon fiber—a material several times stronger than the traditional steel. The "woven building" would have an interior that is completely open (except for elevator shafts) and void of structural support.

Green Buildings

Green is the color associated with energy efficiency and environmental awareness. The clients of many architects seek the design of "green buildings" today to save money, to protect the environment, or, sometimes, to boost a corporate image. Green

11-30 PETER TESTA AND DEVYN WEISER, TESTA ARCHITECTURE AND DESIGN. Carbon Tower.

buildings are efficient in terms of energy, water, and materials. They are constructed with attention to the quality of the indoor air as well as the building's emissions that could prove harmful to the environment. When possible, recycled materials—such as steel, woods, and plastics—are incorporated into design and construction. Converting to "green" is also sometimes facilitated by the location of a building. If residents and employees can access buildings by public transportation, they are less likely to drive to and from home or work, using fossil fuels that contribute to air pollution and greenhouse gases.

Architects employ simple energy conservation measures, such as well-sealed and insulated glass windows. Light-colored roofs reflect heat from the sun in warm climates; dark-covered roofs trap heat from the sun in cold climates. Pine trees can be planted along the north side of a building to protect against icy winds. Along the south side, deciduous trees will provide leafy shade and natural cooling in summer and, in winter, when their branches are bare, admit light and provide warmth. Digging a well to water the lawn or fill the swimming pool conserves water in reservoirs and aquifers. Using appliances with Energy Star ratings decreases the fossil fuels required to make them run. Rooftop solar panels are costly to install but save on electrical costs year after year.

11-32 EMILIO AMBASZ & ASSOCIATES. Fukuoka Prefectural International Hall (1994). Fukuoka, Japan.

Green buildings are not necessarily recognizable as such from the exterior. The Hearst Tower (Fig. **11-31**), designed by Sir Norman Foster, began by preserving the façade of the 1928 stone structure upon which it was built. It is credited with being Manhattan's first green office skyscraper. Walls are coated with vapor-free paint. Floors are made of wood from sustainable forests. About 85 percent of the steel in the building was recycled. Rain is collected on the roof and stored in a basement tank, used in the building's cooling system and to water plants in the ten-story atrium. The triangular planes of glass on the tower's exterior are made of *low-E* glass, which minimizes the loss of heat during winter and the admission of heat during summer. Sensors determine the amount of natural light entering the building and adjust the lighting fixtures accordingly. The building uses 26 percent less energy than the amount deemed desirable by the city and was certified by the LEED (Leadership in Energy and Environmental Design) program of the U.S. Green Building Council.

Some green buildings are decidedly green. The Fukuoka Prefectural International Hall (Fig. **11-32**) was constructed on the last remaining green space in the city center of Fukuoka in Japan. Architects Emilio Ambrasz & Associates managed to keep it green even as they added 600,000 square feet of private and government office space, an exhibition hall, a museum, a 2,000-seat theater, conference facilities, retail shops, and underground parking. One side has the appearance of a conventional steel-and-glass office tower. The other consists of a dramatically descending terraced roof, covered with some 35,000 plants, that culminates in a public park. The literal green roof reduces the building's energy consumption by insulating it from the elements and capturing rainwater for use in the building. The lush terrace has also become home to more than 70 species of birds. Now that's green.

11-31 SIR NORMAN FOSTER. Hearst Tower (2004). NY.

ART TOUR DALLAS/FORT WORTH

ONE HUNDRED YEARS AGO, Will Rogers said, "Fort Worth is where the West begins and Dallas is where the East peters out." His description remains on the money even today. Although the city of Dallas conveys a certain formality and self-conscious sophistication, Fort Worth revels in its "Cowtown" image.

Both cities can claim their skyscrapers, but the creation of an impressive Dallas-type skyline seems not to have been a temptation to the developers of Fort Worth. There things lie closer to the horizon, as shown in the downtown cobbled streets. It is as if the connection with the land wants to be emphasized, or will not be shaken. Dallas and Fort Worth, then, cannot be called twin cities, but one thing they have in common is that they have both lured world-class architects to grace their avenues and their vistas. Although they may be thousands of miles from the coasts and from classic civilizations, civilization has clearly found its way to the Southwest.

Dallas and Fort Worth lie only 33 miles apart. Along with their suburbs, they make up "the Metroplex." If you are visiting them, chances are you drove in on one of the interstates or flew into Dallas/Fort Worth (DFW) International Airport, which sits halfway between the two cities. Although the airport is one of the largest in the world

and entertaining in and of itself, this is Texas, and "big" is where you start.

Downtown Dallas is easy to navigate by subway or on foot, unless you're braving the heat of summer. Most museums and cultural sites can be found within reasonable proximity to one another. I say, get a big-brimmed hat and a bottle of water and "cowboy it up"! You can walk from one end of downtown to the other in an hour.

The Dallas Arts District is 60 acres of museums, a performing arts center, and outdoor sculptures. Its centerpiece is the Dallas Museum of Art—a space that stretches more than 250,000 square feet. The museum's vastness stretches not only over its site but also across continents and eras. It features works from the Americas, Africa, Asia, the Pacific, and Europe. You will find paintings by Frida Kahlo and Frederic Edwin Church, and more Mondrians than in any other museum in the country. The famous Wendy and Emery Reves collection is installed in a setting that recreates the owner–donors' home on the French Riviera. Among the collection's stars are van Gogh, Monet, and Renoir.

Before you get too far, stroll in the Nasher Sculpture Garden (still have your hat on?) adjacent to the Dallas Art Museum. This 2.4-acre site was designed by Renzo Piano, architect of the famed Centre Pompidou in Paris (see the Paris Art Tour), and displays work by artists such as Alexander Calder, Willem de Kooning, Barbara Hepworth, Joan Miró, Richard Serra, and Auguste Rodin.

In the same neck of the woods, you'll find something very different—the Trammel Crow Museum. Once a private collection, it has grown into one of the largest collections of Asian art in the American Southwest. More than 300 objects and works of art from India, Japan, and China (including deities, shrines, scrolls, and vases) are amassed in a 12,000-square-foot space.

As you walk south toward the center of downtown Dallas—finally in dire need of a water break—you will happily come upon Fountain Palace. The fountain, one of Dallas's most popular sites, bears a famous signature; it was designed by I. M. Pei, who created the pyramidal entrance to the Louvre. More than a million gallons of water leap and dance in rhythm, while 172 bubbler fountains shoot water high into the air. Cool. Actually, very cool.

I. M. PEI. FOUNTAIN PALACE. DALLAS, TX.

Elsewhere in Dallas, you'll find quirky and not-so-quirky museums, collections, and sites, including the American Museum of Miniature Arts (fantastic dollhouses, tiny toy soldiers, itty-bitty trains and cars); the African American Museum of Art, History, and Culture (the only one in the Southwest and the largest in the nation); the Meadows Museum (nicknamed "The Prado on the Prairie" with one of the major collections of Spanish art outside Spain); and the Women's Museum: An Institute for the Future (an exhibit that focuses on contributions of women throughout American history). Speaking of the very near future, Dallas will soon be home to the cubic Dee and Charles Wyly Theater, designed by the pioneering Dutch architect Rem Koolhaas.

Pioneer Plaza—the setting for 70 six-foot-tall bronze longhorn steers being driven across a stream by a team of cowboys—is

RENZO PIANO. NASHER SCULPTURE CENTER, VIEW OF THE GARDEN. DALLAS, TX.

probably the largest bronze monument in the world. Speaking of longhorns, the Longhorn Trolley will steer you (pun intended) toward any of the three main districts that make up the metropolitan area of Fort Worth—the Cultural District, downtown/Sundance Square, and the Fort Worth Stockyards National Historic District.

Some of the country's best small museums are lined up like ducks in a row in Fort Worth's Cultural District—the Kimbell Art Museum, the Amon Carter Museum, and the Modern Art Museum. The Kimbell has, in fact, been called "America's best small museum." The initial funding was provided in the will of the industrialist Kay Kimbell, who called for a first-class museum in his name. In the 30 years since it opened its doors, the museum has amassed a diverse collection of art from antiquity to the modern, from Asia to Mesoamerica to Africa. It is best known, however, for its stunning examples of European painting and sculpture from the Renaissance through the twentieth century. You will see works by Caravaggio, El Greco, Vigée-Lebrun, Delacroix, Monet, Renoir, Cézanne, Leger, Miró, and more—wrapped in the extraordinary architecture of Louis I. Kahn, one of the significant modern architects of the twentieth century.

The Amon Carter Museum opened in 1961 as a niche collection of Western art that belonged to the Fort Worth publisher and philanthropist Amon G. Carter. The original 400 paintings have grown to more than 300,000 works of art, and curators have cast a wide aesthetic net to include all styles of American paintings, drawings, prints, photographs, and sculptures.

LOUIS I. KAHN. KIMBELL MUSEUM. FORT WORTH, TX.

More recently, the Carter expanded (tripled!) its exhibition space to do what some museums cannot afford to do—bring their treasures out of storage and into public view.

The nearby Modern Art Museum of Fort Worth amplifies the city's modern and American collections with its mission of collecting and presenting post–World War II art. The roster of artists in its permanent collection reads like a *Who's Who* in European and American art at midcentury and beyond: Pablo Picasso and Hans Hofmann; Jackson Pollock and Willem de Kooning; Agnes Martin and Dan Flavin; Andy Warhol and Jean-Michel Basquiat; Bill Viola and Tony Oursler; and the list goes on and on—at least 2,800 objects in all. But the permanent collection represents only a part of what the museum has to offer. Its vast interior (150,000 square feet) also provides ample space for changing installations of contemporary work in all mediums.

The Fort Worth Stockyards and downtown Fort Worth offer two distinct clusters of tourist sites. As the name suggests, the Stockyards have a long

THE DEE AND CHARLES WYLY THEATER.

and distinct history. If you are in the mood for a close-up look at how "Cowtown" got its name—including Cattleman's Walk, the Fort Worth Livestock Exchange, and the Cowtown (rodeo) Coliseum—this is your destination.

If, on the other hand, the symphony or ballet or opera is your game, blaze your trail to downtown/Sundance Square and visit the Bass Performance Hall. Nancy Lee and Perry R. Bass donated the land for this remarkable space, and it was built by private donations to the tune of $67.5 million. Cowtown architecture it is not. The structure is modeled after the great opera houses of old Europe, complete with an 80-foot-diameter dome and two 48-foot angels flanking a bank of tall, arched windows on the facade. In a bow to pride and tradition, this neo–Beaux Arts design is rendered in homegrown Texas limestone.

Dallas and Fort Worth offer a study in contrasts, but they also share common ground. Both cities, their traditions and their cultural aspirations, aim to preserve their unique identities and balance those identities with awareness of the world and their place in the world—and, of course, in Texas.

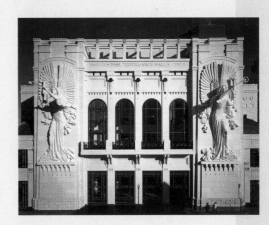

BASS PERFORMANCE HALL, SHOWING THE 48-FOOT ANGELS. FORT WORTH, TX.

TO CONTINUE YOUR TOUR and learn more about Dallas/Fort Worth, go to CourseMate.

I think art can exist within any craft tradition. Craft is just another way of saying means. I think it's a question of conscious intention, finally, and personal gifts, or giftedness. It seems that in art there is a primacy of idea over both means or craft, and function. Idea has to transcend both. I think this is probably why it's so difficult to make art out of something functional, or in a realm where craft has been nurtured for its own sake.

—Martin Puryear

CRAFT AND DESIGN

12

Consider this story concerning one of the Metropolitan Museum of Art's most precious acquisitions, as retold by art critic Arthur C. Danto.[1] According to Thomas Hoving, the director of the museum at the time of the purchase, the vase in Figure 12-1 is "the single most perfect work of art I ever encountered . . . an object of total adoration." In his memoirs, Hoving further described his feelings upon his first encounter with the piece: "The first thought that came to mind was that I was gazing not at a vase, but at a painting." The director was obviously swept off his feet by this masterpiece of Greek art—a terra-cotta vessel painted with the scene of the *Dead Sarpedon Carried by Thanatos and Hypnos* and signed by both the potter and the painter. But why did Hoving diminish the significance of the potter's craft by essentially dismissing the pot as a mere vehicle for the work of an extraordinary painter? Danto suggests that Hoving's reaction is indicative of an art-world prejudice of sorts—one that attaches less importance to functional and decorative objects of any kind. He warns that "the painting [on the vase] is there to decorate an object of conspicuous utility" and cannot be considered without reference to the vase itself. In fact, doing so precludes any real understanding of the work in the historical and artistic context in which it was created.

---

[1] Arthur C. Danto, "Fine Art and the Functional Object," *Glass*, no. 51 (Spring 1993): 24–29.

JENNIFER McCURDY. *Coral Nest* (2009). Porcelain. H: 9".

12-1 EUPHRONIOS AND EUXITHEOS. *Calyx Krater* (1st quarter of 5th century BCE). Ceramic. H: 18"; D: 21 11/16". Villa Giulia, Rome, Italy.

What purpose does this argument have for us who, as students, are trying to understand art? Simply this: The distinction between fine art and functional object is linked to the historical and cultural context in which a work was created. As Danto pointed out, the Greek philosophers placed craftsmen somewhere between artists and philosophers, artists occupying the lowest rung. Danto paraphrases Plato in *The Republic*: "The carpenter knows how to fashion in real life what the painter can merely imitate; therefore . . . artists have no real knowledge at all, trafficking only in the outward appearance of things."[2] More than 2,000 years later, a French philosopher would declare, "Only what serves no purpose is truly beautiful,"[3] suggesting a sure separation between fine art and craft. The mediums of paint and bronze might be used to create works of art in which, to paraphrase Puryear, the idea transcends craft and function. But those materials closest to the artisan—clay, glass, and fiber, metal—these materials were the purview of craft art that prioritized technical skill and utility over the "idea." Today, such lines are often blurred. Miriam Schapiro's *Wonderland* (see Fig. 1-35), according to this distinction, would most certainly be labeled a work of fine art. Yet the composition is a conglomeration of bits and pieces of time-honored craft techniques: quiltmaking, needlework, and crochet. The work does not have a utilitarian function, but it does cast a spotlight on some of the functional objects that provided outlets for artistic expression by women for whom access to the world of fine art was the equivalent of intergalactic travel. As we have seen in Chapter 9, ceramic

artists are creating works of sculpture, and sculptors are finding innovative ways to manipulate clay, wood, and metal. Glassmaking has reached new heights of experimentation while employing centuries-old techniques. Some artists view the distinction between art and craft as artificial, limiting, and even denigrating. Others embrace that distinction, which has, after all, a pedigree going back to Plato.

In this chapter, we take a close look at the functional and artistic aspects of craftmaking and materials traditional to craft—clay, glass, fiber, metal, and wood. We also examine the ubiquity of design in our daily lives through examples of graphic design, industrial design, web design, and urban design. In design, as with craft, the distinction between art for art's sake and art for utility's sake is also sometimes blurred.

CERAMICS

Ceramics are objects made of clay. In the singular, ceramic refers to materials and processes that are used to produce a range of products including familiar **pottery** pots and bowls, clay sculptures, baked bricks, and the tiles that protect the outer surfaces of space shuttles from the intense heat of atmospheric reentry.

Methods of Working with Clay

Ceramics was a highly refined craft in the ancient Middle East and China, but its roots go back further than that. For thousands of years, people have worked wet clay with their

12-2 MARIA MARTINEZ AND JULIAN MARTINEZ. Bowl with plumed serpent (1920–30). Coiled and burnished earthenware. 6" × 9½". Gift of Amelia Elizabeth White, 1937. Newark Museum, Newark, NJ.

[2] Ibid.
[3] Théophile Gautier, Preface to his novel *Mademoiselle de Maupin*, 1835.

1 ft.

12-3 CHERYL ANN THOMAS. *Relic 130* (2008). Porcelain. 22" × 16" × 10".

hands to create functional vessels for such basic things as carrying water or storing grain. Clay was patted and pinched and rolled, well before the invention of the potter's wheel, and these basic hand-built techniques continued (and still do) alongside wheel-thrown pottery. Shaping clay is only part of the process. To achieve hard, durable, and waterproof vessels, clay must be exposed to heat or fire.

Ancient cultures, such as Mesopotamia and Egypt, dried or baked clay and mud bricks in the broiling desert sun. Early ceramics were also hardened by fire in stone pits covered with flammable natural materials such as dried grasses, branches, perhaps even coal. Insulated **kilns**, or ovens, were developed to control temperature and regulate the firing process. Facility with firing techniques—and a growing knowledge of varieties of clay composition and ways to manipulate surface coatings, or **glazes**—culminated in magnificent, complex objects, valued as much for their artistic as utilitarian importance.

The earliest hand-built ceramics are described by their simple techniques. Pinch pots were created by shaping a lump of clay into a small cuplike container, slab pots by seaming together five flat slabs (four for the sides, one for the bottom). Coil pots are built from ropes of clay (you probably remember making snakes in preschool in exactly the same way) that are stacked on one another or coiled like a beehive. After the ropes are stacked, tools can be used to smooth them together, inside and out, or they might be left as is to reveal the coiling process.

These different effects can be seen in two examples of coiling. The perfect contours of the black-on-black, coil-built vessel of Native American potter Maria Martinez (Fig. **12-2**) were

created by smoothing the ridges of the stacked coils into flat, thin walls that belie the process. The surface effect of etched glass was achieved through a complex interplay of burnishing, glazing, and firing techniques. In Cheryl Ann Thomas's work (Fig. **12-3**), by contrast, individual coils retain their shape identity rather than being smoothed together. They are nestled next to one another and then folded and molded into trompe l'oeil objects resembling woven cloth. For Thomas, creating the delicate ropes of clay through the rhythmic movements of her hands forges an intimate connection with her material.

The Potter's Wheel

The potter's wheel (Fig. **12-4**) was first used in the Middle East around 4000 BCE and seems to have come into common use a thousand years later. A pot can be **thrown** quite rapidly and effortlessly on a wheel once the techniques have been mastered, in contrast to the more laborious and time-consuming process of building a pot by coiling. The walls of a wheel-thrown pot tend to be thinner and more uniform in thickness than those of coiled pots, and the outer and inner surfaces are smoother. As we saw in the work of Martinez, however, hand-built pots can be as thin walled and symmetrical as their wheel-thrown counterparts.

Anyone who has been a student of ceramics appreciates the difficulty of getting the rhythm of the potter's wheel. The

12-4 *The Hands of the Potter.*
Conrad Knowles forming a tray and a bowl for his collection of artful pottery.

1 in.

speed of the wheel, placement of the clay, downward pressure of the hands, and force (or delicate touch) of the fingers are an exercise in extreme coordination. The goal, generally, is to achieve perfect symmetry and a smooth contour. How ironic, then, is the work of Jennifer McCurdy (Fig. **12-5**), who begins by throwing on the wheel and then quickly shapes, folds, and slices into her clay with an X-Acto knife. Two firings produce rock-hard porcelain objects that, in the potter's words, "are so durable that they should last 10,000 years." The result subverts the wheel-thrown technique and typically utilitarian function of a clay vessel and blur the boundaries between sculpture and ceramics, fine art and craft.

Glazing

Pottery is glazed for functional and artistic reasons. Without a glaze, a clay pot would remain porous and therefore useless for carrying liquids. Even the simplest glaze—a glassy coating applied to the surface of a vessel—will make it impervious to water. But the variety of glazing techniques and effects devised by potters for aesthetic purposes is rich, diverse, and connected to strong cultural traditions.

Glazing appears on clay bricks that date back to a thirteenth-century-BCE temple in Iran, and both the ancient Egyptian and Mesopotamian river cultures offer sophisticated examples of glazing. The earliest known glaze in Egypt—characteristically blue-green in hue—was found on a nonclay tile from the tomb of the Egyptian pharaoh Menes and dates from about 3000 BCE. In the sixth cen-

tury BCE, ancient Babylonians constructed the Ishtar Gate from glazed bricks in a similar blue-green palette. By the first centuries and millennium CE, glazed ceramics was an accomplished art form across cultures from China and Japan to the Middle East, Southeast Asia, and more.

The surface characteristics of glazed pottery can be glossy or matte, smooth or textured, monochromatic or polychromatic, and simple or complex in pattern or decoration. All of these variations depend on the composition of the glaze, the temperature of the kiln, and sometimes multiple firings.

Glazes usually contain silica, found in sand or quartz, ground metals that facilitate the melting of silica into glass in the presence of heat, and other chemical compounds that produce a range of specific colors. Dry glazes can be rubbed onto clay, and liquid glazes—chemicals combined with ground minerals and liquid—can be brushed, sprayed,

12-6 EMMANUEL COOPER. Bowls, stoneware, thrown and turned, slip, multiple glaze, 12¼" max.

12-7 CHESTER NEALIE. *Bottle* (2000). Celadon glaze. H: 11¾".

scale drip compositions (see Chapter 21). Arneson's Pollock looks as if he stepped out of his Hamptons studio, his face an accidental and unsuspecting "canvas" for his signature drips, whips, and spatters. Arneson's glazed ceramics are purposefully purposefully unrefined and intentionally flawed, mirroring his view of human nature as imperfect.

12-8 ROBERT ARNESON. *Jackson Pollock* (1983). Glazed ceramic.
23" × 13" × 7". Collection of Dr. Paul and Stacy Polydoran. Art © Estate of Robert Arneson/Licensed by VAGA, NY.

poured, or spattered onto the surface. A potter might also dip an object into a bath, so to speak, of liquid glaze.

Contrast the rough textured surfaces of Emmanuel Cooper's earthenware bowls (Fig. **12-6**) with the stunning glasslike finish of Chester Nealie's *Bottle* (Fig. **12-7**). The glaze on Cooper's bowls is reminiscent of volcanic rock or the cratered surface of the moon, while Nealie's pearlescent glaze enhances the sensual, graceful contours of what looks like a fragile glass vessel. These represent only two examples of the degree to which glazing affects the substance and sensibility of a piece, or, as in Robert Arneson's ceramic sculpture, its very meaning. *Jackson Pollock* (Fig. **12-8**) was an Abstract Expressionist painter who shook the art world with his large-

1 in.

12-9 *Krishna Killing the Horse Demon Keshi.* Gupta period (ca. 321–500), 5th century India (Uttar Pradesh). Terra-cotta. H: 21". The Metropolitan Museum of Art, NY.

Types of Ceramics

Ceramics are classified by their clay composition and by the temperature at which they are fired. **Earthenware** is pottery made from slightly porous clay that has been fired at relatively low kiln temperatures (1,000 to 2,000 degrees Fahrenheit). **Terra-cotta**, hard-baked red clay that has been fired at higher temperatures (2,070 to 2,320 degrees Fahrenheit), is used to create pottery, sculpture, building bricks, tile roofs, and architectural ornamentation with a characteristic reddish-brown hue. Utilitarian terra-cotta vessels are common finds in ancient archaeological sites, but the material was also used for sophisticated and large-scale works. The intricately carved and graphically realistic terra-cotta relief (Fig. **12-9**) from India's Gupta period illustrates Krishna, one of the avatars of the god Vishnu, battling and killing a

demon in the guise of a horse. Reliefs such as this one provided sculptural ornamentation on the exterior of stone and brick temples. Other terra-cotta works in your text include a carved sarcophagus from the Etruscan civilization (see Fig. 14-18), the renowned terra-cotta warriors from China's Han Dynasty (see Fig. 1-12), and several examples of pottery in Chapter 14.

Earthenware and terra-cotta span centuries and cultures, and contemporary potters continue to produce works from the same materials. Betty Woodman is described as one of the most important ceramic artists working today, blurring the boundaries between art and craft and conjoining cultural influences—East and West—in her painted vases. Works like *Aztec Vase #06-1* (Fig. **12-10**) belie functionality in their sculptural sensibility even though they are actual vessels. Her glazes and hand-painted decoration show a wide range of artistic references gleaned from her global voyages and

12-10 BETTY WOODMAN. *Aztec Vase #06-1* (2006). Glazed earthenware, epoxy resin, lacquer, and paint. 62" × 42" × 9".

1 in.

12-11 CLAUDI CASANOVAS. *Block #43* (2001). 11¾" × 11¾" × 10¼".

fine, white kaolin clay and contains other minerals such as feldspar, quartz, and flint in various proportions. It is usually fired at 2,400 to 2,500 degrees Fahrenheit, and it is used for fine dinnerware. Chinese porcelain, or **china**, is white and fired at low temperatures. It is vitreous and nonporous, and it may be translucent. It makes a characteristic ringing sound when struck with a fingernail. Porcelain has been used by various cultures for vases and dinnerware for thousands of years, as well as for ceramic sculpture.

Harumi Nakashima's *Porcelain Form* (Fig. **12-12**), with its slippery-smooth surface and meticulously rounded shapes, stands in sharp contrast to the coarse textures often given center stage in other types of ceramics. The repetition in the polka-dotted glaze complements the rhythms found in the budding, biomorphic protuberances. Whereas the colors and textures of Casanovas's *Block* suggest the essence of tactile reality, Nakashima's bulging, morphing, amoeba-like sculpture seems surreal—outside or beyond conscious experience.

One of the fascinating features of clay is its versatility. It is said that one test of the integrity of a work is its truth to its material. In the case

the history of art. Woodman freely adopts shapes and colors from styles she is most drawn to, sometimes mixing and matching them on opposite sides of a vase. Her work is marked by an eclecticism and pluralism that energize her pieces and pay homage to a host of diverse styles.

Stoneware is usually gray or brown—owing to impurities in its clay—and vitreous or semivitreous (glasslike). It is very strong and durable and is therefore commonly used for cookware, dinnerware, and much ceramic sculpture. Claudi Casanovas's *Block #43* (Fig. **12-11**) is a hollow, cubic-form, stoneware sculpture that simulates the crude textures of hardened clay found in nature. The palette of glazes—black, brown, beige, and a hint of gold—deep fissures, and irregular contours combine to create the effect of a naturally occurring rock that has been worn away by time and the elements.

Porcelain is hard, nonporous, and usually white or gray in color. It is made from

1 in.

12-12 HARUMI NAKASHIMA. *Porcelain Form* (2001). Porcelain. Inlaid decoration. 19¾" × 17¾" × 15¾". Den Bosch, Netherlands.

A CLOSER LOOK THE CHANDELIERS OF DALE CHIHULY

*They're going to think we're nuts over there, and of course
we are a little nuts, but we'll get this thing built.*
—Dale Chihuly, about the Icicle Creek chandelier

"A LITTLE BIT NUTS." Artists, and even the rest of us, may have felt this way or been characterized this way at some point or another, especially when we were seeing things in an unconventional way. Glass artist Dale Chihuly has redefined the conventional definition and function of *chandelier* by designing works he describes by this name for public spaces from Venice to Jerusalem, from the world's great museums to the wilderness of the great outdoors. Although many chandeliers, in the traditional sense, are ornamental, they are also functional objects used, with candles or electricity, to illuminate an environment. But Chihuly's chandeliers are a different species. They do not emit light of their own. Rather, they reflect and transform ambient light—batteries not included.

Chihuly's extraordinary glassworks capture, amplify, and channel light. In their unusual stylistic juxtaposition with their surroundings, his chandeliers compel passersby to take another look at the context in which they are set—whether the Byzantine architecture and canals we find in Venice (Fig. 12-13), the ancient ruins in Jerusalem, or in the wilderness, the literal natural state of affairs.

Chihuly designed the chandelier shown in Figure 12-14 for the Sleeping Lady mountain retreat at Icicle Creek in the state of Washington. He erected it on an ancient granite boulder among the grand pines of a primeval setting, surrounded by a river and a profusion of wildlife. The chandelier reflects and amplifies the frosted serenity of the site in winter. It enriches visitors' relationships with the area surrounding the retreat and with nature as a whole. The chandelier also adds Chihuly's—and humankind's—personal stamp to a pristine wooded site. It also says some-

12-13 DALE CHIHULY. *Rio delle Torreselle Chandelier* (1996). A chandelier installation in the Rio delle Torreselle, part of the *Chihuly over Venice* project, Venezia Aperto Vetro. Venice, Italy.

Chihuly is a luminist. He uses glass as a literal and metaphorical prism through which he projects both ambient and intense theatrical light to produce sublime, luminous effects. This connects him to the long history of art in which light is cherished, "otherworldly," and implies divine presence.

—Jack Cowart

thing about the vision and the passion of the artist—unique in this case to Dale Chihuly, though made visual by a team of glassblowers and technicians. Does the work have deeper symbolic meanings—meanings that connect it with the history of art and civilization, meanings that connect it with contemporary technology and modes of expression? Much of the answer to that question lies in you. Perhaps you would like to consider these lines from Wallace Stevens's poem "Anecdote of the Jar":

I placed a jar in Tennessee,
And round it was, upon a hill.
It made the slovenly wilderness
Surround that hill.
The wilderness rose up to it,
And sprawled around, no longer wild.*

---

* From *The Collected Poems of Wallace Stevens* by Wallace Stevens, © 1945 by Wallace Stevens and renewed 1982 by Holly Stevens. Used by permission of Alfred A. Knopf, a division of Random House, Inc.

12-14 DALE CHIHULY. *Icicle Creek Chandelier* (1996). Sleeping Lady Conference Retreat, Leavenworth, WA.

of ceramics, however, one would be hard pressed to point to any one of the products of clay as representative of its "true" face.

GLASS

Glass, like ceramics, has had a long and multifarious history. The Roman historian Pliny the Elder traced the origins of glassmaking to an accidental discovery and an account of Phoenician sailors preparing a meal on a beach. They set their pots on lumps of *natron* (an alkali they had on deck to embalm the dead) and lit a fire, and when the hot natron mixed with the sand of the beach, molten glass flowed. In actual fact, glass predates the Phoenicians and the Romans (earliest examples date back to the civilizations of Mesopotamia and Old Kingdom Egypt), and Pliny's tale is certainly anecdotal and embellished. But the truth is that the recipe for glass is quite simple. Researchers have recreated the Phoenicians' scenario and have come to this conclusion: It could happen.[4] The result may not have been that wondrous substance—transparent or translucent—that has the power to transform light into an ephemeral, jewel-like palette, but it was surely glass. Glass is generally made from molten sand, or **silica**, mixed with minerals such as lead, potash, soda, and lime. Rich hues in glass are achieved by adding metal oxides with distinct color properties to molten silica: copper oxide produces green, and cobalt renders a deep blue.

Methods of Working with Glass

Glassblowing was discovered around 50 BCE, and with that the history of glassmaking was transformed. Earlier techniques included cold-working, in which room-temperature lumps of glass were scratched, ground, or delicately chipped to form objects, and casting, in which molten glass was poured into heat-resistant molds. Like ceramics, glass is a versatile medium. Molten glass can be modeled, pressed, rolled into sheets as it cools, and even spun into threads, as it is for **fiberglass**. Fine filaments can be woven into textiles, used in woolly masses for insulation, or molded into a material that is tough enough to be used for the body of an automobile.

Historically speaking, glassblowing was the game changer. Developed by the Romans, the technique enabled the creation of glass vessels of all shapes, sizes, functions, and colors. Glassblowing begins with a hollow tube or blowpipe that is dipped into molten glass and removed. Air is blown through the tube, causing the hot glass to expand to form a spherical bubble whose contours are shaped through rolling and pulling with various tools.

The *Portland Vase* (Fig. **12-15**), one of the earliest and best-known pieces of Roman glassware, was created in three steps: the body of the vessel was blown from dark blue glass; a coating of semi-opaque white glass was added to the surface of the basic blue vase; and the figures and vegetation that circumscribe the vase were carved in bas-relief on the white glass in subtle gradations of depth. Where the white glass is thinnest and therefore most translucent, the blue of the vase glows through and provides shading to the images. Imagine the

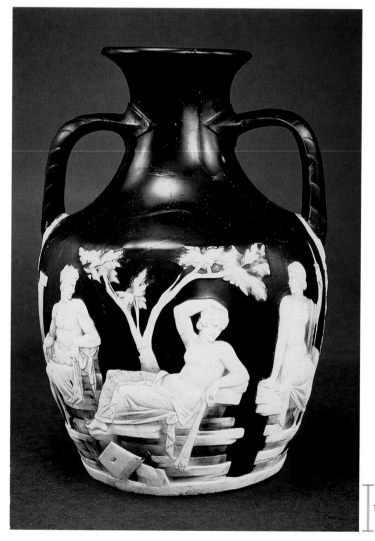

12-15 *Portland Vase* (Roman, 3rd century). Cameo-cut glass. H: 9½"; D: 7". British Museum, London, England.

[4] William S. Ellis, "Glass: Capturing the Dance of Light," *National Geographic* 184, no. 6 (December 1993): 37–69.

delicacy of the handling—glass chipped away from glass, leaving unscratched the brittle blue surface that serves as background for the figures. Roman glassmaking skills were renowned in the ancient world, and cultures that had contact with the Romans—such as the Hindu kingdoms of India and the Arab world—adopted their techniques.

Different world centers became renowned for glassmaking in different eras. During the Middle Ages, stained-glass windows achieved their peak of perfection in French (see Fig. 15-30) and German cathedrals, while in Venice, luxury glass was prized for its lightness and delicacy. In the eighteenth century, on the other side of the Atlantic Ocean in Pennsylvania, Stiegel glass was known for a special hardness and brilliance attributed to the use of flint (lead oxide). **Flint glass** was used to create lenses for optical instruments and for fine crystal. Nineteenth-century Sandwich glass—from the town of Sandwich, Massachusetts—replicated the appearance of carved glass, but its patterns were created by pressing molten glass into molds. Ornamental Sandwich glass pieces in the shapes of cats, dogs, hens, and ducks became common home decorations.

During the second half of the nineteenth century, the name of Louis Comfort Tiffany became synonymous with expert handling of glass as a medium. His studios produced vases whose graceful, attenuated botanical forms married simplicity and exotic refinement, but the real treasures of Tiffany's oeuvre are his stained-glass windows. Large in scale, complex in imagery, and endlessly nuanced in palette, windows such as *Magnolias and Irises* (Fig. **12-16**) exhibit some of the particular material characteristics of much of Tiffany's work. Inspired by ancient glassware and the saturated colors of medieval stained glass, Tiffany sought to create recipes for glassmaking that produced rich color, yes, but also texture, opacity, and surface shimmer. In 1880, he patented **Favrile glass**, a technique of mixing together different colors of hot glass that yielded an iridescent finish. Tiffany described the result: "Favrile glass is distinguished by brilliant or deeply toned colors, usually iridescent like the wings of certain American butterflies, the necks of pigeons and peacocks, the wing covers of various beetles."

12-16 LOUIS COMFORT TIFFANY. *Magnolias and Irises* (c. 1908). Leaded Favrile glass. 60¼" × 42". Anonymous Gift, in memory of Mr. and Mrs. A. B. Frank, 1981 (1981.159). The Metropolitan Museum of Art, NY. Image copyright © The Metropolitan Museum of Art / Art Resource, NY.

1 ft.

TEXTILE ARTS

Textile arts are arts and crafts in which **fibers** are used to make functional or decorative objects or works of art. **Fibers** are slender, threadlike structures that are derived from animals (for example, wool or silk), plants (cotton, hemp, flax, or jute), or synthetic materials (rayon, nylon, or fiberglass). Textile techniques include, but are not limited to, weaving, embroidery, crochet, and macramé.

Weaving

Weaving was well known to the ancient Egyptians and Mesopotamians, although some examples date back to the Stone Age. Weaving was a staple craft in ancient and traditional cultures, including Native Americans of the desert Southwest and South Americans of the Amazon region. Textile art reached a degree of unparalleled accomplishment in Medieval Europe and in Islamic countries, where technological innovations contributed to the development of the craft.

The **weaving** of textiles is accomplished by interlacing horizontal and vertical threads—threads that are on a right angle to each other. The lengthwise fibers are called the **warp**, and the crosswise threads are called the **weft** or **woof**. The particular fiber and weave determine the weight and quality of the cloth. Wool, for example, makes soft, resilient cloth that is easy to dye. Nylon is strong, more durable than wool, mothproof, resistant to mildew and mold, nonallergenic, and also easy to dye.

There are many types of weave structures. The **plain** weave found in burlap, muslin, and cotton broadcloth is the strongest and simplest: the woof thread passes above one warp fiber and beneath the next. In the **satin weave**, woof threads pass above and beneath several warp threads. Warp and woof form broken diagonal patterns in the **twill weave**. In **pile weaving**, which is found in carpeting and in velvet, loops or knots are tied; when the knotting is complete, the ends are cut or sheared to create an even surface. In sixteenth-century Persia, where carpet weaving reached an artistic peak, pile patterns often had as many as 1,000 knots to the square inch.

The *Ardabil Carpet* (Figure **12-17**), completed in 1539–1540, is the oldest *dated* carpet in the history of art, although weaving has been an integral part of Persian culture since ancient times. Persian carpets are refined in technique, ambitious in size, and dazzling in color and complexity. They are classified according to design, pattern, and motif, in traditional and innovative combinations and variations. The *Ardabil Carpet* was woven of short pieces of wool that were knotted onto silk warps and wefts. As each row was completed, it was packed down and the pile trimmed to an even height after the entire rug was finished. The pattern consists of 10 colors. A large field with interlacing flowers and vines provides a backdrop for a central medallion surrounded by 16 pointed ovals. Hanging from the ovals—at 12 o'clock and 6 o'clock—are two lamps, the pointed bottoms of which face in opposite directions. The field is surrounded by four parallel bands of different widths filled with intricate patterns. The carpet, commissioned by an Iranian ruler for the shrine of an ancestor, had as many as 10 weavers working on it at the same time.

The *Ardabil Carpet* was created on a loom. During the Islamic Golden Age, foot pedals were introduced to operate looms, thus facilitating the weaving process. The Alaskan Chilkat robe (Fig. **12-18**), however, was created by Native American weaver Dorica Jackson without a loom. Chilkat women traditionally achieved a very fine texture with a thread

12-17 Ardabil Carpet, Iran (1539–1540). Woolen pile. 34" × 17½". Victoria and Albert Museum, London, England.

made from a core of a strand of cedar bark covered with the wool from a mountain goat. Clan members used robes such as these on important occasions to show off the family crest. Here a strikingly stylized, winged animal occupies the center of a field of eyes, heads, and mysterious symbols.

Traditional weaving techniques may surface in innovative ways in the hands of contemporary artists. Ed Rossbach's wall hanging (Fig. **12-19**), which, in overall shape, is not unlike the Chilkat robe, is worlds apart in its choice of materials and strong political message. Rossbach plaits construction paper in such a manner that his image emerges subtly from an overall mottled background.

The surfaces of fabrics can be enhanced by printing, embroidery, tie-dyeing, or batik. Hand printing has been known since ancient times, and Oriental traders brought the practice to Europe. A design was stamped on a fabric with a carved wooden block that had been inked. Contemporary machine printing uses inked rollers in the place of blocks, and fabrics can be printed at astonishingly rapid rates. In **embroidery**, the design is made by needlework.

Tie-dyeing and batik both involve dyeing fabrics. In **tie-dyeing**, designs are created by sewing or tying folds in the cloth to prevent the dye from coloring certain sections of fabric (Figs. 12-22 and 12-23). In **batik**, applications of wax prevent the dye from coloring sections of fabric that are to be kept light or white. A series of dye baths and waxings can be used to create subtly deeper colors.

Basket Weaving

In **basket weaving**, or basketry, animal or vegetable fibers (such as twigs, grasses, straw, and animal hair) are woven into baskets or other containers. Basket weaving is, like ceramics and textiles, an ancient craft, but because natural materials disintegrate, there is little physical evidence of such early basketry. Yet imprints of the woven patterns of baskets to decorate the surface of clay pots give us a sense of what the craft must have been. As with the other crafts we have considered, basket making crosses time and culture.

Pomo gift baskets, created by Native Americans from Northern California, are woven from materials such as grass, glass beads, shells and feathers (Fig. **12-20**). The Pomo have been described as the finest basket weavers in the world. Baskets such as the one illustrated were not woven for utilitarian purposes but rather served as gifts and treasures.

12-18 DORICA JACKSON. Chilkat robe (1976). Cedar bark warp; sheep's wool wefts. W: 60".

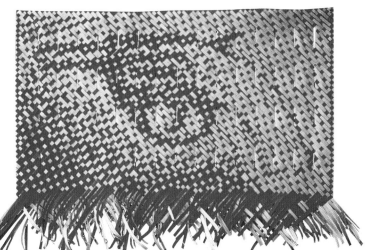

12-19 ED ROSSBACH. *Handgun* (1975). Plaited construction paper. 40" × 54". Craft Alliance, St. Louis, MO.

12-20 Ceremonial feathered basket with bead and shell pendants. Pomo, CA (1900). H: 3½". Phoebe A. Hearst Museum of Anthropology, University of California, Berkeley, CA.

FAITH RINGGOLD WAS BORN in Harlem in 1930 and educated in the public schools of New York City. Raised with a social conscience, she painted murals and other works inspired by the civil rights movement in the 1960s and, a decade later, took to feminist themes after her exclusion from an all-male exhibition at New York's School of Visual Arts. Ringgold's mother, a fashion designer, was always sewing, the artist recalls, and at this time the artist turned to sewing and related techniques—needlepoint, beading, braided ribbon, and sewn fabric—to produce soft sculptures such as those in *Mama Jones, Andrew, Barbara, and Faith* (Fig. 12-21), from her series *The Family of Women*. African garments inspired the clothing of these family members, and the faces are reminiscent of African masks.

More recently, Ringgold is most well known for her narrative quilts, such as the highly acclaimed *Tar Beach* (see Fig. 1-28), which combine traditions common to African Americans and women—storytelling and quilting. *Matisse's Chapel* (Fig. 12-22) is from Ringgold's *French Collection*, which inserts contemporary American artists, other colleagues, and family members into French settings. In one quilt, *Dancing at the Louvre*, friends, including the children of one, are shown in high spirits before the *Mona Lisa*. In *Picasso's Studio*, the famed Spanish artist (literally) draws inspiration for *Les Demoiselles d'Avignon* from a black model. In an ironic twist on Manet's *Luncheon on the Grass* (see Fig. 19-12), a nude Picasso sits on the grass in the company of clothed women. *Matisse's Chapel* places a wedding party composed of the artist's family in the chapel made famous by dint of Matisse's contributions.

Crown Heights Children's Story Quilt (Fig. 12-23) is on permanent display at a Brooklyn public school. The quilt pictures 12 folktales of peoples who have contributed to the life of New York, including Jamaicans and West Africans (the top three on the left), the Dutch (upper right), two Native American peoples, Asians, Puerto Ricans, Italian Americans, and Jewish Americans. True to the genre of quilting, the artist uses her skills to patch together the myths and stories of different peoples in a nation composed of diverse ethnic groups.

12-21 FAITH RINGGOLD. *Mama Jones, Andrew, Barbara, and Faith* (1973). Embroidery and sewn fabric. 74" × 69".

12-22 FAITH RINGGOLD. *Matisse's Chapel* (1991). Acrylic on canvas; tie-dyed, pieced fabric border. 74" × 79½". From *The French Collection* series, Part I, #6.

1 ft.

12-23 FAITH RINGGOLD. *Crown Heights Children's Story Quilt* (1994). Painted and pieced fabric. 108" × 144".

1 ft.

12-24 Pectoral piece from Ordzhonikidze, Russia (4th century BCE). Gold. D: 12". Historical Museum, Kiev, Ukraine.

12-25 BENVENUTO CELLINI. *Saltcellar of Francis I* (1539–1543). Gold and enamel. H: 10"; L: 13¹⁄₁₆". Kunsthistorisches Museum, Vienna, Austria.

METALWORK AND JEWELRY

The process of refining and working with metals is called **metalwork**, a word that encompasses a range of diverse objects and projects from the industrial world to the jeweler's workshop. **Iron** and its alloys were used, in the Iron Age, for arrowheads and, in the Industrial Age, for skyscrapers. **Stainless steel** is used in common kitchen utensils but was also used for the uncommon pinnacle of New York City's Chrysler Building and by postwar American sculptors such as David Smith (see Fig. 21-28). Lightweight **aluminum** is used in cookware and in aircraft; **bronze** has been used for coins, weaponry, farm tools, and sculptural monuments.

Silver and gold have been prized for millennia for their rarity and their appealing colors and textures. They are used in jewelry, fine tableware, ritual vessels, and sacred objects. In jewelry, these precious metals often serve as settings for equally precious gems or polished stones, or their surfaces can be **enameled** by melting powdered glass on them. These metals even find use as currency; in times of political chaos, gold and silver are sought even as the value of paper money drops off to nothing. Threads of gold and silver find their way onto precious china and into the garments and vestments of clergy and kings. Gold leaf adorns books, paintings, and picture frames.

Metals can be hammered, **embossed** with raised designs, and cast using the same techniques described in the section on bronze sculpture in Chapter 9. Each method for working metal has its own tradition and its advantages and disadvantages.

The pectoral piece shown in Figure **12-24** was meant to be worn across the breast of a nomadic chieftain from southern Russia and probably to be buried with him. People and animals are depicted with a realism that renders the fanciful **griffins** in the lower register as believable as the horses, dogs, and grasshoppers found elsewhere in the piece. The open work of the figures is contrasted by the refined gold-on-gold scrollwork in the central register; all are bordered by magnificent, twisted coils.

The Renaissance sculptor and goldsmith Benvenuto Cellini created a gold and enamel saltcellar (Fig. **12-25**) for the French king Francis I that shows the refinement of his art. Its allegorical significance is merely an excuse for displaying the skill of Cellini's craft. Salt, drawn from the sea, is housed in a boat-shaped salt container and watched over by a figure of Neptune. The pepper, drawn from the earth, is contained in a miniature triumphal arch and guarded by a female personification of Earth. Figures on the base represent the seasons and the segments of the day—all on a pedestal only 13 inches in diameter. Unfortunately, the saltcellar is Cellini's sole major work in gold that survives.

12-26 Nose ornament, crayfish, Peru (Loma Negra, 3rd century CE). Gold, silver, turquoise inlay. H: 4¾". The Metropolitan Museum of Art, NY.

Body ornament, ever growing in popularity to this day, spans history and geography. Consider the nose ornament from Peru in Figure **12-26**. The piece is fashioned of gold, silver, and turquoise inlay and is a characteristic example of the ancient Peruvian facility in handling complex metal techniques. Much of the jewelry available for us to see today has been unearthed from tombs of the very wealthy among Peruvian society. The images and their symbolism remain mostly undeciphered, but archeologists have nonetheless constructed a view of these people from such artifacts.

Kiff Slemmons's *Transport* (Fig. **12-27**) is a miniature sculpture that again bridges the supposed gulf between fine art and the functional object. It was constructed for the *Artworks for*

12-27 KIFF SLEMMONS. *Transport* (1990). Sterling silver, aluminum, gauze, mesh, tape, tubing, pearls. 5" × 14" × 4½".

12-28 MELVYN FIRMAGER. *Untitled* (1993). Destroyed in 1994 Los Angeles earthquake. Eucalyptus gunnii. H: 13½"; D: 8".

12-29 DAVID ELLSWORTH. *Vessel* (1992). Norway maple burl. H: 4"; D: 7".

AIDS exhibition that was held in Seattle in 1990. It is a miniature two-wheeled cart that refers to the history of mass deaths. Throughout the ages, such carts have been used in cities to truck away the victims of epidemics. The wheels of the cart are clocks with human hands, seeming to tick away as the number of deaths due to AIDS mounts. Hospital waste and a stylized "progress" chart with an alarming indicator of the rising toll of the epidemic complete the political message.

WOOD

Some relatively sophisticated technology is required to convert glass, metal, and clay into something of use. Wood, however, has only to be cut and carved to form a functional object. Two wood vases hint at the versatility of the medium. The soft, flowing contours of Melvyn Firmager's vase (Fig. **12-28**) highlight the swirling grain patterns of the wood, which almost take on the character of glazing on a ceramic vase. The simple roundness, highly polished surface, and inherent grain patterns in David Ellsworth's vase (Fig. **12-29**) create the illusion of stone.

DESIGN

Design has a multiplicity of meanings. As a discipline or profession, it includes experts in industrial design (objects), fashion design (clothing), graphic design (communication),

and web design (the Internet), to name a few. As a process, it involves the act of designing or creating a concept and product for consumption, communication, or interaction. We refer to the finished product as a design.

Industrial Design: The Object

Objects are three-dimensional products designed for consumer use by industrial designers, also known as product designers. They run the gamut from utilitarian designs (form follows function) to those in which aesthetics override usability (form over function). There are good and bad designs, and then there are objects for which the question "Good or bad?" seems moot. Consider the common houseware item—the citrus juicer—in Figures **12-30** to **12-32**. The first juicer seems to have been designed foremost with utility in mind. The user halves an orange, inverts it onto a conical plastic piece that has pronounced ribs or ridges, and twists it one way or another to release the juice from the orange. The juice flows down the cone between the ridges and into a plastic collection bowl in a quick and tidy fashion. The second juicer is also based on a thoughtful concept. The user presses the orange half onto a ridged cone, twists it back and forth, and the juice is collected in a flat bowl with a spout on one end for pouring. A row of plastic teeth is placed forward of the spout to hold back seeds and unwanted pulp. The only problem is that these teeth are placed exactly where the user's knuckles hit when twisting the orange to extract the juice—a great design

12-31 *Juicer.*

12-30 *Citrus Express.*

12-32 PHILIPPE STARCK. *Juicy Salif.*

in theory, but certainly not in practice. Now take a look at famed French designer Philippe Starck's citrus squeezer titled *Juicy Salif*, purportedly conceived during a meal in which he was squeezing lemon over a squid. A clear example of "form over function," Starck's juicer has become an icon of 1990s design, not because it works well, but because it looks great. In fact, *Juicy Salif*'s manufacturer, Alessi, recommends it for display and not for use.

Although few of us looking for a juicer would actually opt for Starck's product, consumers often make choices based as much on product design and cache as usability. Apple's iPhone (Fig. **12-33**) is a case in point. In terms of function, the iPhone is the electronic equivalent of a Swiss Army knife. You can surf the web; send texts and e-mails; navigate using GPS; record notes; set an alarm to wake up in the morning; take, save, and send photos; and download and play music. You can also make phone calls. However, there are many

"smartphones" on the market, and a fair number of them compete in terms of function and are more economically priced than the iPhone. Even so, sales of the Apple product have swept the globe. In choosing an iPhone, consumers are not only buying a product but also buying into a lifestyle.

FORM AND FUNCTION IN PRODUCT DESIGN A great deal of contemporary product design embraces the philosophy of "form follows function" put forth by the architect Louis Sullivan, whose Wainwright Building we studied in Chapter 11 (see Fig. 11-17). Three of a multitude of examples come from the design collection of the Museum of Modern Art. Rody Graumans's *85 Lamps Lighting Fixture* (Fig. **12-34**) is an unadulterated cluster of naked lightbulbs and wiring that fans out into a more classic chandelier profile as a result of the spherical shapes of the touching bulbs. The "truth in art" that Sullivan sought through his philosophy seems also

12-33 iPhone. Apple, Inc.

Museum of Modern Art. The metal frame and mesh seat and back fully adjust to accommodate bodies of any shape, height, and weight. A tilt mechanism in the chair "floats" users with support no matter which position they are sitting in, and the mesh suspension system distributes weight equally. The quirky appearance of the Aeron Chair, a by-product of its adherence to ergonomic design, has achieved a sort of cult status among trendy office workers. One television commercial advertisement even shows 20-something-year-olds playing office hockey while cruising in their Aeron Chairs.

Graphic Design: Communication

Graphic design is an artistic process used to communicate information and ideas through writing, images, and symbols that are connected to contemporary human experience. Since the beginning of modern history, advances in technology—beginning with the printing press in the early 1400s—have enabled the global dissemination of graphic design products. Components of the graphic design include typography, page layout and book design, and corporate identity. Graphic design

12-34 RODY GRAUMANS. *85 Lamps Lighting Fixture* (1992). Light bulbs, cords, and sockets. H: 39" (100 cm); D: 39" (100 cm). The Museum of Modern Art, NY.

1 ft.

to have inspired Graumans's lighting fixture design: the whole truth and nothing but the truth, in fact.

Many objects of contemporary industrial design take **ergonomics**—the applied science of equipment design intended to minimize discomfort and therefore maximize performance of the user—into account. If your shoulders, neck, elbows, or wrists hurt from the physical stress of prolonged work at your computer, you can purchase an ergonomically designed keyboard that will keep your wrists at a proper angle and a mouse that will support the weight of your arm while mousing. These designs are based on the physiognomy of the human body and typical product use.

The Aeron Chair (Fig. **12-35**), ergonomically designed by Bill Stumpf and Don Chadwick, has emerged as the Porsche of office chairs and is also part of the design collection at the

12-35 BILL STUMPF AND DON CHADWICK. Aeron Chair. The Museum of Modern Art, NY.

mediums include photography, printmaking, computer-aided design, and digital design. The history of graphic design can be traced back to marks made by humans on the walls of caves and the earliest forms of writing. In this section, we will consider contemporary examples of graphic design as it is the most ubiquitous of art forms, entering our consciousness and our lives in a steady stream on a daily basis.

TYPOGRAPHY **Typography** is the technical term for designing and composing letterforms. Until the digital age, printing was done with movable pieces of metal (or wood) cast or carved with letters raised above the surface of the piece. These pieces were put together into strings of words and lines by typesetters. Today typesetting is done on computers, as is type design. Designers can choose from hundreds of typefaces and can manipulate things like scale, color, perspective, and the overlapping of letters and other images. A designer will use type to communicate with optimal clarity—a variant of form follows function—or with expressiveness. It is an eye-opener to realize that any and all type that we come into contact with as consumers originated with a graphic designer who was skilled in typography.

The clearest, most utilitarian form of typography is probably the pictogram, which is widely used in signage. From the simplified shapes of a woman in a dress and man in trousers, we can figure out which restroom is intended for whom, even if we find ourselves in a foreign country where we don't speak the language (Fig. **12-36**). So-called barrier-free communication is also seen in the now-familiar graphic design of a red circle with a line drawn through it signifying "NO!"—whatever *no* may apply to. The pictogram in Figure **12-37** consists of simple, easily understood symbols designating areas in which smoking is forbidden.

LAYOUT A **layout** is a way of organizing the design elements in a printed work such as a poster, book, or magazine. Layouts typically consist of visual elements, including type and pictures, which may be drawings and photographs. The layout of children's books may also contain buttons to press, a variety of textures to feel, and speakers that make sounds.

12-36 Signage for women's and men's restrooms.

12-37 Signage for nonsmoking and smoking areas.

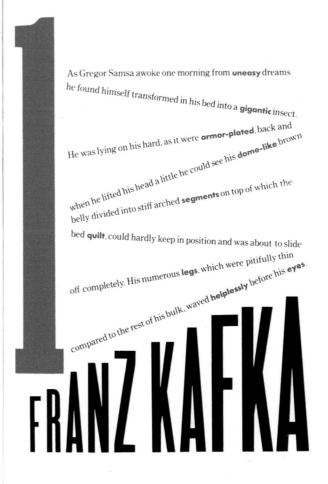

12-38 PAULA SCHER. "Great Beginnings" spread for Koppel & Scher promotional booklet (1984).

The design of this book generally includes two columns of text which are "justified" (vertically aligned on both left and right). Photographs and drawings are interspersed throughout in various locations in an effort to provide aesthetic appeal and to have works of art displayed on the same page on which they are discussed. "Running feet" display the page numbers, the names of the chapters (on the left) and the names of the sections (on the right). Major and minor heads are distinguished both by color and size. Boxed features, such as "A

Closer Look" and "Compare + Contrast," are placed on what are called *screens* or *tint panels* to help set them apart from the main text. You are not expected to be thinking about all this as you read, but the layout is intended to be stimulating yet refined, to complement the subject matter, and to assist the reader in navigating the material.

Figure **12-38** shows the layout for a spread for a promotional booklet, "Great Beginnings," by Paula Scher. Because of a tight budget, she limited her palette to three colors: black, red, and a putty color. She turned to rarely used typefaces and to features of Art Deco and Russian Constructivism (see Chapters 19 and 20) three to four generations after their passing. Put more simply, her typefaces went from thick to thin; her colors, like her subject, alternated; she worked her key letters and numbers like columns; and her horizontal lines of text ramped uphill then down, but always left to right, requiring dizzying backward leaps. Even the red and the black work like shocking figures against the calming putty-colored background. The layout is all "metamorphosis," or change, as is the title of the work.

Gitte Kath's poster for the Sydney Paralympics (Fig. **12-39**) required her to collect materials such as the athletic shoe, glove, and feathers, post them on a worn, discolored wall in her home, paint and photograph them, then apply the graph-

12-40 HENRI DE TOULOUSE-LAUTREC. *Le Divan Japonais* (1892). Color lithograph. 31⅝" × 23⅞". Musée Toulouse-Lautrec, Albi, France.

12-39 GITTE KATH. Poster for the Sydney 2000 Paralympics.

ics. The condition of the elements in the poster suggest the poignancy of the transitory nature of living things. There is nothing heroic about this poster; there is only the suggestion of loss and caring. The colors are muted, the positioning of the objects and the graphics are balanced, and the allover grid and decay provide unity.

Henri de Toulouse-Lautrec, a late-nineteenth-century French artist, is seen by some as the father of the color lithograph poster. Toulouse-Lautrec dwelled in nighttime Paris—its cafés, music halls, nightclubs, and brothels. The posters that he designed for concerts and other performances are among the most well known in the history of art. His designs (Fig. **12-40**) are successful because they capture, in a single image, the spirit and personality of the establishment and the performer. Areas of unmodulated color and high-contrast values in the poster design evoke theater lighting and costuming. The lyrical market research. When former vice president and Nobel Prize recipient Al Gore sought to promote his nonprofit advocacy group for the prevention of global warming (Alliance for Climate Protection), he hired a wellknown advertising firm to design an ad campaign, including a logo. The result was a simple green circle inscribed with white letters forming the word we (Fig. **12-43**). Answering questions about the concept, lead designer Brian Collins explained that the bright green color best expresses the idea of *green*—a word used to describe efforts to conserve and restore energy and the planet's environment and resources. The color is symbolic, but also uplifting and optimistic. The typeface used for the word *we*, turned upside down, reads *me* backward, and was created by typographer Chester Jenkins specifically for the Gore alliance's logo. The *we-me* inversion is intended to signify human cooperation to achieve a solution to the climate crisis. Finally, according to Collins, the circular shape of the logo symbolizes the earth and draws attention to the fact that the climate crisis affects all of its inhabitants.

shapes and undulating lines, coupled with an oblique perspective and bold patterns influenced by Japanese prints, combine to catch the eye and draw the patron to the party.

12-42 Google Logo. http://www.google.com.

Logos

A **logo** is an emblematic design used to identify and advertise a company or an organization. The most successful corporate identity designs—like Apple's instantly recognizable apple minus a single bite (Fig. **12-41**)—are inseparable from the entities they represent. The logo for the Internet search engine Google (Fig. **12-42**) features broadly spaced letters of intense—mostly primary—colors. The simplicity of the design and the straightforwardness of the color scheme suggest an ease of use (even a child can do it) that the company would want to promote.

Logos are well conceived and deliberately designed symbols that are decided upon after much consideration and

12-43 Alliance for Climate Protection logo. Courtesy Alliance for Climate Protection.

Web Design

Websites are an inextricable part of the information superhighway. Any of us cyberspace surfers can go online, access the website of a popular consumer magazine, and get the latest reviews on the new car we're drooling over. We can research without books, order DVDs, make reservations, or bid on a special reserve wine. And a big part of what keeps us attached to our PC's mouse at the end of an electronic umbilical cord is the visual feedback we get when we click. The better the design of the website, the more tantalizing the product or service—a clear fact not lost on the thousands of businesses, organizations, agencies, and individuals for whom the website is the new face and first face to the consumer in the age of electronics.

Web design consists of multiple tasks. One is technical and involves programming—how users click their way around a web page, how links to other pages and sites are established, and how to insert still images or animated clips and sound. Other tasks concern aesthetics and marketing, where the main priority is designing a home page that will have the greatest visual impact, and thus entice the user to discover more by digging deeper into the site, or to buy whatever it is that is being sold.

As you surf the web, you have no doubt been struck by the endless variety, quality, and quantity of web design. I, like you, come across interesting websites almost every day, so it was hard to settle on just one or two to highlight in this chapter. Some current favorites include the website for the Alvin Ailey American Dance Theater in New York City (known for its brilliant mind- and body-stretching choreography) (Fig. **12-44**). Another is the site for Squared Design Lab (Fig. **12-45**). These, like other websites, feature icons or zones that the user can click on to navigate the site for more images or related web pages and information.

Squared Design Lab is a multidisciplinary design studio working with two- and three-dimensional animation, photomontage, graphic design, and other services. They are

12-44 Website: Alvin Ailey American Dance Theater. www.alvinailey.org.

also known for their 3D digital visualization, as seen in this screen shot from their website; they have used a variety of techniques to create a visualization of a completed National September 11 Memorial and Museum at Ground Zero in Manhattan (also see Fig. 11-28 on page 229) as it was under construction. Run your mouse over the narrow bands that bracket the central image; as you do, each multicolored band converts to a white one that features the name of a site or a project. Click on one and the center screen will switch to a photograph, a bit of animation, or, in this case, a 3D visualization of that project. Click elsewhere and you will find an animation depicting the construction of a futuristic apartment building, or a rendering of gas-sipping minicars.

Art museums are also among the untold number of organizations that can be accessed through websites. In fact, you can engage in virtual museum visits by clicking your way through the world's most renowned collections: the Louvre in Paris, the Vatican Collection in Rome, the State Hermitage museum in St. Petersburg, Russia, or—closer to home—The Metropolitan Museum of Art in New York or any one of the collections featured in the Art Tours in your textbook.

Website design is a burgeoning business, but the ability to create sites does not reside exclusively among professionals. Students take courses that feature web design, software and templates for websites are widely available, and online tutorials give detailed information on how to "create your own." Like much related to the Internet, access is becoming universal.

Fashion Design

It has become routine for me to enter a classroom on any given day to overhear a play-by-play analysis of a previous night's episode of the Lifetime network's *Project Runway*. A reality TV program that pits established and up-and-coming fashion designers against one another in a series of challenges leading to a single winner, *Project Runway* has engendered a near cult-like following. So wide-ranging and popular is its appeal that in the wake of an early 2008 season of the show, *Saturday Night Live* writers created a skit around the winning designer Christian Siriano (Fig. **12-46**), who, along with his skinny jeans and signature hair-sprayed coif, brought the words *fierce* and *hot mess* into contemporary parlance. *Project Runway* has raised the consciousness of the realities of the world of fashion design from initial design sketches through the construction of a garment to a completed piece. It has also introduced terms like *haute couture*, *ready-to-wear*, and *mass-market apparel*.

Haute couture is the French term for "high fashion." Haute couture designs are technically made-to-measure for individual customers from expensive materials combined with meticulous stitching, detail work, and finishing. Runway shows feature many haute couture designs that are impressive for their innovation and aesthetics as artforms (Fig. **12-47**).

On the opposite end of the spectrum from haute couture is mass-market apparel, designed for ordinary consumers to be more universal in style and more affordable in price. Fabrics are generally of a lesser grade in terms of quality, and detailed hand-stitching is replaced by machine work that both expedites the execution and thus makes large quantities of an item possible. Designs for mass-market fashion often follow in the footsteps of couture designs, and it is not uncommon to find high-end designers creating product lines that are more accessible to department store shoppers. Ready-to-wear is a fashion category that straddles haute couture and mass-market fashion. Fabrics used for ready-to-wear are of high quality, and the workmanship is careful and often complex. Because apparel is created in smaller quantities, price tags are high. Ready-to-wear lines of the couture industry appear in major European and American cities during Fashion Week runway exhibits.

Fashion design has always reflected the culture and society of its time as much as it has contributed toward contemporary

12-46 Christian Siriano, left, stands with a model on the runway during the Christian Siriano Fall 2008 Collection, part of Bravo Network's *Project Runway* final show during Mercedes-Benz Fall 2008 Fashion Week, in New York.

12-47 Haute couture design, Christian Dior, Autumn/Winter 2007–2008.

12-48 *Himation. Eirene, Daughter of Zeus and Themis.* Roman copy of a Greek original of the 4th century BCE. The Metropolitan Museum of Art, NY.

12-49 J MENDEL. A model walks the runway during the J Mendel Spring 2008 Fashion Show at The Promenade in Bryant Park during Mercedes-Benz Fashion Week on September 7, 2007, in New York City.

taste. And fashion has been inspired by history as much as it has anticipated the look of the future. One particular style that has been characterized by a remarkable longevity is one inspired by ancient Greece. The *chiton* (a loose-fitting gown pinned at the shoulders), *himation* (a mantle that was draped over one shoulder and sometimes wrapped around the body; see Fig. **12-48**), and *peplos* (a gown pinned at the shoulders and cinched at the waist; see Fig. 14-8) have been mimicked and interpreted by costume and fashion designers stretching back to the Napoleonic era in France forward to today (Fig. **12-49**).

On the opposite end of the chronological and fashion spectrum, consider the Hyper Space Couture Design Contest held in Tokyo in 2006. Participating designers focused on a couture line of personal fashions for space travel and habitation (Fig. **12-50**).

Urban Design: The Realm of the "Space in-Between"

Perhaps it is in urban design that our desire for order and harmony achieves its most majestic expression. Throughout history, most towns and cities have more or less sprung up. They have pushed back the countryside in all directions, as necessary, with little evidence of an overall guiding concept.

12-50 A model wears futuristic makeup and clothing at the Hyper Space Couture Design Contest held at Tokyo University on November 2, 2006.

Urban planners and designers "are the 'city builders' whose realm is 'the space in between,'
'in between' the buildings that are the province of architecture, and 'in between'
the neighborhoods, cities and regions, the planning for which plays an often-under-
appreciated role in the healthy development of our urban centers."
—Skidmore, Owings and Merrill

As a result, cities around the globe have experienced "the pollution of vital land, air, and water resources, shortages of food, energy, and potable water, inadequate housing, killing commutes, impersonal highrise districts, and aesthetically mind-numbing residential wastelands."[5] The Rome of the early Republic, for example, was an impoverished seat of empire, little more than a disordered assemblage of seven villages on seven hills. Later, the downtown area was a jumble of narrow streets winding through mud-brick buildings. Not until the first century BCE were the major building programs undertaken by Sulla and then the Caesars.

The new towns of the Roman Empire were laid out largely on a rectangular grid. This pattern was common among cen-

trist states, where bits of land were parceled out to the subjects of mighty rulers. The gridiron was also found to be a useful basis for design throughout history—from the ancient Greeks to the colonial Americans. Many cities of the Near and Middle East, such as Baghdad, have a circular tradition in urban design, which may reflect the belief that they were the hubs of the universe. The throne room of the palace in eighth-century Baghdad was at the center of the circle. The palace—including attendant buildings, a game preserve, and pavilions set in perfumed gardens—was more than a mile in diameter, and the remainder of the population occupied a relatively narrow ring around the palace.

WASHINGTON, D.C. Few urban designs are as simple and rich as Pierre-Charles L'Enfant's plan for Washington, D.C. (Fig. **12-51**). The city is cradled between two branches of the Potomac River, yielding an uneven, overall diamond shape.

---

5 Skidmore, Owings and Merrill. http://www.som.com/content.cfm/services_urban_design_and_planning (accessed March 18, 2011).

12-51 PIERRE-CHARLES L'ENFANT.
Plan for Washington, D.C. (1792).

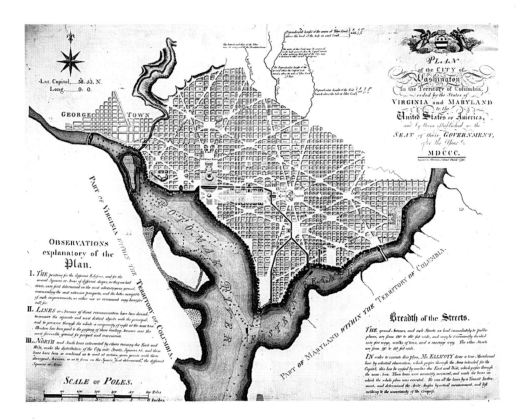

12-52 Rendering of the framework plan for Alexandria, Egypt, to complete the historic Eastern Harbor.

Within the diamond, a rectangular grid of streets that run east-west and north-south was laid down. Near the center of the diamond, with its west edge at the river, an enormous Mall or green space was set aside. At the east end of the Mall is the Capitol Building. To the north, at its west end, is the president's house (which is now the White House). Broad boulevards radiate from the Capitol and from the White House, cutting across the gridiron. One radiating boulevard runs directly between the Capitol and the White House, and other boulevards parallel it.

The design is a composition in which the masses of the Capitol Building and White House balance one another, and the rhythms of the gridiron pattern and intersecting diagonal boulevards create contrast and unity. The Mall provides an open central gathering place that is as much a part of American culture as it is respite from the congestion of the city. We see more of Washington, D.C., in the Art Tour at the end of the chapter.

ALEXANDRIA, EGYPT Alexandria, the ancient center of the Western cultural world, is now a city of 4 million. It was founded around 331 BCE by Alexander the Great. Its lighthouse, a hallowed beacon on the Mediterranean Sea, now gone, was one of the Seven Wonders of the Ancient World. Its library, built by the Greeks and accidentally burned down by Julius Caesar in 48 BCE, was the largest in the world. Alexandria was also a major center of shipping because of its overland proximity to the Red Sea, but with the building of the Suez Canal, completed in 1869, the city's importance as a transportation hub was diminished. The historic library has been replaced with the Bibliotheca Alexandrina, completed in 2002 at a cost of $220 million, but the once-beautiful harbor itself has remained underused and somewhat in decay.

The Master Plan by Skidmore, Owings and Merrill (Fig. 12-52) is intended to bring new life to the Eastern Harbor and to help re-establish the city as a leading cultural center. New museums, cultural facilities, and hotels are intended to serve as magnets for the tourism industry. The design connects the harbor to various city districts via new rail lines and green pedestrian walkways, while sidewalks and tunnels lead to underwater archeological sites. In the plan, beaches are expanded and passenger boat terminals will be constructed. One of the design's most striking elements—a new breakwater—will improve the quality of the water in the city. What time and history have torn away, urban design can perhaps create anew.

ART TOUR WASHINGTON, D.C.

ON JULY 14, 1789, in what became the defining symbolic moment of the French Revolution, the Bastille prison was stormed by revolutionaries who freed a grand total of seven prisoners. Four years later, with the founding of a new Republic, the doors of the Louvre Museum (containing about 200 works that had belonged to the king) opened to the public.

The point to this story lies in its contrast with the next: In 1936, Andrew Mellon (an American statesman and financier) gave his art collection to the United States of America and built the National Gallery of Art in Washington, D.C., to house it. In subsequent years, other collectors followed suit until the "nation's collection" outgrew its space. Unlike many of the world's great art museums, such as the Louvre, the museums you will see in Washington, D.C., did not begin as private royal collections made accessible to the public only after revolution and democratization. The core of Washington's holdings came from entrepreneurs who willingly, even affectionately, gave their art to their fellow citizens. Much of what you will see in Washington, D.C., is yours by virtue of your U.S. citizenship. And seeing just about all of it costs you nothing.

If you're coming to Washington by train, come hungry. You will arrive, most likely, at Union Station—a fine example of the Beaux Arts architectural style. From the three main archways that define the entry (based on the Arch of Constantine in Rome!) to the magnificent gilded barrel-vaulted ceiling, Union Station is not simply a transit center to move through—linger and look. It opened in 1907, and for more than 50 years this station was the largest in the world. After careful and costly restoration in 1988, this is now the second most visited site in Washington, D.C. Union Station is home to one of the most fantastic food courts you will ever come upon, with selections to entice every palate. Take a spin around the stalls before you commit to that Maryland crab-cake sandwich.

Union Station is a well-situated starting point for your art tour of the capital. From there, a short stroll along Delaware or Louisiana Avenue will bring you to the U.S. Capitol and the Mall, the site of many museums and memorials. Here you will experience the feeling of the nation's capital—its Classical architecture (inspired, as was the new democratic government, by Greek and Roman ideals), expanses of tree-lined grassy lawn, reflecting pools, and marble and granite monuments. The Capitol Building (see Fig. 3-9) is at the "top"—or eastern end—of the Mall and has much to offer to the art seeker. The dome, designed by Thomas U. Walter, is one of the largest in the world. The rotunda (the large, circular space in the interior beneath the dome) contains many paintings and sculptures and is capped by Constantino Brumidi's mural depicting the Apotheosis of Washington (bring your binoculars and your sense of humor).

Outside the Capitol, the Mall is arrayed before the visitor, offering a perspective toward the Washington Monument on the west end and all that lies between. The Mall was designed by the French architect Pierre L'Enfant, who imported many of his

elements of city planning (grand boulevards, elegant residences, well-situated monuments) from Paris. The first museum on your tour is the National Gallery of Art. The collection is divided between two buildings—East and West. The West (Neoclassical) Building is the earlier museum—the one financed by Andrew Mellon and designed by John Russell Pope. Here the visitor will find Western art spanning the thirteenth through the nineteenth centuries, featuring stellar examples of works by such artists as Giotto, Botticelli, Leonardo da Vinci, Raphael (*The Alba Madonna*), Rembrandt, Rubens (*Daniel in the Lion's Den*), El Greco, Monet (*Woman with a Parasol—Mme Monet and Her Son*), Cassatt, Cézanne, Toulouse-Lautrec (*Quadrille at the Moulin Rouge*), Homer (*Breezing Up*), and Whistler (*Symphony in White, No. 1: The White Girl*), among many, many others of fame and note. And that's just the west wing. The entire East Building, designed by I. M. Pei and one of the few Modernist works of architecture in the city, houses the country's collection of twentieth-century art. A dramatic, soaring atrium, featuring an enormous mobile by by Alexander Calder (see Fig. 2-70) and works by Henry Moore, Joan Miró, and Andrew Goldsworthy, is flanked by balconies and galleries in which one will find works from the permanent collection as well as traveling exhibitions. Both museums (connected underground) have wonderful restaurants and bookshops.

One of the highlights of the Mall is the Sculpture Garden of the National Gallery of Art, poised between the West Building and the National Museum of Natural History. Works of modern sculpture pepper the sections of lawn surrounding a refreshing fountain in summer and delightful skating rink in winter. Viewers can walk among and around pieces by Claes Oldenberg,

Roy Lichtenstein, Louise Bourgeois, Joan Miró, and others. And from these fun-filled, art-filled surroundings, one can cross over a broad expanse of lawn to another collection of outdoor sculpture belonging to the Hirshhorn Museum, a private-turned-public collection displayed in a cylindrical building affectionately referred to as "the doughnut." Rodin's *The Burghers of Calais* (see Fig. 19-36) finds itself in equally prestigious company in this collection.

The Mall contains a staggering number of museums, galleries, and monuments. The old Smithsonian Castle, the building that once housed works that are now found in other sites along the Mall (don't miss wandering through its splendid gardens); the spectacular National Air and Space Museum; and such small jewels as the Arthur M. Sackler Gallery of Asian Art, the National Museum of African Art, and the United States Holocaust Memorial Museum just beyond the Washington Monument merely scratch the surface of what one might discover on an art tour of the capital. And to these we must add artistic memorials such as the Vietnam Veterans Memorial (see "A Closer Look," page 211), the Korean War Vet-

MAYA YING LIN. *Vietnam Veterans Memorial, Names and Reflections on the Wall.*

SMITHSONIAN CASTLE.

erans Memorial, and the Franklin D. Roosevelt Memorial, all of which have altered the very concept of meaningful memorials for Washington, D.C., and the country.

For many students in the United States, "the family trip to Washington" was viewed as essential to child rearing. For others, "the school trip to Washington" was the first independent trip away from home—traveling on a rowdy bus with one's peers to take in the sights and watch history come alive. Memories of these experiences traverse generations. We have always understood the importance of symbols to American history. Our own art tours of the nation's capital enable us to understand the importance of art to American people.

TO CONTINUE YOUR TOUR and learn more about Washington, D.C., go to CourseMate.